PRESENTED TO

_____

DATE/OCCASION

_____

PERSONAL NOTE

_____
_____
_____
_____
_____
_____
_____
_____
_____

This is the Day!
Copyright © 2013 by Deborah S. Glover

Unless otherwise indicated, all Scripture quotations are taken from the KJV—King James Version. The author has adapted the KJV by capitalizing nouns and pronouns referring to God, replacing Old English pronouns with modern English spelling (ex. thy to your), and spelling verbs with the modern English ending (ex. Saith to says).

All rights reserved. This book is protected under the copyright laws of the United States of America and may not be reproduced, stored in a retrieval system, or transmitted in any form or by any means—electronic, mechanical, photocopy, recording, scanning, or any other—except for brief quotations in critical reviews or articles, without the prior written permission of the author.

The front cover photo was purchased from: © Kamchatka | Above the Clouds photo from Dreamstime.com – https://www.dreamstime.com/stock-photo-above-clouds-beautiful-sunset-hill-image59703053#res16534329

The photos printed before the beginning of each month were photographed and donated to this project from the private portfolio of Rita Barnett of Memphis, Tennessee.

Book design by Debbi Stocco, MyBookDesigner.com

Library of Congress Control Number: 2017900466

ISBN: 978-0-9984392-0-4

## *Testimonials*

"There are those few who pay the price to hear the riches and priceless treasures of what the Lord whispers. Time alone with the Lord produces an abundant, life giving harvest proven here in the unfolding intimacy of, *This Is the Day!* This devotional was forged from a crucible of suffering, obedience, and a life seeking first the Kingdom of God. It is a gift, not from flesh and blood, but from a beautiful collaboration of the Divine and His faithful handmaiden. It is rich and satisfying."

~*Rita Barnett, Intercessor*

"Deborah's Devotional Book, *This is the Day!* is a combination of several things:

The sound of Deborah's wise counsel, the Scripture, the sound of worship, the Command of The Lord, a reminder to worship at all times, and a fleshing out of the scripture back into wise counsel with direction to proceed into the day with The Lord.

Some days begin without the desire to "worship at all times" for some of us. But, Deborah starts each page with the reminder, the admonition, the encouragement and blessing to join into that holy encounter, shifting the start of the day, coming into alignment with the command and resting in that place of worship within the confines of Scripture and its expansion into the supernatural Divine transaction which comes only by Holy Spirit.

Liturgical passages are woven into the Scriptural passages she has put into the thoughts for each day, before the reminder that our focus is to be on The Lord, the burden is to be on The Lord, the Glory is The Lord's, the Joy is in The Lord, and Holy Spirit is here to help us shift the focus onto Him Who Is, and Who Was, and Who will be.

It is a reminder, an instruction, an encouragement that we do not walk into the day alone. She has done a wonderful job bringing The Lord into the first part of my day when I am not sure I am ready to relinquish my own thoughts before my coffee."

~*Gail Weaver, Missionary and Author*

"Each of the devotional writings in *This is the Day!* begins with this statement from Scripture, "I will rejoice and be glad in it." How many days I have read these words at the beginning of the day, and felt anything but the ability to rejoice. And many days, I have read these words and been full of joy.

One of the reasons I love *This is the Day!* devotional, is the daily inclusion of God's Word, making the content always fresh and alive.

I also know, through reading Deborah's testimony, that God is faithful in the worst of circumstances; that knowledge for me, brings great comfort as I face life's daily challenges.

For the past three years, I have been admonished, comforted and edified through adding *This is the Day!* to my daily time with the Lord, and I look forward to continuing to read it for many years to come."

*~Susan Blackburn, Director of Project Management*

"After Thanksgiving of 2016, I received a copy of *This is the Day!* from Deborah Glover …God's perfect timing … A time of great turmoil in my life ~ attacks one after the other ~ lies of the enemy ~ broken to think, that those I love, thought evil…

Thankfully, God helped me recognize the real enemy…

\*\*\*For we wrestle not against flesh and blood… SOoooo, right after the devotional arrived, I began reading a little here, a little there… (more than 1 a day ~ 3 times a day ~) *More ~ More ~ More…*

Aughhhh *His Peace came…* Supernatural Strength @ a Time when I was weak, Yet *He sent His Love ~ His Grace in the form of a Book…*

The Words lined up w/ what Father was showing me…

Knowing my Sister n Christ, 4 we have labored together for many years, I Know these Words are as Fresh Manna from Father's Throne Room of Grace…

I am SOooo very Thankful 4 the Life she Lives…\*\*\*Holy set apart, a forerunner in the Kingdom of God… *Come … Become immersed in the PRESENCE of GOD. Come … Drink from FATHER'S Life giving well as HIS WORD* purifies your soul, strengthens your Spirit man…

I invite You to come… Be Blessed as You come and dine @ *the Master's table…"*

*~Deborah Newman, Washed By The Word Ministries*

# THIS IS *the* DAY!

*365 Day Devotional*

DR. DEBORAH S. GLOVER

# DEDICATION

*I want to dedicate this devotional to my Father who loves me beyond words can express and human emotions can experience. I dedicate it to Him for His guidance and His grace of confidence to complete this book. I forever hold Him in reverence for His great love for me and all His children!*

*Lastly, I dedicate it to my daughter, Valerie, who is now living the blessed life prepared for her in Heaven. Thank you, Valerie, for always being a mighty encourager to me as I witnessed you following your heart with full passion in obedience to your Lord. May I, may we all, follow that same path of passion and see you soon!*

## INTRODUCTION

*I was about nine years old when the Holy Spirit pierced my heart to accept Jesus as my Savior and Lord. I stepped out of the aisle in that Baptist church and walked to the front. A real conversion! Since then it has never been too difficult for me to step out of an aisle to find my way to the front of a church for prayer. Thank God for Baptist churches!*

*Then the teenage years and rebellion came, leading me down a hard path until the age of 34 in 1982. At that time, the Good Shepherd had seen His perfect timing. He went out to find this lost sheep and carried me back into the fold. I have been there ever since, because of His mercy, grace, and love.*

*Later that year, Jesus baptized me in His Holy Spirit and I became zealous about the things of the Spirit! Everything about God, Jesus, and the Holy Spirit was heightened and exploded within me! No experience is quite like it on earth. Ever since then the journey with God has been beyond what words can describe!*

*In April of 1996 I believed the Lord was leading me to write a daily devotional. During my quiet time with the Lord, I began to write once a day what I sensed the Holy Spirit was saying to me. When I received inspiration from God which I heard in my inner man in the first person, I have printed these words in bold type. The other words were inspired by His Spirit, but not in the sense of a direct quotation from Him. When the devotion is read, one must discern for himself using Holy Scripture as the ultimate authority to its truthfulness and applicability to one's own life. The book you are holding in your hands is that devotional written throughout 1996–1997, day by day and edited more recently in the past few years. May these daily words encourage you to press on and in, to know Him and the life He has planned for you—your destiny.*

*I would like to comment on the cover picture. When I saw the movie entitled, "Unconditional," (2012, written and directed by Brent McCorkle) I was given the idea to print a copy of the sun rising above the clouds for the cover of this book. There was a story written and told by the heroine in the movie about an oriole baby bird, named Firebird. He loved basking in the sun and lived for sunshine. When the clouds, rain, and winds came, he complained to his mom saying, "Why does God give the storm clouds power to take away the sun?" She always replied, "You'll know someday, when you take a walk on the clouds."*

*Then the day came when her answer was different. On that stormy day when he asked the same question, she said to him, "It's up there waiting for you. You just have to see it for yourself." Firebird began to climb the sky up and up, but there were only dark and darker clouds. He was scared! As he went up into the unknown, instead of answers, he met with lightening, thunder, and wind. He was about to turn back when it happened. He broke through the clouds and there it was—more beautiful than ever. In that moment, it became clear. No storm could take the sun away. The sun was always shining as constant as his mother's love. He just needed to take a walk on the clouds.*

*This is my hope and prayer for you—that you will always be walking on the clouds, as you diligently look to God every day as the morning breaks and the sun sets. The Son*

✝

*is always shining in and on your life. Look to Him and rise above the circumstances of your life to see the Son shining. These devotions will encourage you to see the Son in everything! You can rejoice and be glad in the day that He has made for you!*

*~Deborah S. Glover*

# JANUARY

"*In the midst of the street of it, and on either side of the river, was there the tree of life, which bare twelve manner of fruits, and yielded her fruit every month: and the leaves of the tree were for the healing of the nations.*"

REVELATION 22:2

## JANUARY 1
### THIS IS THE DAY THAT THE LORD HAS MADE. I WILL REJOICE AND BE GLAD IN IT.

*Hallelujah! The blood is sufficient. Satan truly is under our feet. The battle has been won. The war is over. Stand. And having done all, STAND.*

*But how we waiver and toddle when the enemy of our flesh and soul comes to knock.*

*Know the Word and in knowing the Word, he flees—backs down—and retreats.*

*Do you get tired of standing? Can you find someone to hold up your hands like Aaron and Hur did for Moses? (Exodus 17:12)*

*The Word works. So use the Word. Remember Jesus is the Word.*

\*\*\*

*"Submit yourselves therefore to God. Resist the devil, and he will flee from you." James 4:7*

*"Wherefore take unto you the whole armor of God, that you may be able to withstand in the evil day, and having done all, to stand." Ephesians 6:13*

## JANUARY 2
### THIS IS THE DAY THAT THE LORD HAS MADE. I WILL REJOICE AND BE GLAD IN IT.

*Jesus came to set us free from the original curse of eating from the tree of the knowledge of good and evil. When we ate from that tree, we acted in pride. We thought we could make decisions outside of God's counsel which would lead to prosperity. We acted in rebellion, because we disobeyed God. When we ate of that tree, we realized we could do wrong and be punished, so we experienced fear. All the curses were manifested at this time, stemming from pride, rebellion, and fear.*

*"Let not your heart be troubled," Jesus says to us. Jesus came to redeem us from the curse; to put us back in our position in which we stood before the trespass. We can now live as Adam and Eve did before they sinned. They did not fear making a mistake. They were like two-year-old children, who go about their day with no fear of reprisal. They just go. If the child gets out of hand, his parent gently corrects him. And that is exactly how we as adults can live. We do not have to fear making decisions or making mistakes. God will gently correct us.*

*As for the repercussions of wrong-doing, Jesus paid the price. It is all over—done—settled. You cannot do anything for which Jesus has not already paid the price. That is why we can walk in freedom and not fear. We have been redeemed from fear. Perfect Love has cast out fear (I John 4:18).*

*He has also redeemed us from rebellion. As newborn babes filled with the Holy Spirit, we have the power to obey God.*

*And what about pride, the initial cause of our trouble? God tells us to humble ourselves. <u>We</u> have to humble ourselves. If we do not, He will arrange circumstances that will humble us. This is His goodness and mercy to keep us close.*

✝

*What a wonderful Father we have! Thanks be to God!
He has saved us from pride, rebellion, and fear.*

\*\*\*

*"Christ has redeemed us from the curse of the law,
being made a curse for us: for it is written, Cursed is
every one that hangs on a tree:" Galatians 3:13*

## JANUARY 3
### THIS IS THE DAY THAT THE LORD HAS MADE. I WILL REJOICE AND BE GLAD IN IT.

*Hallelujah! The debt has been paid. The Lord is no longer angry with us. He will no longer rebuke us.*

*"For this is as the waters of Noah unto me: for as I have sworn that the waters of Noah should no more go over the earth; so have I sworn that I would not be wroth with thee, nor rebuke thee." Isaiah 54:9*

*Walk in freedom! Walk in joy! He has done all things well. Provided for all situations. If you don't believe so, just lean on Him and see His provision. He is enough. Go for it! Live life to the fullest extreme. Lengthen your cords, and strengthen your stakes.*

*You shall not be ashamed nor will you be confounded, for the Lord is your husband whether you are a male or a female. Rejoice for He is your Provider!*

\*\*\*

*"Fear not; for thou shalt not be ashamed: neither be thou confounded; for thou shalt not be put to shame: for thou shalt forget the shame of thy youth, and shalt not remember the reproach of thy widowhood any more." Isaiah 54:4*

*"For your Maker is your husband; the LORD of hosts is His name; and your Redeemer the Holy One of Israel; The God of the whole earth shall He be called." Isaiah 54:5*

## JANUARY 4
### THIS IS THE DAY THAT THE LORD HAS MADE. I WILL REJOICE AND BE GLAD IN IT.

*He has everything under control.*

*Why worry?*

*Because we don't know Him. We trust the bank, a friend, a chair, etc., etc. Because we know them well enough, we trust them. We've used a bank, a friend, a chair, etc.*

*We, in this day, trust ourselves more than God. Therefore we don't know Him nor trust Him. Sometimes God must allow things to run out or fail before we seek to know Him and trust Him.*

*How many people turn to God to learn about Him after a loved one's death, a financial difficulty, or a sickness?*

*Seek Him NOW with ALL your heart, soul, and body, while He may be found. Do not be "ho-hum" about KNOWING GOD!*

\*\*\*

*"Then shall you call upon Me, and you shall go and pray unto Me, and I will hearken unto you. (13) And you shall seek Me, and find Me, when you shall search for Me with all your heart." Jeremiah 29:12–13*

## JANUARY 5

### THIS IS THE DAY THAT THE LORD HAS MADE. I WILL REJOICE AND BE GLAD IN IT.

*Be glad in all you do, for He is watching you.*

*Watching in pleasure and joy, for He rejoices over you in love. He loves you.*

*Have you ever loved a child? Have you ever desired the best for your child? Do you want to make your child happy and prosperous? Well, if you being evil, desire their well-being, how much more does your Heavenly Father desire blessings for you? (Matthew 7:11)*

*Make yourself available to Him, and He will renew your mind with truth and not error. We have spent enough years in half-truths.*

*Dwell with the Father and He will uncover the lies you live in, replacing them with His truth that removes the burden and destroys the yoke (Isaiah 10:27).*

*GO TO HIM.*

*Find out who He is. The truth will set you free.*

\*\*\*

*"The LORD your God in the midst of you is mighty; He will save, He will rejoice over you with joy; He will rest in His love, He will joy over you with singing." Zephaniah 3:17*

## JANUARY 6
### THIS IS THE DAY THAT THE LORD HAS MADE. I WILL REJOICE AND BE GLAD IN IT.

*Who is responsible for you?*
*"I AM," says the Lord God Almighty.*

*He is responsible for you. When you surrender yourself to Him, desiring in your soul's heart to be molded and guided by Him, then He has the responsibility to do the work. However your life turns out, it is to His credit or His discredit. How many know that God never fails?! The burden is on His back to make us succeed when we surrender all to Him.*

*He knows the deepest desire of your soul's heart. Since we are not perfect in manifesting our surrender but desire to be, He calls this perfect; and at the same time continues to work out perfect manifested surrender. Rejoice, the battle is His!*

**Isn't that what I told Jehoshaphat when he began to praise Me. So praise Me, and stand back to see Me work. Praise Me, and I'll show Myself worthy. Praise Me, and see the enemy flee. Praise Me, and see Me hold back no good thing from thee.**

\*\*\*

*"And when he had consulted with the people, he appointed singers unto the LORD, and that should praise the Beauty of Holiness, as they went out before the army, and to say, Praise the LORD; for His mercy endures for ever. (22) And when they began to sing and to praise, the LORD set ambushments against the children of Ammon, Moab, and mount Seir, which were come against Judah; and they were smitten." II Chronicles 20:21–22*

## JANUARY 7
### THIS IS THE DAY THAT THE LORD HAS MADE. I WILL REJOICE AND BE GLAD IN IT.

*Yes, God has provided all things for our health and wealth. It is by trusting Him; walking in faith and withstanding the pressures of fear and doubt that we shall inherit the promise. But we ask ourselves,*

*"How? How shall He bring this to pass? Have I sinned? Have I done wrong, by stepping out in faith?"*

*All these emotions are wrapped up in fear and doubt. Fear that we will be wrong. Well, the fear of being wrong was a curse from the garden. Eve wanted to know all and evil entered into the earth.*

*When Jesus died on the cross, He destroyed that curse of the knowledge of good and evil and provided us with faith in God.*

*When Jesus was following God to the cross, it did not make sense.*

*Maybe what you are doing now does not make sense. What I am doing now does not make sense!*

*"Father God, can You once again reassure us that we are walking in Your way and not off in 'La La Land.'"*

*Have you ever been accused of going there?*

*Without a need, there is no struggle. That problem is a small one for Me, but a large one for you. Without this problem, you would not be looking to Me for a solution. I wanted you in a place beyond your ability, so I could build faith and trust in you.*

*Now walk—not as a man of this world, but as a man in heavenly places where you are seated*

† 

*with Christ empowered by the same power that raised Christ, My Son, from the dead!*

\*\*\*

*"For our light affliction, which is but for a moment, works for us a far more exceeding and eternal weight of glory; (18) While we look not at the things which are seen, but at the things which are not seen: for the things which are seen are temporal; but the things which are not seen are eternal." II Corinthians 4:17–18*

*"But God, who is rich in mercy, for His great love wherewith He loved us, (5) Even when we were dead in sins, has quickened us together with Christ, (by grace you are saved;) (6) And has raised us up together, and made us sit together in heavenly places in Christ Jesus: (7) That in the ages to come He might show the exceeding riches of His grace in His kindness toward us through Christ Jesus." Ephesians 2:6–7*

## JANUARY 8
### THIS IS THE DAY THAT THE LORD HAS MADE. I WILL REJOICE AND BE GLAD IN IT.

*It is a great day when we follow His Spirit and not our soul's desires.*

*"Oh! the soul is good and perfect as it submits to Your Spirit, but how evil it can be when it submits to the flesh, Satan, or the world!*

*"Let us lean forward into Your Spirit for moment by moment leadership."*

*It is in walking in the Spirit that WE FULFILL THE THINGS OF GOD in our lives. He has caused us to do all things well as we walk in His Spirit.*

*This means our spirit taking guidance from the Holy Spirit; and the soul and flesh surrendered.*

*All things work together for good for those who are called according to His purpose. Just don't fall into the purposes of the flesh and soul which have not surrendered (Romans 8:28).*

*Seek to know Him in Spirit and in truth!*

\*\*\*

*"For they that are after the flesh do mind the things of the flesh; but they that are after the Spirit the things of the Spirit." Romans 8:5*

## JANUARY 9
### THIS IS THE DAY THAT THE LORD HAS MADE. I WILL REJOICE AND BE GLAD IN IT.

*Have you any unconfessed sins? Only the LORD knows.*

*Have you any prayers that have been long in manifesting?*

*Turn your face to God and cry out,*

*"Search me, O God, and know my heart; try me and know my thoughts; and see if there be any wicked way in me, and lead me in the way everlasting."*
*Psalm 139:23–24*

*"Oh God, uncover our sins known and unknown that we may confess them and turn from them toward You. Oh God, let us not continue in our waywardness, but be merciful and bring us to repentance. We cry out for the truth to be revealed in our lives as the deceptions are disclosed and brought to light.*

*"Have mercy on us! Have mercy, for we are but dust, and depend entirely upon Your mercy and lovingkindness. Have mercy!"*

\*\*\*

*"Turn unto me, and have mercy upon me; for I am desolate and afflicted." Psalms 25:16*

## JANUARY 10
### THIS IS THE DAY THAT THE LORD HAS MADE. I WILL REJOICE AND BE GLAD IN IT.

*It is time to rejoice and cry! Cry out for the lost and rejoice in your crying out. For in crying out I have initiated the preparation for revival. So cry out and continue to cry. Let your heart have no rest. Cry out day and night for revival. Cry out for My Spirit to bring conviction of sin. Before revival comes, conviction comes. With cleansing, comes power.*

*My bride is every whit whole. Oh come unto Me! Come unto Me! For I have refreshing for your soul. No matter the circumstances, those who keep their mind on My Son shall have peace.*

*Practice walking in trust, and you'll walk in trust in the storm.*

*Storms are no different from calmness, if you're walking in the Spirit.*

*That means your eyes are on Jesus!*

*Come unto Me.*

\*\*\*

*"Their heart cried unto the Lord, O wall of the daughter of Zion, let tears run down like a river day and night: give yourself no rest; let not the apple of your eye cease. (19) Arise, cry out in the night: in the beginning of the watches pour out your heart like water before the face of the Lord, lift up your hands toward Him for the life of your young children, that faint for hunger in the top of every street:" Lamentations 2:18–19*

## JANUARY 11
### THIS IS THE DAY THAT THE LORD HAS MADE. I WILL REJOICE AND BE GLAD IN IT.

*Oh hallelujah! Those that keep their mind on Jesus are at peace (Isaiah 26:3).*

*When fear comes in like a flood, raise up the Word of God and fear flees! (Isaiah 59:19)*

*It is written, Trust in the LORD with all your heart, lean not on your own understanding and He will direct your path (Proverbs 3:4–5).*

*It is written, I am always with you (Matthew 28:20).*

*If God is with you, what could there be to fear? (Romans 8:31)*

**My right hand upholds you. My right hand is victorious. My right hand is exalted. My right hand is valiant. You are in My right hand! And you hold My right hand. (Psalm 118:15–16)**

\*\*\*

"The voice of rejoicing and salvation is in the tabernacles of the righteous: the right hand of the LORD does valiantly. (16) The right hand of the LORD is exalted: the right hand of the LORD does valiantly." Psalm 118:15–16

## JANUARY 12
### THIS IS THE DAY THAT THE LORD HAS MADE. I WILL REJOICE AND BE GLAD IN IT.

*Oh, that we would come and worship the Most High God! It is He that has conquered the sins of this world, overcoming Satan and hell. He has the keys, and He has given us the keys. One of the keys is praise and worship. Oh, sing unto the LORD! Offer Him sacrifices of praise and thanksgiving.*

*"It is You we adore and upon whom we meditate. It is You who has bought us and given us unto righteousness and justification. How is it You have loved us so much?! It brings tears to my eyes and a constriction to my heart that cries out, 'I am loved!'*

*"Oh come into us, Lord Jesus! Still our minds and bodies. Speak forth and send forth Your love into our hearts. I know this is Your desire. Thank You for filling us with Your love!"*

\*\*\*

*"Let Him kiss me with the kisses of His mouth: for Your love is better than wine." Song of Solomon 1:2*

## JANUARY 13
### THIS IS THE DAY THAT THE LORD HAS MADE. I WILL REJOICE AND BE GLAD IN IT.

*It is you who I love, and for whom I gave My Son. He is My most precious possession, and I gave Him up for you. How much more will I do whatever is necessary to bless you?*

*Does it not appear as a blessing today? It is! No matter what the situation looks like. What did it look like when My Son died on the cross? When Joseph was thrown into the hole? When David was in front of a giant? When the Israelites were at the Red Sea? Do you get the picture?*

*When the picture is the darkest, the glory will be the most glorious, the victory the grandest, the deliverance the most thorough. So when going through the valley of the shadow of death, I will be with you and I never fail. I never mean for harm, but for good.*

*So rejoice as the Israelite boys did in the fiery furnace; as Paul and Silas did in prison, and watch Me act on your behalf. You will see the goodness of the LORD in the land of the living. Wait, I say, wait on the LORD and be of good courage. (Psalm 27:14)*

\*\*\*

*"He that spared not His own Son, but delivered Him up for us all, how shall He not with Him also freely give us all things?" Romans 8:32*

## JANUARY 14
### THIS IS THE DAY THAT THE LORD HAS MADE. I WILL REJOICE AND BE GLAD IN IT.

*Come unto Me all ye who labor and are heavy laden and I will give you rest.*

*Come and drink from My cup and eat My bread. It is enough that you should come to Me everyday. I will come to you also. We shall meet and sup together. We shall break bread together.*

*Seek Me and I shall be found in the breaking of the bread. It is enough that you should come. I will do the rest.*

*Your presence will be enough for Me to work; to melt and mold you into the image of My Son. You shall be like Him, if you persist and faint not; looking neither to your right nor left, but looking unto the Author and Finisher of your faith.*

*It is enough to come!*

*So come.*

\*\*\*

*"Behold, I stand at the door, and knock..." Revelation 3:20a*

## JANUARY 15
### THIS IS THE DAY THAT THE LORD HAS MADE. I WILL REJOICE AND BE GLAD IN IT.

*Be quiet and listen.*

*I shall speak a word to you today that can and will change your life.*

*Be quiet and listen.*

*Put away your books and recordings and just listen.*

*You will hear for I have ordained it.*

*I have spoken It.*

\*\*\*

*"Be still, and know that I am God:" Psalms 46:10a*

## JANUARY 16
### THIS IS THE DAY THAT THE LORD HAS MADE. I WILL REJOICE AND BE GLAD IN IT.

*Has the word of the LORD to you on the 15th changed your life? Please write this word down in your journal and nurture it. Do not let it get choked out or dried up. Meditate on it and do not let go of it, until it is rooted well. Continue to care for it.*

*My word was "Only believe."*

*Then the song came to mind, "Only believe, only believe, all things are possible, only believe." (Song by Paul Rader, 1921)*

*"God, we ask for Your faithfulness in helping us to nurture the word given so that it grows into a big tree that birds from all around can be given a home."*

\*\*\*

*"Which indeed is the least of all seeds: but when it is grown, it is the greatest among herbs, and becomes a tree, so that the birds of the air come and lodge in the branches thereof." Matthew 13:32*

*"And all things whatsoever you shall ask in prayer, believing, you shall receive." Matthew 21:22*

## JANUARY 17
## THIS IS THE DAY THAT THE LORD HAS MADE. I WILL REJOICE AND BE GLAD IN IT.

*He has called us to love. (I would say the hardest commandment we have.) But we can only love to the extent He has loved us, and we have experienced this love.*

*He loves us completely, but how much have we experienced? In Ephesians 3:19, Paul prays that we would experience His love. Oh! to be overcome with His love!*

*"Embrace us, Father. Overshadow us with Your love as You did Mary with the conception of Jesus. Paul prays for us to be filled with God's love. Oh! how we need this in order to be light and salt, in order to love our enemies."*

*Seek not to love, but seek first the kingdom of God and all these things will be added.*

*You try to grow up too fast, and you become impatient and disheartened at your behavior and your heart. Keep seeking Me and love will be a fruit of My life in you and your life in Me.*

\*\*\*

*"But the fruit of the Spirit is love, joy, peace, longsuffering, gentleness, goodness, faith, meekness and temperance: against such there is no law." Galatians 5:22–23*

## JANUARY 18
### THIS IS THE DAY THAT THE LORD HAS MADE. I WILL REJOICE AND BE GLAD IN IT.

*All things are known by God, our Father. It is up to us to rely on Him to reveal the plans of our life. Can we trust Him above all else and everyone else?*

*Yes.*

*So rest in His plans as they unfold. Trust Him and not your eyes to orchestrate the moments in your day.*

*Trust Him. This is resting.*

*TRUST.*

*Totally*

*Relying*

*Upon the*

*Savior's*

*Touch*

\*\*\*

*"Trust in the LORD with all your heart; and lean not unto your own understanding. (6) In all your ways acknowledge Him, and He shall direct your paths." Proverbs 3:5–6*

## JANUARY 19

### THIS IS THE DAY THAT THE LORD HAS MADE. I WILL REJOICE AND BE GLAD IN IT.

*This is the day. He says that to us every day.*
*This is the day...LIVE...REJOICE...*

*He gives us new days for new ways. Is it not exciting when you think of the wonders He will reveal today, tomorrow! Each day is brand new, never before written upon. It is our day for new beginnings, new ideas, new ways, new words, new beliefs, new loves, new passions.*

*Today, He is busy unraveling who you are, who I am.*

*Follow His Spirit.*

*Seek to know Him, and you will be led by Him.*

*(Do not neglect your journal. It will be a forever testimony of His love.)*

\*\*\*

*"And He that sat upon the throne said, Behold, I make all things new. And He said unto me, Write: for these words are true and faithful." Revelation 21:5*

*"Then they that feared the LORD spoke often one to another: and the LORD hearkened, and heard it, and a book of remembrance was written before Him for them that feared the LORD, and that thought upon His name." Malachi 3:16*

## JANUARY 20
## THIS IS THE DAY THAT THE LORD HAS MADE. I WILL REJOICE AND BE GLAD IN IT.

*How many times must I say rejoice?! Begin to make a record of all My words that can cause you to rejoice and then meditate on these.*

*You have grown up with enough words that cause doubt and worry. Now replace all these falsehoods with the truth. It will indeed set you free.*

*Renew your mind with truth. Replace the old with new wine skins.*

*Oh! Hallelujah! My salvation has come nigh unto thee and you would not. Please accept My salvation of love and peace; joy and rest; healing and provision. These are all yours for the receiving!*

*Just receive. Just believe and yours shall be the kingdom and the power and the glory.*

*I have made you to share in My kingdom. I have made you to share in the inheritance of Jacob.*

\*\*\*

"He shall choose our inheritance for us, the excellency of Jacob whom He loved. Selah. (5) God is gone up with a shout, the LORD with the sound of a trumpet. (6) Sing praises to God, sing praises: sing praises unto our King, sing praises. (7) For God is the King of all the earth: sing you praises with understanding." Psalm 47:4–7

# JANUARY 21

## THIS IS THE DAY THAT THE LORD HAS MADE. I WILL REJOICE AND BE GLAD IN IT.

*Without faith, it is impossible to please God. For by faith Abraham received Isaac, and Enoch was taken up.*

*By faith, what have you received? Your eternal life for starters. But from your salvation what have you received by faith?—a baby, a healing, clothes, souls, a business.*

*The new year is upon us. Let us begin to ask our Father to reveal His plans for us; to open our eyes to our future so by faith we too can receive His life for us.*

*Let us not wander through life, but let us have before us goals. Yes, there will be long term goals and short term goals—spiritual and physical goals.*

*"Lord, we ask You to begin to formulate our goals so we will have concrete goals to which we can aspire."*

\*\*\*

*"I will stand upon my watch, and set me upon the tower, and will watch to see what He will say unto me, and what I shall answer when I am reproved. (2) And the LORD answered me, and said, Write the vision, and make it plain upon tables, that he may run that reads it." Habakkuk 2:1–2*

## JANUARY 22
### THIS IS THE DAY THAT THE LORD HAS MADE. I WILL REJOICE AND BE GLAD IN IT.

*Let's make a vow to rejoice today, to be glad today. He has called us to such a time as this to rejoice and be glad! Let us be happy today with a smile on our face as if we had nothing to worry about, but only thoughts of well-being. Thoughts that say, "Everything is going well. Everything is being taken care of. Nothing is being forgotten, neglected, or overlooked. But all things are covered with perfect protection." This is His shalom!*

*Does this not sound like what a loving earthly father would do for his children? Well, if we being evil, then how much more does our heavenly Father take good care of us. You can individualize scripture and your relationship with God. God's relationship with each of us is one-on-one. He is interested in how you as one person, individually relates to Him. Christianity is a one-on-one relationship.*

*What are you doing to walk in the way the Lord is leading you? You must be true to whom He has made you to be, regardless of your surrounding circumstances.*

*This is not a lonely walk, because He often gives you someone who stands beside you. However, there can be times you are standing alone with Him. At those times He is establishing a strong foundation in Him alone!*

\*\*\*

*"If you then being evil, know how to give good gifts unto your children, how much more shall your Father which is in heaven give good things to them that ask Him?" Matthew 7:11*

## JANUARY 23
### THIS IS THE DAY THAT THE LORD HAS MADE. I WILL REJOICE AND BE GLAD IN IT.

*Come unto Me all ye who labor and are heavy laden and I will give you rest.*

*A Sabbath rest He will give you, as He speaks of in the book of Hebrews. Come to Him. He has a rest in which He wants you to walk. How can you enter your destiny, your "promised land," unless you are walking in rest? When resting, there is trusting. In trusting, there is believing in God and what He said and says.*

*The children of Israel did not enter their Promised Land because of unbelief. God calls unbelief disobedience.*

*In Deuteronomy 28, God says to listen to His voice and obey and all these blessings will follow you.*

*Now choose you this day whom you will serve, belief or unbelief, rest or labor, obedience or disobedience, trust or doubt, faith or fear. Let us choose the God of Abraham, Isaac, Jacob and His Son, Jesus Christ of Nazareth through the power of His Holy Spirit.*

*"We say by the power of Your Spirit and with Your grace and mercy working in us, 'We choose You, Lord! We walk in rest today!'"*

\*\*\*

*"And to whom swore He that they should not enter into His rest, but to them that believed not? (19) So we see that they could not enter in because of unbelief." Hebrews 3:18–19*

## JANUARY 24
### THIS IS THE DAY THAT THE LORD HAS MADE. I WILL REJOICE AND BE GLAD IN IT.

*Let us rejoice that we have authority over every evil thing. At His Name, the name of Jesus, demons flee.*

*Let us ponder: "Have I been washed in the Blood? Letting the Blood wash me on the inside. Evil cannot cast out evil. First I must be made clean, and then I can help to clean out the other person. The log that is in my eye hinders me from helping my neighbor get the speck out of his. Satan must not find any of himself in me. As long as I am harboring his friends, the Holy Spirit's ability to use me is weakened. But once I allow the Holy Spirit to search me and know me—to see if there be any wicked way in me, I will experience His power flowing through me in a more profound way to set the captives free!"*

*Today is the day of salvation and it begins with judgment in the house of God (I Peter 4:17). I am, you are, the house of God. Judgment of our enemies means uncovering evil within us—confessing, repenting, asking forgiveness, expelling of evil, and destroying their strongholds. Evil has a harvest. We do not want to experience the harvest Satan desires to reap.*

\*\*\*

*"See, I have this day set thee over the nations and over the kingdoms, to root out, and to pull down, and to destroy, and to throw down, to build, and to plant." Jeremiah 1:10*

*"You hypocrite, first cast out the beam out of your own eye; and then shall you see clearly to cast out the mote out of your brother's eye." Matthew 7:5*

## JANUARY 25
### THIS IS THE DAY THAT THE LORD HAS MADE. I WILL REJOICE AND BE GLAD IN IT.

*What is rejoicing? What is forgetting about ourselves and getting our eyes upon the Lord Jesus Christ, His Father and their Spirit? That is rejoicing!*

*We become so bogged down with the things we see with our physical eyes. Let us try walking around with our eyes blindfolded, our ears plugged up, and our mouth taped shut. That is walking in the Spirit. He wants us so sensitive to His Spirit that we are like the blind, deaf, and dumb. We are to walk by faith, not by sight. How can we do that? Therein lies a lot of transforming of the mind! A lot! For we have grown up using our physical eyes, ears, and mouth. There is a lot of transforming as Paul talks about in Romans 12, before we know the perfect will of God.*

*Oh, may we and our children not be so deceived as to walk by sight and not by faith! Our prayer—*

*"Oh Lord, have mercy upon us as we know You are merciful. Have mercy and continue to lead us into a life lived in Your Spirit and not according to our flesh. Oh Lord, have mercy! Christ, have mercy!*

*"Lord, have mercy!"*

\*\*\*

*"And be not conformed to this world: but be you transformed by the renewing of your mind, that you may prove what is that good, and acceptable, and perfect, will of God." Romans 12:2*

*"(For we walk by faith, not by sight.)" II Corinthians 5:7*

## JANUARY 26
### THIS IS THE DAY THAT THE LORD HAS MADE. I WILL REJOICE AND BE GLAD IN IT.

*Let us talk about being happy. Some Christians say that Scripture does not say that we should be happy, but should have joy. Well, let us consider these Scriptures:*

*"Happy is that people, that is in such a case: yea, happy is that people, whose God is the LORD." Psalm 144:15*

*"Happy is he that hath the God of Jacob for his help, whose hope is in the LORD his God:" Psalm 146:5*

*"Happy is the man that finds wisdom, and the man that gets understanding." Proverbs 3:13*

*"He that handles a matter wisely shall find good: and whoso trusts in the LORD, happy is he." Proverbs 16:20*

*"Where there is no vision, the people perish: but he that keeps the law, happy is he." Proverbs 29:18*

*"But and if you suffer for righteousness' sake, happy are you: and be not afraid of their terror, neither be troubled;" I Peter 3:14*

*"If you be reproached for the name of Christ, happy are you; for the spirit of glory and of God rests upon you: on their part He is evil spoken of, but on your part He is glorified." I Peter 4:14*

*It appears from the Scriptures of God that we Christians can be HAPPY!*

\*\*\*

*"So shall My word be that goes forth out of My mouth: it shall not return unto Me void, but it shall accomplish that which I please, and it shall prosper in the thing whereto I sent it." Isaiah 55:11*

## JANUARY 27
### THIS IS THE DAY THAT THE LORD HAS MADE. I WILL REJOICE AND BE GLAD IN IT.

*"Let us see the sin and suffering surrounding us, and let us cry out to You for mercy. Let us cry out for You to burn within us love for our brothers and sisters. Oh! Father, that our hearts would burn with Your compassion which would propel us into Your arms for help and mercy.*

*"Oh God, burn in our hearts a fire that will not be quenched until we are walking in Your peace, joy and love; a fire that will not be quenched until our hearts and minds are consumed with desire for You—to know You, to serve You, to bless You, to seek You, to follow You, to please You, to extol You, to praise, thank, and to worship You, to talk with You, to know Your voice!*

*"Leave us not alone until You have us— heart, soul, and body. Amen."*

\*\*\*

*"A new heart also will I give you, and a new spirit will I put within you: and I will take away the stony heart out of your flesh, and I will give you a heart of flesh." Ezekiel 36:26*

## JANUARY 28
### THIS IS THE DAY THAT THE LORD HAS MADE. I WILL REJOICE AND BE GLAD IN IT.

*Forgive that your sins may be forgiven you. Who has sinned as much as I? Yet, God forgives, because He accepts Jesus' sacrifice of Himself. No one knows his own heart, but God.*

*We have all sinned and come short of the glory of God. All our works are as filthy rags. Oh woe is me! Who can deliver me from my shortcomings? Christ has delivered me. He loves me, adores me, takes care of me. He has made a way for me, and it is the cross. I too must carry my cross daily.*

*What is that cross? It is the thing you wish would go away and stop bothering you. It is attached to some part of your self you are hanging unto. Go ahead, raise your arms in surrender and let go!*

*Jesus let go in the garden when He said, "Not My will, but Yours be done." It meant His death on a cross. You have to make the same decision to surrender your life and all your fears to your Father. That thing that continues to hinder your walk, carry it to the cross of Jesus, let go of it, lay it down at the foot of the cross and follow Him. This is not a one-time occurrence. He said, "Daily."*

*Carrying your cross daily means to continue to walk in a dependent, surrendered position with your Father God. From this position of surrender comes peace that passes your understanding.*

\*\*\*

*"Then said Jesus unto His disciples, If any man will come after Me, let him deny himself, and take up his cross, and follow Me."*
*Matthew 16:24*

## JANUARY 29
## THIS IS THE DAY THAT THE LORD HAS MADE. I WILL REJOICE AND BE GLAD IN IT.

*This day is a day for celebrating the Lord. Worshiping Him and recalling all His marvelous deeds to His children.*

*Bless Him with a recorded testimony of His deeds toward you. Recall His marvelous acts of deliverance. Recall His marvelous acts of tender love toward you.*

*Oh, can you praise His name for the difficult situations He has taken you through?! Thanking Him for His marvelous gifts to you and mankind.*

*You cannot praise Him simply for the things He's done for you. Your praise will automatically overflow concerning the mighty acts for others. Consider not yourself as a lone ranger of blessings. His blessings spill over to others in your vicinity. God's flow never stops.*

*Seek Him and His blessings will follow. Seek blessings and disappointments will follow.*

\*\*\*

*"I will bless the LORD at all times: His praise shall continually be in my mouth." Psalm 34:1*

## THIS IS THE DAY THAT THE LORD HAS MADE. I WILL REJOICE AND BE GLAD IN IT.

*Every day has its own anxieties. So don't think about the anxieties of tomorrow.*

*But for today think on these things...*

*"Trust in the Lord with all your heart; and lean not unto your own understanding. In all your ways acknowledge Him, and He shall direct your paths." (Proverbs 3:5–6)*

*Say to the Lord:*

*"You are my Shepherd, I shall not want for anything. You cause me to lie down in green pastures. Those are places of plenty.*

*"You lead me beside still waters. Those are peaceful places.*

*"You restore my soul. You heal my emotions and my mind.*

*"You lead me in paths of righteousness for Your name sake. Those are paths that keep me in right standing with You.*

*"And even as I walk through the valley of the shadow of death, Your rod and Your staff shall comfort me. Blessed are they who mourn for they shall be comforted.*

*"You prepare a table before me in the presence of my enemies. I am prepared to win against my enemies.*

*"You anoint my head with oil. I have been given Your yoke-destroying, burden-removing power.*

*"And my cup runs over. I shall bless others too. You have blessed me so I can be a blessing.*

*"Surely goodness and mercy shall follow me all the days of my life.*

✝

*"You make me say, 'Good things happen to me everyday and mercy is with me every day.'*

*"And I shall dwell in the house of the Lord forever. The house of the Lord is my reborn spirit and that is where I live.*

*"I walk in the Spirit and not in the flesh."*

\*\*\*

*"The LORD is my Shepherd; I shall not want. (2) He makes me to lie down in green pastures: He leads me beside the still waters. (3) He restores my soul: He leads me in the paths of righteousness for His name's sake. (4) Yea, though I walk through the valley of the shadow of death, I will fear no evil: for You are with me; Your rod and Your staff they comfort me. (5) You prepare a table before me in the presence of my enemies: You anoint my head with oil; my cup runs over. (6) Surely goodness and mercy shall follow me all the days of my life: and I will dwell in the house of the LORD for ever."*
*Psalm 23*

## THIS IS THE DAY THAT THE LORD HAS MADE. I WILL REJOICE AND BE GLAD IN IT.

*This is the last day of the month, very much like the last day of the year. Take stock of goals, and determine what should be happening in the next month.*

*Pray and seek the Lord with diligence today. Renew your passion for Him.*

*Stay up all night and pray (Luke 6:12). It will help you to return to a narrower path. Narrow is the way to life and broad is the path to destruction (Matthew 7:14).*

*Keep your life disciplined (I Corinthians 9:27).*

*Do not be caught without oil in your lamp, when the bridegroom comes (Matthew 25:1ff).*

*Do not be caught doing bad things, when the owner of the house returns (Luke 20:9ff).*

*And do not have buried your treasure, when the Boss returns to receive His returns (Matthew 25:18).*

*Awake! Awake! Do not be found wanting. But be found ready and waiting "with a full tank of gas" (Romans 13:11).*

*Watch! for you do not know the day or time of His return (Mark 13:35).*

\*\*\*

*"And that, knowing the time, that now it is high time to awake out of sleep: for now is our salvation nearer than when we believed."*
*Romans 13:11*

# FEBRUARY

*And He said unto them, "If any man will come after Me, let him deny himself, and take up his cross daily, and follow Me."*

LUKE 9:23

## FEBRUARY 1
### THIS IS THE DAY THAT THE LORD HAS MADE. I WILL REJOICE AND BE GLAD IN IT.

*Oh, Hallelujah! Sing unto the Lord. He has given us a new month with new goals to meet.*

*"Oh Lord, burn in our hearts what we can do to propel Your coming forth on earth, as well as in each heart."*

*"So that you come behind in no gift; waiting for the coming of our Lord Jesus Christ:" I Corinthians 1:7*

*"A strong force is many united peoples. Let us come together and unite our voices in cries for our hearts to be turned to You, O Lord!"*

*So many are wandering…some with unfounded hope, but hope none the less…some without hope, which may be better than unfounded hope. The Hope of the world has come into the world and we knew Him not.*

*"Oh, open our eyes that we may see! Open our ears! Turn our hearts to You, O Lord!"*

\*\*\*

*"He was in the world, and the world was made by Him, and the world knew Him not." John 1:10*

## FEBRUARY 2
## THIS IS THE DAY THAT THE LORD HAS MADE. I WILL REJOICE AND BE GLAD IN IT.

*Give thanks unto the Lord for He has triumphed gloriously.*

*If you feel defeated, it is a lie from Satan. Do not believe his fairy tales. The truth will set you free. Seek the God of Abraham, Isaac and Jacob and you shall receive the truth, which will displace the lies (deceptions) you are living in and under.*

*Arouse yourself! Do not sleep in the midst of the battle. Do not lie down and sleep. It is time for arousal! It is time to fall back into His arms of love and mercy, surrendering to Him, trusting Him in all things. That is the battle we fight—surrendering—falling back into His arms—trusting Him—trusting His goodness. It is time to be busy searching for our God of love. For He said, "Those that seek Me with all their heart shall find Me." (Jeremiah 29:13) "And those that put their trust in Me shall never be put to shame." (Psalm 25:20)*

*"Father, individually we say, 'I fall back into Your arms of Love! I surrender to You, to Your goodness, mercy and lovingkindness.'"*

\*\*\*

*"Show Your marvelous lovingkindness, O You that save by Your right hand them which put their trust in You from those that rise up against them." Psalm 17:7*

*"How excellent is Your lovingkindness, O God! Therefore the children of men put their trust under the shadow of Your wings." Psalm 36:7*

## FEBRUARY 3
### THIS IS THE DAY THAT THE LORD HAS MADE. I WILL REJOICE AND BE GLAD IN IT.

*He is calling us to a Sabbath Rest. If we rest in Him, we receive His Holiness for He is Holy.*

*Relinquish your members to Him in the morning. Throughout the day fall back into His arms with assurance that He will inhabit your life, if you have given Him permission.*

*Now go forward with faith and assurance that He will be faithful to lead you. This is walking in trust and rest.*

*Our Father is big enough to grab hold of us, if we're going the wrong way. That is exactly what He will do.*

*Yes. Yes. Yes.*

**Come unto Me, all ye who labor and are heavy laden, and I will give you rest.**

\*\*\*

"For he that is entered into his rest, he also has ceased from his own works, as God did from His. (11) Let us labor therefore to enter into that rest, lest any man fall after the same example of unbelief." Hebrews 4:10–11

"Cause me to hear Your lovingkindness in the morning; for in Thee do I trust: cause me to know the way wherein I should walk; for I lift up my soul unto Thee." Psalm 143:8

## ✝
### FEBRUARY 4
## THIS IS THE DAY THAT THE LORD HAS MADE. I WILL REJOICE AND BE GLAD IN IT.

*"Come unto Me, all ye that labor and are heavy laden, and I will give you rest." (Matthew 11:28)*

*Oh, hallelujah! He will give rest. There is no one else who will give rest.*

*His love is free and unconditional. He wants only what is needed to bless us.*

*He does not take from a dry well, but replenishes it. He does not ask for what is not there, except in faith believing.*

*He knows your heart intimately. He knows your strength and when your strength is gone, His strength kicks in (II Corinthians 12:10).*

*Oh give thanks to the Lord! He is our supplier of plenty. He supplies all things. He made all things. He receives all things. He loves all things. He sees all things. He abides in all things. He is everywhere and in everything.*

*There is nowhere you can go that He is not.*

*Oh, give thanks to the Lord! He is good. His mercy endures forever, and His mercy is available right now.*

\*\*\*

*"O give thanks unto the LORD, for He is good: for His mercy endures for ever." Psalm 136:1*

*"You are good, and do good; teach me Your statutes." Psalm 119:68*

# FEBRUARY 5
## THIS IS THE DAY THAT THE LORD HAS MADE. I WILL REJOICE AND BE GLAD IN IT.

*Do you not stand amazed at how good and faithful God is? He is faithful all the time, for He is Faithful. Just as He is Love, He is Faithful.*

*He takes care of us when we do not know we need taking care of. Just like parents take care of their children when the children are too young to know they need taking care of.*

*You do not walk this earth alone. He is always with you, so when you feel fretful, worried, and anxious, remember He is right there—beside you, in you, with you! And if He's right there, then you have the wisdom available to know whatever you need to know.*

*Please, whatever your problem, come to Me. Keep coming to Me. I have the solution. I have the life-giving answers to all problems, and from My solutions will come help for others also. Trust Me.*

\*\*\*

"And I will betroth you unto Me for ever, yes, I will betroth you unto Me in righteousness, and in judgment, and in lovingkindness, and in mercies. (20) I will even betroth you unto Me in faithfulness: and you shall know the LORD." Hosea 2:19–20

"Cause me to hear Your lovingkindness in the morning; for in You do I trust: cause me to know the way wherein I should walk; for I lift up my soul unto You." Psalm 143:8

## FEBRUARY 6
### THIS IS THE DAY THAT THE LORD HAS MADE. I WILL REJOICE AND BE GLAD IN IT.

*What gain is there in trusting the Lord when everything in your physical world is taken care of and everything is done and in order? It's like the verse that says, "even sinners love those that love them." ("For if you love them which love you, what thank have you? for sinners also love those that love them." Luke 6:32) Anyone can trust when there are no problems in sight.*

*But to trust the Lord Almighty when the money is not there... the time is not there... the love is not there... the affirmation is not there... the health is not there... that is REAL trusting.*

*To rely upon completely is trusting. When there seems to be no way, and you still walk in peace; when you're thrown into the fiery furnace and you still trust, that's the trust God wants from us, and the trust we want to walk in.*

*How does one develop this trust? By walking in uncertain circumstances. Circumstances that appear to have nothing good about them. In other words, there's a storm. There's no way to get to the other side or survive. You cry out to Jesus. He calms the storm, and immediately you're at the other side. Or better yet, you are sleeping in the back of the boat with Jesus. Read about it in Mark 4:35–41 and John 6:17–21.*

\*\*\*

*"And He was in the hinder part of the ship, asleep on a pillow: and they awake Him, and say unto Him, Master, do You not care that we perish? (39) And He arose, and rebuked the wind, and said unto the sea, Peace, be still. And the wind ceased, and there was a great calm." Mark 4:38–39*

## FEBRUARY 7

### THIS IS THE DAY THAT THE LORD HAS MADE. I WILL REJOICE AND BE GLAD IN IT.

*How do I love you?*

*Let Me love you. Let Me caress you, hold you safely in My arms.*

*Feel My strength that makes void any attacks at you. Rest in My arms. My Body supporting you as you lean completely upon Me. I AM there.*

*You have to come in touch with the Spirit world. Those who live all their time in this physical world will miss Me. They'll never know My embraces, My strong support.*

*I wait for My children to come to Me. But they're running to and fro, to and fro. Satan has so deceived My children that they hardly know Me.*

*They have no idea how easy it is to commune with Me, but not as long as the world makes up 90% of their time.*

*I AM waiting to love you.*

\*\*\*

*"For thus says the Lord GOD, the Holy One of Israel; In returning and rest shall you be saved; in quietness and in confidence shall be your strength: and you would not… (18) And therefore will the LORD wait, that He may be gracious unto you…" Isaiah 30:15 & 18a*

## FEBRUARY 8
## THIS IS THE DAY THAT THE LORD HAS MADE. I WILL REJOICE AND BE GLAD IN IT.

*Enter His gates with thanksgiving and His courts with praise.*

*Sing aloud unto the Lord and sing in your heart to the Lord. He has triumphed o'er your foes.*

*Give a joyful noise unto all you see. He has given you enough victories over which to rejoice.*

*And the victories that have yet to be manifested, you can by faith rejoice in those also.*

*Trust in God.*

*Do you not think that it pleases God, when He sees His child rejoicing in bad circumstances; because the child knows His Father is going to bring victory in it. That is why we can always rejoice.*

*Rejoice!*

*And again I say rejoice!*

\*\*\*

*"And at midnight Paul and Silas prayed, and sang praises unto God… (26) And suddenly there was a great earthquake, so that the foundations of the prison were shaken: and immediately all the doors were opened, and every one's bands were loosed."*
*Acts 16:25a, & 26*

## FEBRUARY 9

### THIS IS THE DAY THAT THE LORD HAS MADE. I WILL REJOICE AND BE GLAD IN IT.

*He is worthy to be praised—no matter the condition of your heart. It matters not that you are downcast, worried, distraught, distracted, overcome...Praise Him! He is worthy of praise— not because you feel good, but because He is good! Don't look at your heart. Look at His! Don't look at your circumstances. That's what Satan wants you to do. Look at Him.*

*Those that keep their mind on Him are in perfect peace! (Isaiah 26:3) If you're not in peace, your mind is on something or someone besides Jesus.*

*Now change your course. You have the ability. Jesus provided that ability by His Spirit that is in you. Don't say you cannot praise Him or think about Him. That's a lie from Satan. If God said to praise Him, then you can. If only you will.*

*"Lord, have mercy upon us! Come to us with Your great love and overcome, over-shadow all that is within us that keeps us from experiencing Your great love! In the mighty name of Jesus, amen!"*

\*\*\*

*"Finally, brethren, whatsoever things are true, whatsoever things are honest, whatsoever things are just, whatsoever things are pure, whatsoever things are lovely, whatsoever things are of good report; if there be any virtue, and if there be any praise, think on these things." Philippians 4:8*

## ✝
### FEBRUARY 10
### THIS IS THE DAY THAT THE LORD HAS MADE. I WILL REJOICE AND BE GLAD IN IT.

*It is time to rejoice! We have been ignorant long enough.*

*"Oh, Father! Establish in us Your joy, and we thank You for it."*

*It is a work of grace.*

*He continues to seek for a praying, interceding human to bring forth His will on earth.*

*It is through God and each of us that His will is brought forth. Seek His face so you can be His hand on earth.*

*We seek Him not just for His will to be done on earth, but because we want to know Him, as a friend knows a friend and a wife knows a husband.*

*Our Father is more interested in a relationship with us individually than accomplishing His will on earth. He loves us. Adores us. We are the apple of His eye and He has provided all things for us. Hallelujah! Our God is good and He does good! All the Time!*

\*\*\*

*"And you shall love the Lord your God with all your heart, and with all your soul, and with all your mind, and with all your strength: this is the first commandment." Mark 12:30*

## FEBRUARY 11
### THIS IS THE DAY THAT THE LORD HAS MADE. I WILL REJOICE AND BE GLAD IN IT.

*How is it so many of My children are restless and tormented by time?*

*I have given them everything that pertains to life and godliness.*

*Come unto Me all who are weary and heavy laden and I will give you rest. I give rest. Only I give rest.*

*Sleep gives rest to your body, but not your soul. It is a temporary rest for your soul that needs replenishing over and over.*

*But the rest that I give to your soul is eternal. It is a restoring of your soul that I spoke of in Psalms. Come to Me—I'll give you rest.*

*It can be found nowhere else. No where!*

*The enemy of your soul has distracted you with much good. Will you turn from your wicked ways and return to Me? Selah.*

\*\*\*

"Many will say to Me in that day, Lord, Lord, have we not prophesied in Your name? And in Your name have cast out devils? And in Your name done many wonderful works? And then will I profess unto them I never knew you: depart from Me, you that work iniquity."
Matthew 7:22–23

## FEBRUARY 12
## THIS IS THE DAY THAT THE LORD HAS MADE. I WILL REJOICE AND BE GLAD IN IT.

*Come.*

*The Father continues to call His children.*

*Come.*

*Who will answer His call?*

*Come to the quiet, the calm, the still, so you can hear, feel, and experience your Father, your Savior and Brother, the Lover of your soul. He calls out to, "Come," only so He can bless you, heal you, save you, restore you, prosper you, endue you with power. And most of all, He yearns to enable you to receive His love.*

*Will you come?*

*Will you separate yourself from the world including the worldly church? He waits to be gracious to you.*

*Will you come?*

*Say, "Yes, I come."*

\*\*\*

*"My Beloved spoke, and said unto me, Rise up, My love, My fair one, and come away." Song of Solomon 2:10*

## FEBRUARY 13
### THIS IS THE DAY THAT THE LORD HAS MADE. I WILL REJOICE AND BE GLAD IN IT.

*It is right for us to give Him praise and thanksgiving.*

*For no matter the appearance of the situation, our Father has a way out that is good.*

*His ways are good. Every good and perfect gift comes from above (James 1:17).*

*Come unto Him. He continues to call His children to come. What shall we say except, "I come." What Father is lonely that does not call for His children? God has prepared the way, shown the way, and made the way to His heart. It is Jesus.*

*It is in silence you shall hear Him, see Him, feel Him and know Him.*

*How He longs to heal and deliver, but you would not.*

*This is the day to come.*

*Will you?*

\*\*\*

*"For thus says the Lord GOD, the Holy One of Israel; In returning and rest shall you be saved; in quietness and in confidence shall be your strength: and you would not." Isaiah 30:15*

## FEBRUARY 14
### THIS IS THE DAY THAT THE LORD HAS MADE. I WILL REJOICE AND BE GLAD IN IT.

*Come unto Me all ye who are weary and heavy laden and I will give you rest.*

*Rest for your soul and your body.*

*Restoration for both.*

*For it is I who heals and restores. How can I take care of you if you never or rarely succumb to the Master's touch?*

*It is I who restores, redeems the years the locusts have eaten. How can I do that, if I never or rarely have My hands upon you?*

*It is I who loves you, created you and destined you for greatness—everyone—not just a few.*

*Come unto Me and learn of Me. Stop learning of you and him and her and it.*

*Stop! And come unto Me.*

\*\*\*

*"I sleep, but my heart wakes: it is the voice of my Beloved that knocks, saying, Open to Me, My sister, My love, My dove, My undefiled: for My head is filled with dew, and My locks with the drops of the night." Song of Solomon 5:2*

## FEBRUARY 15
### THIS IS THE DAY THAT THE LORD HAS MADE. I WILL REJOICE AND BE GLAD IN IT.

*Today we consider to whom we submit.*

*As far as possible we are to live at peace with all men (Romans 12:18).*

*We submit to those in authority over us (Hebrews 13:17). However first and foremost is our obedience and submission to the Lord Jesus Christ (Mark 12:30).*

*Who is lord in your life?*

*How can you determine who is lord of your life? Is it Jesus Christ? Your husband? Your wife? Your job? Your health? The health of your loved ones? Your friend, whose feelings you do not want to hurt, even at the cost of disobedience to God's instructions to you?*

*Think about it. Who do you fear? Who or what do you consider and give most of your thoughts and emotions to?*

*Is it someone or something else other than your Father?*

*Selah.*

\*\*\*

*"The fear of man brings a snare: but whoso puts his trust in the LORD shall be safe." Proverbs 29:25*

## FEBRUARY 16
## THIS IS THE DAY THAT THE LORD HAS MADE. I WILL REJOICE AND BE GLAD IN IT.

*O come unto Me, you who are weary and seek to be comforted by your Father.*

*I am here to love you and tend to you. You are the apple of My eye and all that I have is yours. All that I desire is you. I have made you for My praise and for My praise you shall live.*

*Come unto Me, when fear tries to intrude upon your mind.*

*Come unto Me, when doubt and discouragement come to you, you come to Me. My presence will annihilate them.*

*You see, no evil can remain in My presence and My presence rides in on the wings of praise!*

*Listen to the birds.*

*They sing praises to Me, and I do not forget them.*

*Look at the flowers.*

*They lift their heads to Me in praise, and I clothe them.*

*And look at the young children, they walk in quiet assurance of My care.*

*Can you be like a child?*

\*\*\*

*"Verily I say unto you, Whosoever shall not receive the kingdom of God as a little child shall in no wise enter therein." Luke 18:17*

# ✝
## FEBRUARY 17
### THIS IS THE DAY THAT THE LORD HAS MADE. I WILL REJOICE AND BE GLAD IN IT.

*This is the day that the Lord has made.*

*Is He the Lord of your day?*

*Can He do with you as He pleases?*

*Are you supple in His Hands?*

*Have you relinquished to Him your rights?*

*Then, yes, He is the Lord of your day.*

*What does all this mean?*

*Say to Him, "Father, my body is Yours today. I want it to go, do, see, say, eat, think, feel, what You would if You were living now on earth. I am at Your disposal."*

*Say this to Him with as much sincerity as you have and He will accept it. Your offer and His grace will fill in what is lacking. A willing heart is what our Father is looking for.*

*Please surrender yours to Him today, and see what a day in the Spirit will do!*

\*\*\*

*"But now, O LORD, You are our Father; we are the clay, and You our potter, and we all are the work of Your hand." Isaiah 64:8*

*"Then said I, Lo, I come (in the volume of the book it is written of Me,) to do Thy will, O God." Hebrews 10:7*

## FEBRUARY 18
### THIS IS THE DAY THAT THE LORD HAS MADE. I WILL REJOICE AND BE GLAD IN IT.

*Oh, listen you who seek righteousness. There is none righteous, but My Son. So seek Him and all these things will be added unto you.*

*You think you know what is going to happen in the future, but be aware; My plans for you are for good, to give you a future. My plans are for a future. Your perceptions are short and narrow, but I have eternity in view!*

*Do you think that you can perceive the things of God? My ways are higher than your ways! Rejoice and be glad for My ways are higher than your ways and My ways are the way in which you shall go.*

*I have plans from the beginning of time that shall come to pass.*

*I will have My way.*

\*\*\*

*"For I know the thoughts that I think toward you, says the LORD, thoughts of peace, and not of evil, to give you an expected end." Jeremiah 29:11*

## FEBRUARY 19
### THIS IS THE DAY THAT THE LORD HAS MADE. I WILL REJOICE AND BE GLAD IN IT.

*Let us rejoice as the Holy Spirit expends His work of conviction. Without cleansing, we cannot receive the holiness of God. We must seek His mercy daily of searching our hearts and seeing if there is any wicked way in us and leading us into paths of righteousness (Psalm 139:23–24).*

*Without His mercy and grace turning us from our wicked way, we cannot and will not turn.*

*Oh, we cry out for a Spirit of repentance to be shed abroad in this country among believers and unbelievers. We must cry out in reliance, total humility, before God for Him to turn us and we will be turned.*

*We must be made aware of our own wickedness or we will continue in ignorance, believing we are doing well.*

*"Oh, Father, send Your Spirit of Truth to set us free from the deceptions we live under.*

*"Unless You move, we are lost and undone."*

\*\*\*

*"Nevertheless I tell you the truth; It is expedient for you that I go away: for if I go not away, the Comforter will not come unto you; but if I depart, I will send Him unto you. And when He is come, He will reprove the world of sin, and of righteousness, and of judgment:" John 16:7–8*

## FEBRUARY 20
### THIS IS THE DAY THAT THE LORD HAS MADE. I WILL REJOICE AND BE GLAD IN IT.

*Oh, give thanks to the Lord! He is in control. Think on Him. Do not give worry or concern a moment's pleasure. Cast all your cares upon Him for He cares for you. Let all your petitions be known to Him with thanksgiving. Tell Him all your problems and then say "Thank You," because you know He's your Father and He cares for you and takes care of you.*

*Is anything too hard for God? Is anything too small for God?*

*No. No. He will restore to you the years the locusts have eaten. He will renew your youth and make your light shine.*

**Oh, come to Me, My children. As I see you wail and groan under the rule of a hard taskmaster, I cry for you.**

**Oh, come to Me. I own You. You are Mine. You do not have to live under Satan's reign. My Son has forever defeated him. Do not linger in his arena or you will find yourself aligned with him—loving him and not knowing the difference between truth and deception.**

*Come to Me. I continue to call and few answer.*

\*\*\*

"Be careful for nothing; but in every thing by prayer and supplication with thanksgiving let your requests be made known unto God. (7) And the peace of God, which passes all understanding, shall keep your hearts and minds through Christ Jesus." Philippians 4:6–7

"For many are called, but few are chosen." Matthew 22:14

† 

## FEBRUARY 21

## THIS IS THE DAY THAT THE LORD HAS MADE. I WILL REJOICE AND BE GLAD IN IT.

*This is the day to rejoice—not tomorrow—not when issues are settled. Rejoice, today!*

*Lighten the frown on your face with a smile. Relax the tension on your face with a smile.*

*Get alone with God. He misses you and would like to spend some time with you. Read a spiritual book, take a walk outside to simply enjoy His creation, or watch a funny movie!*

*Oh, you don't have time to be quiet and still, or just relax and daydream? Well, ask yourself this, "Do you have time to live?"*

*Seriously, God has given His all to us, may we be given His grace to give back to Him. Not having time for God only reveals our lack of love for Him, and the lack of His love working in our lives.*

*Do you have time to read the Bible, pray, listen, praise?*

*If you don't, please know that your Father misses you, and desires above all else to see you and talk with you, for He wants to shower you with blessings! There may be many lessons to learn before receiving any rewards. Remember the five wise virgins, and the five foolish ones.*

*Which one are you?*

\*\*\*

*Matthew 25:1–13*

## FEBRUARY 22
### THIS IS THE DAY THAT THE LORD HAS MADE. I WILL REJOICE AND BE GLAD IN IT.

*God is not a forceful taskmaster. He is a loving Father, Husband and Judge. One Who loves with an everlasting love.*

*See… we cannot do or say or think anything that would stop Him from loving us. He is Love!*

*He loves no matter the state of the person. However, and this is a big however, you can stop His love from coming to you. This is done by not receiving His love. His love is there. Will you receive it?*

*If you don't or can't receive it, you will not know His great love for you. It is like electricity being in the outlet, but no receptacle plugged into it. The electricity is always there, but nothing is plugged in to receive the flow of electricity.*

*How do we get plugged into God? Ask Him to plug you in. Tell Him of your desire to know Him and His love. He will answer that prayer. Some of the ways that He has led me to get plugged in are: by my spirit communing with His Spirit in quietness and stillness; talking to Him, He talks to me; I wait upon Him, He comes to me; I read His Word, meditate on His Word, sing His Word, and He develops an uninterrupted wide flow of His love, power, mercy, kindness, gentleness, patience, thoughtfulness! Whatever I need!*

*Hallelujah! His mercy is all we need, and His mercy He has given!*

\*\*\*

*"Surely goodness and mercy shall follow me all the days of my life: and I will dwell in the house of the LORD for ever." Psalm 23:6*

## FEBRUARY 23
### THIS IS THE DAY THAT THE LORD HAS MADE. I WILL REJOICE AND BE GLAD IN IT.

*Oh, hear the words of the Lord! He commands us, instructs us, and encourages us to rejoice in all circumstances. In knowing God, we can rejoice easily, because He is a good God!*

*Good, we understand. And bad, we know and we don't like.*

*How can the bad things in our life reconcile with God's goodness? I heard the Spirit say to me,*

*There is evil and the protection of the blood is sufficient.*

*Plead the blood of My Son. It is sufficient to repel evil from your midst. Once My Son's blood is pled, the enemies of your flesh and soul have no authority or power to harm you! It is pleading the blood that denies the attacks of Satan. It is pleading the blood that renders your enemies helpless and harmless. They cannot, and have no right, and are acknowledged as impotent to carry through their claims.*

*They come with accusations and the blood rises up and says, "It's already been tried and the case is closed and the penalty has been declared and already paid! The judgment made and the debt paid. You cannot come and exact further payment for crimes and sentences already satisfied! The judgment was decided! The sentence to pay for the crime has been finished. A person cannot serve another sentence for the same crime or crimes that have already been paid for. The case is closed! You have no right to come against this person!"*

\*\*\*

*"And they overcame him by the blood of the Lamb, and by the word of their testimony; and they loved not their lives unto the death." Revelation 12:11*

## FEBRUARY 24
### THIS IS THE DAY THAT THE LORD HAS MADE. I WILL REJOICE AND BE GLAD IN IT.

*It is I who has called you. You did not choose Me until I chose you.*

*Therefore whatever I have called, I will equip.*

*Why worry?*

*Why be concerned about yourself? It is I Who work and you who rest. As a matter of fact, I have already worked and My work is finished.*

*Obey My commandment to love Me with all your heart, soul, and body, and your neighbor; and you shall know My will and follow in My ways.*

*For My yoke is easy and My burden is light. Is that not good news!*

*Learn of Me.*

\*\*\*

*"You have not chosen Me, but I have chosen you, and ordained you, that you should go and bring forth fruit, and that your fruit should remain: that whatsoever you shall ask of the Father in My name, He may give it you. (17) These things I command you, that you love one another." John 15:16–17*

# FEBRUARY 25

## THIS IS THE DAY THAT THE LORD HAS MADE. I WILL REJOICE AND BE GLAD IN IT.

*Oh, the peace of God comes from knowing our God! In knowing Him comes confidence to know all things work together for good to those that love Him and are called according to His purpose (Romans 8:28).*

*He is forever in our midst and in the midst of our circumstances. Isn't it good to know He is working all things for our good and to His glory? He is looking for those who can believe and those who will believe in Him and His goodness.*

*All things are possible to those who believe. The manifestation of the "all things" may not look like what you were or are believing. His ways are higher than ours. We must look at this earthly life from an eternal perspective, a heavenly vision, God's viewpoint (Colossians 3:1–2). He knows the end from the beginning. Jesus came to save the world and destroy the works of Satan. The cross did not look like victory. It was. Your situation may not look like "all things are possible." Trust and wait for the eternal outcome orchestrated by your Father.*

*It was unbelief in Father God that kept the Israelites out of the Promised Land. We cannot relieve ourselves of the responsibility of believing. But in knowing God (Who He is and what He does), it is easier to believe.*

*Seek to know the Most High God, and in knowing, believing will follow.*

\*\*\*

*"Jesus said unto him, If you can believe, all things are possible to him that believes." Mark 9:23*

*"And to whom swore He that they should not enter into His rest, but to them that believed not? (19) So we see that they could not enter in because of unbelief." Hebrews 3:18–19*

## FEBRUARY 26
### THIS IS THE DAY THAT THE LORD HAS MADE. I WILL REJOICE AND BE GLAD IN IT.

*Oh, give thanks to the Lord! But know for what and to whom you are giving thanks.*

*Ignorance is no excuse in the law, as well as in the Kingdom of God.*

*We must seek to know the Most High God. He has made Himself known in nature and more preeminently in His Son. We have no excuse (Romans 1:19–20) for not knowing God.*

*Let us seek to know Him. "And this is eternal life that they might know You the only true God, and Jesus Christ whom You have sent." (John 17:3)*

*His Spirit is wooing us to Himself. But we are looking in all directions of the physical for love, peace and joy; until the physical proves itself not to be sufficient.*

*Why must we seek in all other areas before we will come to the Most High God? Let us save ourselves some time and trouble, and come first to the Most High God.*

\*\*\*

*"But seek ye first the kingdom of God, and His righteousness; and all these things shall be added unto you." Matthew 6:33*

*"That all the people of the earth may know that the LORD is God, and that there is none else." I Kings 8:60*

## THIS IS THE DAY THAT THE LORD HAS MADE. I WILL REJOICE AND BE GLAD IN IT.

*Oh, come unto the Most High! Rejoice and be glad!*

*He has worked out all things for your good. When evil comes lurking, you can laugh at it. God does!*

*Oh, come and see the goodness of God! Search the Scriptures. His goodness is unsearchable. Search and keep searching. You cannot and will not exhaust His goodness.*

*Get to know Him and all things—all things crumble under His goodness.*

*Have faith in God. Have the God kind of faith.*

**When I spoke, "Let there be light," it did not appear instantaneously, but it did appear. You just don't know Me nor My ways. But you can. Seek Me and you will find Me when you seek Me with ALL your heart.**

\*\*\*

*"He that sits in the heavens shall laugh: the Lord shall have them in derision." Psalm 2:4*

*"And you shall seek Me, and find Me, when you shall search for Me with all your heart." Jeremiah 29:13*

## FEBRUARY 28
### THIS IS THE DAY THAT THE LORD HAS MADE. I WILL REJOICE AND BE GLAD IN IT.

*There is no fear.*

*There is no fear!*

*Hallelujah! There is no fear.*

*Why should there be fear when God is your husband, father, mother, brother, sister, lover, companion, protector, enlightener, mediator, way-maker, divider of the sea, leader in the desert.*

*He is the Answer. He has the answer.*

*Draw nigh unto God. Ask, seek, knock, fast, groan, cry, pant, yearn for God's presence.*

\*\*\*

"Oh, that You would rend the heavens, that You would come down, that the mountains might flow down at Your presence, (2) As when the melting fire burns, the fire causes the waters to boil, to make Your name known to Your adversaries, that the nations may tremble at Your presence!" Isaiah 64:1–2

"Draw nigh to God, and He will draw nigh to you. Cleanse your hands, you sinners; and purify your hearts, you double minded. (9) Be afflicted, and mourn, and weep: let your laughter be turned to mourning, and your joy to heaviness. (10) Humble yourselves in the sight of the Lord, and He shall lift you up." James 4:8–10

## FEBRUARY 29
## THIS IS THE DAY THAT THE LORD HAS MADE. I WILL REJOICE AND BE GLAD IN IT.

*For has He done that which cannot be done again?*

*Jesus has shown us the way to live—quietly for 30 years and then baptized in the Spirit—then victory over Satan—then public ministry.*

*Do you think I would send you out ill-prepared, ill-equipped? Mine is not the job of failure. My Son said, "Count the cost," and We meant it. I shall not graduate one of My children and put them in public ministry only to have them eaten up, chewed up and thrown down.*

*Look to Me the Author and Finisher. I am not in a hurry, and you must not be either. Please trust your Father, Mentor, and Enabler. We know what We are doing.*

*Trust and obey for there is no other way for success. Be faithful in little things, and I will make you responsible for big things. For all things are big to Me. It is you who differentiate between things—days, jobs, circumstances, situations, moments, duties, etc.*

*Be content in whatsoever and wheresoever you may find yourself!*

\*\*\*

*"He has made every thing beautiful in His time: also He has set the world in their heart, so that no man can find out the work that God makes from the beginning to the end." Ecclesiastes 3:11*

# MARCH

"Come unto Me, all ye that labor and are heavy laden, and I will give you rest."

MATTHEW 11:28

# MARCH 1
## THIS IS THE DAY THAT THE LORD HAS MADE. I WILL REJOICE AND BE GLAD IN IT.

*Have I not said?!*

*Will I not perform My Word to you! Yea and amen.*

"God is not a man, that He should lie; neither the Son of man, that He should repent: hath He said, and shall He not do it? Or hath He spoken, and shall He not make it good?" Numbers 23:19

*I have spoken once and twice, power belongs to God.*

"God hath spoken once; twice have I heard this; that power belongs unto God." Psalm 62:11

*So why not follow the powerful One. I will cause all things to come to pass.*

"The LORD of hosts hath sworn, saying, Surely as I have thought, so shall it come to pass; and as I have purposed, so shall it stand:" Isaiah 14:24

\*\*\*

"Ah Lord GOD! behold, You have made the heaven and the earth by Your great power and stretched out arm, and there is nothing too hard for Thee:" Jeremiah 32:17

"My sheep hear My voice, and I know them, and they follow Me: (28) And I give unto them eternal life; and they shall never perish, neither shall any man pluck them out of My hand. (29) My Father, which gave them Me, is greater than all; and no man is able to pluck them out of My Father's hand. (30) I and My Father are One." John 10:27-30

> ## THIS IS THE DAY THAT THE LORD HAS MADE. I WILL REJOICE AND BE GLAD IN IT.

*Oh, hallelujah from the depths of my soul!*
*It is He who has set us free.*

*Free to be—not do.*

*Free to be—not do.*

*He is the God of I AM. He is not the God of I DO.*
*Doing denotes laboring. Being denotes flowing.*

***Abide in Me.***

***Abide in Me.***

***Abide in Me and life will flow.***

*Living*

*In the*

*Flow of*

*Elohim*

*Abiding in the Creative One.*

***Come unto Me. Come.***

\*\*\*

*"Abide in Me, and I in you. As the branch cannot*
*bear fruit of itself, except it abide in the vine; no more*
*can you, except you abide in Me." John 15:4*

> **THIS IS THE DAY THAT THE LORD HAS MADE. I WILL REJOICE AND BE GLAD IN IT.**

*Sing! It is the tune of the Spirit to sing! Life is a flow. It is not interruptions. That is why interruptions are so destructive, damaging to your soul.*

*Life was meant to be a flow—singing a tune of*

*PEACE—a*

*Place*

*Ever*

*Abiding in*

*Christ*

*Eternally.*

*Life is a flow. It is being, not doing. Because doing must at some point end, but being continues forever.*

*Where are you? I am always here. Come. Dwell. Abide. You shall experience life. Life without fear—without fear. No abrupt interruptions. Read the Scriptures. You see and hear the Word of the Lord saying, "Come. Rest. Receive."*

\*\*\*

*"The thief comes not, but for to steal, and to kill, and to destroy: I am come that they might have life, and that they might have it more abundantly." John 10:10*

*"My Beloved spoke, and said unto me, Rise up, My love, My fair one, and come away." Song of Solomon 2:10*

## MARCH 4
## THIS IS THE DAY THAT THE LORD HAS MADE. I WILL REJOICE AND BE GLAD IN IT.

*It is I who awakens this love in you. You must know My love for you or how else can you share it with others?*

*But if there were no others, I still desire to let you know (actually through experience) My love for you. It is My desire—it is My heart—it is My existence.*

*It was My love that created. Love creates. Love is not stagnant. It is constantly moving and creating. It is creating good. The opposite—hate—is creating bad.*

*I must get My love to earth. That is why I sent My Son. Then I sent My Spirit. What more can I do?*

*I continue to woo and woo and woo. Who will come and receive?*

Definition of woo: 1. To seek the favor, affection, or love of, especially with a view of marriage. 2. To seek to win. (http://www.dictionary.com)

Oh! how He loves us with a persistent love! Love that cannot be satisfied until it is being received and experienced by His beloved—you.

He is your Lover, your Provider, your Protector, your Way-Maker.

He is your Everything!!!

Rejoice in His love. Turn your face to Him.

His is always toward you!

\*\*\*

"And to know the love of Christ, which passes knowledge, that you might be filled with all the fullness of God." Ephesians 3:19

## MARCH 5
### THIS IS THE DAY THAT THE LORD HAS MADE. I WILL REJOICE AND BE GLAD IN IT.

*Let us follow after the Lord, looking not to the right nor left.*

*"Lead on, Oh, King Eternal! Our steps are in Your steps. May we not linger long on the road of destruction where moth and rust do corrupt."*

*We have looked in many places for love, attention, and peace. Where do all these things originate?*

*Jesus.*

*Yes, you're right. He is love and He is the attention of the universe. Be in Him and you will get all the love and attention you can stand.*

*Be in Him and watch the peace manifest before your eyes.*

*What does His peace look like?*

*The order you experience in your surroundings and in your heart. Where is the hurry, scurry? Where's the rush? Where are the messes? Where are they?*

*Jesus has put your life in order, and it is good.*

\*\*\*

*"And He arose, and rebuked the wind, and said unto the sea, Peace, be still. And the wind ceased, and there was a great calm." Mark 4:39*

*"You are good, and do good; teach me Your statutes." Psalm 119:68*

## MARCH 6
### THIS IS THE DAY THAT THE LORD HAS MADE. I WILL REJOICE AND BE GLAD IN IT.

*What is there to be glad about? That's a good question. Are you not reading a devotional book pointing the way to Jesus?*

*Are you not focusing upon some form of spirituality?*

*Yes, to both questions.*

*Just the fact that you have some desire to hear from God is great news, wonderful news! Were you not at one time on the road to destruction? Jesus being nowhere in sight? As a matter of fact, Jesus was of no account in your life.*

*And now... now you have turned some part of yourself toward life. This is a rejoicing! This is a grand rejoicing!*

*His eyes are roaming back and forth, looking for anyone with an eye toward Him. He is lonely and you have brought pleasure and comfort to Him. Rejoice He has brought you out of darkness into His glorious light.*

*Rejoice, you are His and He is yours.*

\*\*\*

*"For the eyes of the LORD run to and fro throughout the whole earth, to show Himself strong in the behalf of them whose heart is perfect toward Him..." II Chronicles 16:9a*

## MARCH 7
### THIS IS THE DAY THAT THE LORD HAS MADE. I WILL REJOICE AND BE GLAD IN IT.

*Write what you hear, My child. I love you. Ever adore you. Always on My mind. Can never forget you, but always forgive you. Seek not that which fades. Seek that which lightens the world with My Glory and Light.*

*(I Peter 1:4)*

*Seek Him. Seek My Son.*

*(Colossians 3:1, Matthew 6:33)*

*It is He Who sustains the worlds and each molecule is at His beck and call. He it is for whom the worlds were made. I love you only because you are in My Son. For God so loved the world that He gave His only begotten Son. It was the world I made for Him and He ended up saving the world.*

*Each person has their own destiny. And to reach it, he will have to die on a cross just as My Son did. The disciple is not above his master, nor the student above his teacher. (Luke 9:23–24, Matthew 10:24)*

*Find that thing that you fear most and know that it will have to die. Die so I can resurrect it in purity—not tainted by the world. It is for you that I seek to save the lost. Selah.*

\*\*\*

*"And He said to them all. If any man will come after Me, let him deny himself, and take up his cross daily, and follow Me. (24) For whosoever will save his life shall lose it: but whosoever will lose his life for My sake, the same shall save it." Luke 9:23–24*

> THIS IS THE DAY THAT THE LORD HAS MADE. I WILL REJOICE AND BE GLAD IN IT.

*It is for you that I died and rose again. Rose again to new life. Life in Christ, the born again One.*

Those whose lives have died in Christ will be raised from the dead to live lives eternally. Eternally. Forever. Never to fade, nor end.

Think about the glorious forever existence with the ever existent One!

What can it be like? Let us begin our journey now.

Basking in His presence as we forget ourselves and all else. To focus on Him—Him alone…To desire Him—Him alone…To wait on and for Him. Let our hearts, our eyes cry with yearning for Him.

"Oh, that we had wings like a dove and could fly off to You!" (Psalm 55:6)

*Settle down My little one and I will come to you. Be still, and you will find Me waiting on you.*

\*\*\*

"And therefore will the LORD wait, that He may be gracious unto you, and therefore will He be exalted, that He may have mercy upon you: for the LORD is a God of judgment: blessed are all they that wait for Him." Isaiah 30:18

## THIS IS THE DAY THAT THE LORD HAS MADE. I WILL REJOICE AND BE GLAD IN IT.

*Let us rejoice and be glad in it.*

*I am here for you, My little one.*

*Come unto Me.*

*I have many, many words to speak to you—words that will soothe your soul.*

*Words that will fit like the last puzzle piece fits.*

*My presence is like none other.*

*Be still.*

*Be quiet.*

*I will come. Shhhhh.*

*Selah.*

\*\*\*

*"…and, lo, I am with you always, even unto the end of the world. Amen" Matthew 28:20b*

> **THIS IS THE DAY THAT THE LORD HAS MADE. I WILL REJOICE AND BE GLAD IN IT.**

*Oh, the loss of a loved one. What do we do with this loss?*

*Come to Me.*

*I am the lost and found department. I have the lost parts. I have the missing pieces. I have your healing balm. I have the words that soothe the broken heart and sets it free to dance and sing again in the midst of trauma and terror.*

*Sounds unbelievable?*

*I AM. Try Me.*

*I AM all that you need. From Me flows fellowship.*

*When I AM lifted up, I bring all men unto Me. All men.*

*Oh, the heartbreak!*

*But did I not come to heal the broken heart?*

\*\*\*

*"The Spirit of the Lord is upon Me, because He has anointed Me to preach the gospel to the poor; He has sent Me to heal the brokenhearted..." Luke 4:18a*

## MARCH 11
### THIS IS THE DAY THAT THE LORD HAS MADE. I WILL REJOICE AND BE GLAD IN IT.

*What more is there to say than to say, "Let us rejoice"? It is in giving thanks that all things can be yours.*

*How can that be?*

*It is in giving thanks that the enemy of your soul and body is left helpless. You see, he cannot stand to be around a person that is giving thanks in the midst of horror and seeming defeat.*

*But all things—ALL—things do work for good to those who love Me and have given themselves to Me, for My care of them. Have you given and given yourself to Me? Yes, and again I say, Yes. Then fall back on the truth of Scripture that says, I AM your Husband, and Redeemer, and Provider, and Shepherd, and Father, and Protector and your LORD GOD.*

*No matter the circumstances, take time to think upon Me. I will keep you in perfect peace as you keep your thoughts stayed on Me.*

*Now it is time to believe. It is time to trust.*

*It is time to have faith that I AM who I say that I AM and you are My child!*

\*\*\*

*"For you are all the children of God by faith in Christ Jesus." Galatians 3:26*

† 

## MARCH 12

## THIS IS THE DAY THAT THE LORD HAS MADE. I WILL REJOICE AND BE GLAD IN IT.

*The meaning of the word, rejoice, in this verse means to spin around; to be under the influence of any violent emotion. This rejoicing that we can do is a violent spinning around emotion, not some calm rejoicing.*

*How different is our life than this commandment of the Lord?*

*Psalm 118:22–24 is part of the Jewish Passover celebration. Jesus would have quoted verse 24, "This is the day which the LORD has made, we will rejoice and be glad in it," during His Passover celebration just prior to His Crucifixion. Have we suffered unto blood yet? No, most of us have not.*

*In I Thessalonians 5:16–18, God says for us to, "Rejoice evermore. Pray without ceasing. In every thing give thanks: for this is the will of God in Christ Jesus concerning you."*

*Now we know God's will. We shall always rejoice, pray continually, and give thanks in ALL circumstances.*

*Oh hallelujah! His name shall forever be praised on earth as in heaven. If we do not praise, the stones will cry out!*

\*\*\*

*"And He answered and said unto them, I tell you that, if these should hold their peace, the stones would immediately cry out." Luke 19:40*

## MARCH 13
### THIS IS THE DAY THAT THE LORD HAS MADE. I WILL REJOICE AND BE GLAD IN IT.

*What I want to say today is that I AM is in control. Now what are you going to do with this information and indeed the truth as it relates to your life? Will you go about wondering what to do or will you look to Me like a lamb following its shepherd?*

*I am your Shepherd and I care for you—be about Our business. But you cannot be about Our business, because of the years and years of operating from your head. So…it is time to retrain your thinking, and the only way to do that is to think on My words and to keep your mind on Me with thankfulness and joy.*

*Be light-hearted, like a child who gets up in the morning and goes about his business with no cares. No cares. Be light-hearted, My child. So you are thinking, "But I am an adult." In order to enter the kingdom of heaven you must become like a little child. So come on and BECOME. I will assist you. That is My job, among others.*

*Keep your gaze upon Me. And whenever your gaze is upon worries, fears, yourself, gently turn your thoughts to the Goodness of the Lord. And if finding the Goodness of the Lord is hard to find, go to the Psalms and read about My goodness.*

*Seek…and you will find Me.*

\*\*\*

*"Who is among you that fears the LORD, that obeys the voice of his servant, that walks in darkness, and has no light? Let him trust in the name of the LORD, and stay upon his God." Isaiah 50:10*

## THIS IS THE DAY THAT THE LORD HAS MADE. I WILL REJOICE AND BE GLAD IN IT.

*How are you coming along in your quest to find the goodness of God?*

*Has your life experiences made you think differently of Me?*

*Can you corral those thoughts of abuse and put them under your feet?*

*Apply the Blood of My Son to your mind, emotions, and desires.*

*Apply the Blood of My Son to your body for healing and restoration. Commune with Him in His Body and Blood. You will see the enemy of your body and soul begin to recede into the background and finally fade from view.*

*But you must be persistent, consistent, unwavering, and undaunted in your trust of Me. For in due season you will reap if you faint not and do not lose your confidence in*

*ME.*

\*\*\*

*"Cast not away therefore your confidence, which has great recompense of reward. (36) For you have need of patience, that after you have done the will of God, you might receive the promise. (37) For yet a little while, and He that shall come will come, and will not tarry. (38) Now the just shall live by faith: but if any man draw back, My soul shall have no pleasure in him. (39) But we are not of them who draw back unto perdition; but of them that believe to the saving of the soul." Hebrews 10:35–39*

**THIS IS THE DAY THAT THE LORD HAS MADE. I WILL REJOICE AND BE GLAD IN IT.**

*Notice, God does not force us to rejoice, but He invites us to rejoice. He asks us only to believe. All things are possible to those who believe.*

*What needs have you in your life? Why not believe that your kind and compassionate Father will provide the answer? His will is for your body to be healthy. Do not let go of your Father, until He has supplied the manifestation of a healthy body.*

*All who came to Jesus for healing were healed. If we come to Him, will He not heal us too? Did He love those people in His earthly walk better than He loves us? He is willing.*

*Are you willing to continue to keep on asking, seeking, and knocking? (Luke 11:9–10) Are you willing to be like the widow with the unjust judge (Luke 18:2–8) or the friend asking for bread at midnight? (Luke 11:5–8)*

*Jesus said, "Surely He will answer His elect who cry out to Him day and night and that right soon." (Luke 18:7–8)*

\*\*\*

*"And we desire that every one of you do show the same diligence to the full assurance of hope unto the end: (12) That you be not slothful, but followers of them who through faith and patience inherit the promises." Hebrews 6:11–12*

## MARCH 16
## THIS IS THE DAY THAT THE LORD HAS MADE. I WILL REJOICE AND BE GLAD IN IT.

*Come unto Me all you who labor and are heavy laden. I will give you rest.*

*But what is rest? Rest is:*

*Relinquishing*

*Everything,*

*Surrendering*

*Totally*

*When nothing is yours, then you have no responsibility for anything. For without ownership, there can be no responsibility.*

*Stress comes when you feel the responsibility to do something or change something or correct something; but in all reality you do not have the ability to do such, because you are not responsible for the situation. If you were responsible, then you would have the power to do, change, or correct.*

*Rest, My child, in the finished work of Jesus. Go to Jesus and learn of Him. Learn of His meekness and lowliness of heart. Who came not to do His will, but the will of Him Who sent Him. You are no different from My Son. I have sent you and you are Mine.*

*The problem comes, because you do not see rightly. Learn of My Son and you shall see rightly.*

\*\*\*

*"There remains therefore a rest to the people of God. (10) For he that is entered into his rest, he also has ceased from his own works, as God did from His. (11) Let us labor therefore to enter into that rest, lest any man fall after the same example of unbelief." Hebrews 4:9–11*

*Rejoice! You are not your own! You do not hold the strings to life—yours nor anyone's.*

*Rest in His care.*

*He has taken care of all things in the past. He will do it again.*

*Refuse, refuse, refuse to worry and pine away over whatever it is that is causing unrest within your soul.*

*Speak to your soul and say,*

*"Peace, be still. I will trust my Daddy, the One who loves me beyond any emotion and action that I can imagine."*

*Rejoice in having Someone who loves, cares for, watches over, and died for you.*

\*\*\*

*"He that spared not His own Son, but delivered Him up for us all, how shall He not with Him also freely give us all things?" Romans 8:32*

## MARCH 18
### THIS IS THE DAY THAT THE LORD HAS MADE. I WILL REJOICE AND BE GLAD IN IT.

*Let all things lead to Me. I AM the Alpha and the Omega.*

*How is it that all things lead not unto Me?*

*Because man has placed himself on the throne, and I have been taken down.*

*It is not easy, but someone has to reign and faith is not a likely candidate for reigning.*

*Come unto Me all ye who labor and are heavy laden.*

*But this takes faith, of which is in short supply upon earth. Man would rather be in charge than leave it to a self-existent God—one he cannot see with his eyes, nor touch with his hands.*

*No wonder that without faith it is impossible to please Me. Anything other than faith is man-made and thus tainted with sin. Thomas had to feel my hands and side. Blessed are you who see not, but believe.*

\*\*\*

*"Jesus says unto him, Thomas, because you have seen Me, you have believed: blessed are they that have not seen, and yet have believed." John 20:29*

## MARCH 19
### THIS IS THE DAY THAT THE LORD HAS MADE. I WILL REJOICE AND BE GLAD IN IT.

*"I must taste You, Lord!"*

*Taste and see that the Lord is good (Psalm 34:8).*

*"How do we taste You, Lord?"*

*Eat My Words. They are life and health to your flesh, soul, and spirit.*

*Eat and be satisfied. Eat and rejoice.*

*Eat and be free of many transgressions.*

*For it is in the eating that you are nourished for life everlasting. Taste with your mouth of faith and see with your eyes of faith. Feel with your hands and walk in My steps.*

*You shall know Me if you go on to know Me.*

\*\*\*

*"Then shall we know, if we follow on to know the LORD:" Hosea 6:3a,*

*"O taste and see that the LORD is good: blessed is the man that trusts in Him." Psalm 34:8,*

*"My son, attend to My words; incline your ear unto My sayings. (21) Let them not depart from your eyes; keep them in the midst of your heart. (22) For they are life unto those that find them, and health to all their flesh." Proverbs 4:20–22*

## MARCH 20
## THIS IS THE DAY THAT THE LORD HAS MADE. I WILL REJOICE AND BE GLAD IN IT.

*It is the will of God that all be made whole.
It is the will of God that all be saved.*

*Now what is your will?*

*Now that you know God's will, what do you say
that your will is? Is it any less than God's?*

*Why?*

"And He did not many mighty works there, because of their unbelief." (Matthew 13:58) All things are possible for those who believe (Mark 9:23). All that followed Him were healed (Matthew 12:15). If God did not want you physically healed, why did Jesus heal all those who came to Him? He turned no one away. There is no record or example of someone coming to Jesus for healing and Him saying, "No." Even the Syrophenician woman was denied at first, but her faith prevailed and Jesus healed her daughter (Matthew 15:21–28).

What is your ailment? God can heal you, and God's will is to heal you. His healings take many forms. They may not line up with your perception of what healing looks like. But press in to know Him, and His love for you. Look to Him and He will make all things clear. He is the Answer! Let us trust Him to reveal His way of healing.

\*\*\*

"And besought Him that they might only touch the hem of His garment: and as many as touched were made perfectly whole." Matthew 14:36

## MARCH 21
### THIS IS THE DAY THAT THE LORD HAS MADE. I WILL REJOICE AND BE GLAD IN IT.

*For He has triumphed gloriously over our enemies of sickness, complacency, lack, fear, doubt and whatever our enemies are.*

*If God healed all who came to Him in His days on earth, how much more does He heal now that Jesus has accomplished our redemption? Is God a liar? Does God change? No. No. No. Do not be tossed about like the ocean waves. "For let not that man think that he shall receive any thing of the Lord." (James 1:7) The testing of your faith is more precious than gold (I Peter 1:7). So linger in this testing with pure joy (James 1:2), for He Who has called you is able to bring you to completion. He lives inside of you. He has the power to deliver you. Therefore you have His power within you to be healed, delivered, and set free.*

*Look to Him for His manner of healing, delivering and setting you free. It may look different from your vision. Ask Him to enable you to see as He sees. Ask Him to help you see your life from His perspective.*

*Give Him praise, honor, and glory! Sing praises unto His name, for He has triumphed gloriously, and because He has, we have! Amen and amen.*

\*\*\*

*"Being confident of this very thing, that He which has begun a good work in you will perform it until the day of Jesus Christ:" Philippians 1:6*

*"For it is God which works in you both to will and to do of His good pleasure." Philippians 2:13*

*This is the day to glory in His wisdom for your life. He came to set you free. Freedom is meant for His children. With the Spirit of God dwelling in you and you walking in Christ, freedom is inevitable. God is ultimate freedom. He came to set us free. Galatians 5:1 says,*

*"Stand fast therefore in the liberty wherewith Christ hath made us free, and be not entangled again with the yoke of bondage."*

*Revel in this knowledge, "I am Free!" Free to do whatever I want, because the Spirit of God dwells in me (Romans 8:9). He constrains me to follow Him and not my mind (flesh). Those who walk after the flesh are subject to the law, but those walking after the Spirit have been set free from the law, and are subject to the Holy Spirit.*

*It is the Holy Spirit that convicts the world of sin, righteousness and judgment (John 16:8). Oh, hallelujah! He convicts the world of unbelief, convicts it of righteousness in Jesus, and convicts it of the powerlessness of the ruler of this world (John 16:8–11). Satan has been rendered null and void by the finished work of the cross. We overcome him by the word of our testimony, the blood of Jesus, and our fearlessness of death.*

\*\*\*

*"And they overcame him by the blood of the Lamb, and the word of their testimony, and they loved not their lives unto death." Revelation 12:11*

> MADE. I WILL REJOICE AND BE GLAD IN IT.

*"How can I ever let You know how much I love You? I can take consolation in the fact that You know my heart.*

*"Each step with You makes my love for You greater and greater. Every trial, temptation, or sin leads me into a stronger, closer relationship with You. Therefore whenever anything negative comes into my life, I can rejoice, because it only strengthens my love for You and my brethren. As my love deepens for You, I subsequently am enabled to love others in a more agape way.*

*"Oh, how great is the majesty of Your love for me, for us! It fills the deepest point in the sea and reaches to the highest heaven where You are.*

*"Oh! Father, thank You for Your Son and Holy Spirit that reside in me and in the world.*

*"Oh, come Holy Spirit and fill us with Your love and compassion that we with You may cry, 'Come, Lord Jesus.'"*

\*\*\*

*"Whither shall I go from Your Spirit? Or whither shall I flee from Your presence? (8) If I ascend up into heaven, You are there: if I make My bed in hell, behold, You are there. (9) If I take the wings of the morning, and dwell in the uttermost parts of the sea; (10) Even there shall Your hand lead me, and Your right hand shall hold me. (11) If I say, Surely the darkness shall cover me; even the night shall be light about me." Psalm 139:7–11*

† 

## MARCH 24

### THIS IS THE DAY THAT THE LORD HAS MADE. I WILL REJOICE AND BE GLAD IN IT.

*Follow Me where I may go.*

*Do not be afraid. I never force (coerce).*

*I am gentle and peaceful.*

*My way is never out of order.*

*I have plans. I follow My plans, and I take you along with Me.*

*So do not fear. The Creator of the universe is your personal guide or "itinerary setter."*

*I make your plans and order your steps for blessings and hope.*

*So fear not! The Lord thy God is with thee.*

*Fear not for the Lord thy God is at thy right hand to stay thee in the time of trouble.*

\*\*\*

*"God is our refuge and strength, a very present help in trouble. (2) Therefore will not we fear, though the earth be removed, and though the mountains be carried into the midst of the sea; (3) Though the waters thereof roar and be troubled, though the mountains shake with the swelling thereof. Selah." Psalm 46:1–3*

## MARCH 25

### THIS IS THE DAY THAT THE LORD HAS MADE. I WILL REJOICE AND BE GLAD IN IT.

*Be glad for I am with you.*

*What can happen to a person who has God with him? It is like having the perfect bodyguard. Whereas earthly bodyguards can make mistakes and cannot be everywhere at all times, your heavenly Father has sent the Holy Spirit to be everywhere at all times. He is the perfect bodyguard. He is also the perfect planner, director, and supervisor. He leads us into God's plans. He directs our actions moment by moment, and He supervises our actions to keep us on course.*

*Why are so many lives askew? Our flesh (the brain, our mental thoughts) reigns in our lives instead of the Holy Spirit. Make the decision today to strive to enter into the Holy Spirit's rest. We do this by desiring and consciously looking to our spirit for guidance instead of our brain.*

*Try it today when you are wondering what to do next, ask the Holy Spirit for His desire. It will be frightening to follow the Spirit versus your brain, but it is very rewarding. For the Lord said, "I do nothing except what I see the Father doing." (John 5:19) Walk according to the Spirit today and do not fulfill the desires of the flesh. And remember the desires of the flesh can be good (not always evil), but following the flesh will not be pleasing to God nor will it produce fruit that remains.*

\*\*\*

*"So then they that are in the flesh cannot please God. (9) But you are not in the flesh, but in the Spirit, if so be that the Spirit of God dwells in you. Now if any man have not the Spirit of Christ, he is none of His. (10) And if Christ be in you, the body is dead because of sin; but the Spirit is life because of righteousness." Romans 8:8–10*

**THIS IS THE DAY THAT THE LORD HAS MADE. I WILL REJOICE AND BE GLAD IN IT.**

*It is for freedom that I have come to set you free. It is for freedom that I came to set you free. It is for freedom that I come to set you free. It is like ask and keep on asking. I come and keep on coming to set you free for freedom's sake.*

*Unless a person is free they have nothing to offer others and the world. Only what you have can you give away. Only what you freely have can you give away.*

*It is an endless source, for freedom comes from Me. All bondage, inhibition, and holding back are from the devil once you are born again. Yes, this is a bold statement and a scary one for humans, but the truth will set you free. There is that word again, "free."*

*Ponder upon this freedom I speak of and it shall be sown in good ground.*

*Galatians 5:1, "It is for freedom that Christ has set us free. Stand firm, then, and do not let yourselves be burdened again by a yoke of slavery." NIV*

\*\*\*

*"Stand fast therefore in the liberty wherewith Christ has made us free, and be not entangled again with the yoke of bondage." Galatians 5:1*

*Rejoice for the Lord is at hand. The Lord of life, the Holy Spirit. He was with and in Jesus while He lived on earth. He is with and in you. Rejoice! The same Spirit that raised Jesus from the dead is residing in you.*

*Is anything too hard for Him? In that case, is anything too hard for you? No, nothing is too hard for you. Whatever He is calling forth in your life, He is able to bring it forth.*

*Rejoice you cannot be defeated in Christ. It may look like a defeat. Temporal visions do not move a child of God to disbelieve His Word. Our understanding may be lacking… BUT God.*

*Keep looking to Him. He will satisfy you. He is your satisfaction in all things earthly and heavenly.*

*The Christ that bleed, suffered physical beating, hung on the cross naked did this for your victory. He said there will be tribulation in the world, but be of good cheer, He has overcome the world (John 16:33) and so we have too.*

*Do not stop until you have your victory for which Christ suffered to provide for you. And do not presume what this victory will look like. You will know it by the love, joy, and peace that is evident in your life. Do not let His suffering be for naught.*

\*\*\*

*"O death, where is your sting? O grave, where is your victory? (56) The sting of death is sin; and the strength of sin is the law. (57) But thanks be to God, which gives us the victory through our Lord Jesus Christ. (58) Therefore, my beloved brethren, be you steadfast, unmovable, always abounding in the work of the Lord, forasmuch as you know that your labor is not in vain in the Lord." I Corinthians 15:55–58*

**THIS IS THE DAY THAT THE LORD HAS MADE. I WILL REJOICE AND BE GLAD IN IT.**

*The Sun of righteousness shall come with healing in His wings (Malachi 4:2).*

*He has come and returned to the Father. He has accomplished our healing. Who has believed our report? (Isaiah 53:1–5)*

*God is revealing Himself to believers.*

*ALL things are possible to those who believe (Mark 9:23).*

*What is God asking, leading, guiding you to believe? Find out what He is saying concerning a situation in your life and believe.*

*Do not give up on God, but persist in your belief; and like the widow with the unjust judge, He will avenge your enemies and give you victory in this world.*

*He is more than willing to manifest His many blessings upon His children. His timing is perfect. Look to Him, the Author and Finisher of your faith (Hebrews 12:2). We do not know how these blessings shall appear, nor when they shall appear. Our sight is limited, short-sighted, and often very earth bound. The Word of God is true. However, we see through a glass darkly (I Corinthians 13:12). Trust Him to carry out your healing as He sees best. He will avenge you against your enemies!*

\*\*\*

*"And shall not God avenge His own elect, which cry day and night unto Him, though He bear long with them? I tell you that He will avenge them speedily. Nevertheless when the Son of man comes, shall He find faith on the earth?" Luke 18:7–8*

*Come unto Me all ye who labor and I shall give you rest.*

*Do not neglect to preach the gospel or heal the sick or fight for the right.*

*When Satan comes against the Word of God, you come against Satan with the Word of God. Jesus did.*

*Do not back down. Do not doubt. Do not stop standing!*

*Do not let down your strength of battle against the enemy. Your strength of battle is rejoicing in the Lord, falling back in His arms of love, and surrendering to Him—trusting Him with your life and the outcome.*

*Do not give up, but go forward with even more determination to trust Him no matter the appearance of circumstances. He is good and He does good (Psalm 119:68).*

*The Word of God is true and does not return void. Satan is a liar and a deceiver.*

*Hallelujah! The victory is ours in Jesus Christ!*

\*\*\*

*"And Jesus answered him, saying, It is written, That man shall not live by bread alone, but by every word of God." Luke 4:4*

*"You are of your father the devil, and the lusts of your father you will do. He was a murderer from the beginning, and abode not in the truth, because there is no truth in him. When he speaks a lie, he speaks of his own: for he is a liar, and the father of it." John 8:44*

## MARCH 30
### THIS IS THE DAY THAT THE LORD HAS MADE. I WILL REJOICE AND BE GLAD IN IT.

*What makes you think I have stopped doing My miracles?*

*Can anyone or anything else do miracles? Why would I, the Miracle Working God, stop doing miracles?*

*If I needed to perform miracles when I, the Son, lived on earth, why would I not need to perform miracles when I, the Spirit, now live on earth?*

*Do not doubt, only believe.*

*Is it not enough that there are needs?*

*No, there must be resolution to those needs and I AM the RESOLUTION; look to Me.*

*I AM the Resolution.*

*I resolve the problem(s).*

*Look unto Me.*

*Lift up your eyes... know Me... seek Me.*

*Is there anyone who seeks Me?*

\*\*\*

"And call upon Me in the day of trouble; I will deliver you, and you shall glorify Me." Psalm 50:15

"I love them that love Me; and those that seek Me early shall find Me." Proverbs 8:17

"And shall not God avenge His own elect, which cry day and night unto Him, though He bear long with them? (8) I tell you that He will avenge them speedily. Nevertheless when the Son of man comes, shall He find faith on the earth?" Luke 18:7–8

## MARCH 31
### THIS IS THE DAY THAT THE LORD HAS MADE. I WILL REJOICE AND BE GLAD IN IT.

*Speak to the clouds of your life and command them to move. The clouds may be sad thoughts, grief, fear, anger, presumption. Speak to these and say, "Move. I am clearing the way to my Father. I'm preparing the way of the Lord." Now put your thoughts and emotions upon the Lord. Ephesians 5:19–20 says, "Speaking to yourselves in psalms and hymns and spiritual songs, singing and making melody in your heart to the Lord; (20) Giving thanks always for all things unto God and the Father in the name of our Lord Jesus Christ."*

*Our power and authority in Jesus Christ has been weakened by sin. But we can rebuild our most Holy Faith by praying in the Holy Ghost (Jude 1:20).*

*So begin today and speak to your clouds, command them to move. Replace them with songs of the Lord, praying and singing in the Holy Spirit. His presence comes on the wings of praise. And if He doesn't, keep praising Him, for He is worthy of our praise whether anything moves or not!*

*"Arise, Oh Spirit of God, and show Yourself mighty on behalf of Your needy children."*

\*\*\*

*"And He arose, and rebuked the wind, and said unto the sea, Peace, be still. And the wind ceased, and there was a great calm." Mark 4:39*

# APRIL

*"Jesus said unto her, I am the resurrection, and the life: he that believes in Me, though he were dead, yet shall he live."*

JOHN 11:25

## THIS IS THE DAY THAT THE LORD HAS MADE. I WILL REJOICE AND BE GLAD IN IT.

*Has it not been said, "Give to the poor, give to the needy and give to the worthy."*

*But I say unto you, "Give and it shall be given unto you, pressed down, shaken together, running over shall men put into your bosom."*

*Give to Me. And I shall make men give to you. Give to Me and watch Me cause men to give to you.*

*It will be as Peter caught the fish, after he had let Me use his boat. He gave to Me, and then I caused men to give to him by buying his fish. I give seed to the sower.*

*Come unto Me all ye who are weary and heavy laden.*

*I keep saying that to you, because you seldom come unto Me for rest and release, but you are always and forever proactive.*

*There comes a time daily for you to fall irretrievably into My arms.*

*Do it now!*

*Do it daily!*

\*\*\*

*"While it is said, Today if you will hear His voice, harden not your hearts, as in the provocation." Hebrews 3:15*

## APRIL 2
## THIS IS THE DAY THAT THE LORD HAS MADE. I WILL REJOICE AND BE GLAD IN IT.

*Have you read Ephesians 3 recently?*
*Read it and pray this prayer.*

*It has been prayed for centuries and I want you to join into the prayers of the saints that you too may know the love of Christ, the anointed One.*

*To know His love is to know Me.*
*To know Me is to have eternal life.*

*Seek to know Me that you may do the works My Son did and even greater works, that My wisdom may be made known to the rulers and authorities.*

*You see, My purpose in sending My Son was not only to save you, but to make known My manifold wisdom to the rulers and authorities.*

*So seek to know Me, and your joy will be full.*

\*\*\*

"And to make all men see what is the fellowship of the mystery, which from the beginning of the world has been hid in God, who created all things by Jesus Christ: (10) To the intent that now unto the principalities and powers in heavenly places might be known by the church the manifold wisdom of God." Ephesians 3:9–10

## APRIL 3
### THIS IS THE DAY THAT THE LORD HAS MADE. I WILL REJOICE AND BE GLAD IN IT.

*For I have said and will I not perform it? The inheritance of the righteous will be right standing within My gates.*

*I have called forth righteousness in abundance, and My children shall share in this righteousness that My Son has accomplished.*

*He performed these mighty deeds for your sake so you would believe, and hold fast that He is My Son; and if My Son, then an heir to My Kingdom that many would be made righteous and join Him in His reign.*

*I have done these mighty acts that you would believe, and in believing would act upon My Word and make it your word.*

*So speak My thoughts and it shall come to pass.*

*Waver not in unbelief, but be a doer of My Word.*

*Be a doer and not a hearer only, saith the Lord of Host.*

\*\*\*

*"But be you doers of the word, and not hearers only, deceiving your own selves. (23) For if any be a hearer of the word, and not a doer, he is like unto a man beholding his natural face in a glass: (24) For he beholds himself, and goes his way, and straightway forgets what manner of man he was." James 1:22–24*

## APRIL 4

### THIS IS THE DAY THAT THE LORD HAS MADE. I WILL REJOICE AND BE GLAD IN IT.

*Judge not that ye may not be judged, for according to your judgment shall ye be judged.*

*This makes a barrier between Me and thee when you judge. This is the work of My Spirit and My Spirit only.*

*Seek not what I can do for you, but seek ye first the Kingdom of God.*

*For all things have been added unto you, and I have placed you in My hands never to be removed.*

*So do not leave voluntarily.*

*It is I who keeps you.*

\*\*\*

"Who shall lay any thing to the charge of God's elect? It is God that justifies. (34) Who is he that condemns? It is Christ that died, yes rather, that is risen again, who is even at the right hand of God, who also makes intercession for us." Romans 8:33–34

## APRIL 5
### THIS IS THE DAY THAT THE LORD HAS MADE. I WILL REJOICE AND BE GLAD IN IT.

*All things are possible with God—ALL things (Matthew 19:26).*

*Look to Him, the Author and Finisher of your faith (Hebrews 12:2); for it is impossible to please God without faith (Hebrews 11:6).*

*Walk by faith and not by sight (II Corinthians 5:7).*

*Trust in the Lord with all your heart and don't lean on your own understanding; in all your ways acknowledge Him and He will direct your paths (Proverbs 3:5–6).*

*He will watch over whatever concerns you (I Peter 5:7), for you are the apple of His eye (Zechariah 2:8).*

*The Lord of hosts is with us (Psalm 46:11).*

*If God be for us, who can be against us? (Romans 8:31) Walk by faith and not by your sight.*

\*\*\*

"Looking unto Jesus the Author and Finisher of our faith; who for the joy that was set before Him endured the cross, despising the shame, and is set down at the right hand of the throne of God." Hebrews 12:2

*There is nothing, absolutely nothing that can happen today that we are not commanded to rejoice! Rejoice in all things.*

*I Thessalonians 5:16–18, God says, "Rejoice evermore. Pray without ceasing. In everything give thanks: for this is the will of God in Christ Jesus concerning you."*

*Psalm 91:1–2, 10, God says, "He that dwells in the secret place of the most High shall abide under the shadow of the Almighty. (2) I will say of the LORD, He is my refuge and my fortress: my God; in Him will I trust... (10) There shall no evil befall thee, neither shall any plague come nigh thy dwelling."*

**When evil approaches you and your dwelling, look to Me. I am there. Trust Me. I am trustworthy. Just as a child runs to his parent when afraid, run to Me. I will not disappoint. Yes, rest even as My Son did in the back of the boat when the storm was raging. In due time, I gave Him the word to say, "Peace, be still." I shall give you the word also to bring down the enemy advancing toward you.**

\*\*\*

*"Who has believed our report? And to whom is the arm of the LORD revealed? ... (4) Surely He has borne our griefs, and carried our sorrows: yet we did esteem Him stricken, smitten of God, and afflicted. (5) But He was wounded for our transgressions, He was bruised for our iniquities: the chastisement of our peace was upon Him; and with His stripes we are healed." Isaiah 53:1, 4–5*

*And it shall come to pass that I shall speak and My children shall obey. Up unto this point, I have spoken and I speak, but no one answers nor responds.*

*Will I find faith when I return? Yes, I will. I will find faith for My Spirit convicts you of unbelief—I do not fail. My Spirit does not fail, for Love never fails.*

*Am I a man that I should lie? No. Let every man be a liar, but God be true.*

*It is impossible for Me to lie, because when I open My mouth and speak it comes to pass. It comes into existence.*

*So, you see, you may as well agree with Me, for what I say... IS.*

\*\*\*

*"I tell you that He will avenge them speedily. Nevertheless when the Son of man comes, shall He find faith on the earth?" Luke 18:8*

*"So shall My Word be that goes forth out of My mouth: it shall not return unto Me void, but it shall accomplish that which I please, and it shall prosper in the thing whereto I sent it." Isaiah 55:11*

*"And God said unto Moses, I AM THAT I AM: and He said, Thus shall you say unto the children of Israel, I AM has sent me unto you." Exodus 3:14*

## MADE. I WILL REJOICE AND BE GLAD IN IT.

*We are robed in righteousness, right standing with God.*
*Isaiah 61:10*

*All things are possible with Him.*
*Matthew 19:26*

*We wear a helmet of salvation and our thoughts are brought under the submission to the obedience of Him.*
*Ephesians 6:17*

*Our thoughts are high and lifted up thoughts of heavenly matters and not of earthly things.*
*Colossians 3:1–2*

*We wear the breastplate of righteousness purchased for us by our Savior and Redeemer.*
*Ephesians 6:14*

*Nothing can separate us from God's love.*
*Romans 8:39*

*It is finished.*
*John 19:30*

*We wear the belt of truth and we know the truth and it sets us free.*
*Ephesians 6:14, John 8:32*

*For our feet are shod with the gospel of peace and we shall walk in peace this day—not strife nor confusion.*
*Ephesians 6:15*

*The Word of God in our hand defeats all attacks of the enemy, and whatsoever lifts itself up against us shall be confuted by*

†

*His Word in our mouths.*
*Ephesians 6:17 & Isaiah 54:17*

*It is written, The shield of faith we carry repels the attacks of the enemy, so they fall to the ground and we tread upon serpents and snakes (Luke 10:19). All attacks are refuted by His Word and no weapon formed against us today will prosper!(Isaiah 54:17) For His Word says so!*

*It is a day of rejoicing and being made glad by His presence which is always with us.*
*Psalm 32:11, Matthew 28:20*

**Be not afraid nor weary in well doing, for I shall come with vengeance to recompense My holy ones. No weapon formed against you shall prosper. Just as I did for My servants of old, I shall do for you.**

\*\*\*

*"Say to them that are of a fearful heart, Be strong, fear not: behold, your God will come with vengeance, even God with a recompense; He will come and save you." Isaiah 35:4*

## APRIL 9
### THIS IS THE DAY THAT THE LORD HAS MADE. I WILL REJOICE AND BE GLAD IN IT.

*It was good when they said unto me, "Let us go into the house of the Lord." Psalm 122:1*

*Sing a joyful song unto the Lord, for He is good and His mercy endures forever. Psalms 95 & 136*

*Just as Jehoshaphat and his company of men sang praises unto our God, we shall sing and be victorious over the enemy. (II Chronicles 20)*

*He has conquered, so we can be conquerors. He has overcome, so we are overcomers. Praise be to God! Thanks be to God!*

*"Come unto Me all ye who labor and are heavy laden and I will give you rest." (Matthew 11:28) And His rest is not temporary. His rest is a Sabbath rest that is continuous.*

*Our Lover has so many good things for us. Can we not come into His presence to receive and give adoration to Him? He is worthy of all that we can give to Him.*

*Let us pray,*

*"Only enable us, Father, to pour out upon You the blessings You desire from us. Our heart, soul, and body are Yours."*

\*\*\*

*"And when he had consulted with the people, he appointed singers unto the LORD, and that should praise the Beauty of Holiness, as they went out before the army, and to say, Praise the LORD; for His mercy endures for ever." II Chronicles 20:21*

## APRIL 10

## THIS IS THE DAY THAT THE LORD HAS MADE. I WILL REJOICE AND BE GLAD IN IT.

*Sing praises unto Him! He has provided for all our needs. He has provided for all our wants. Sometimes patience has to have its perfect way (James 1:4), but God has provided.*

*He is a good Husband.*

*He is our All in all. He is sufficient. He is overflowing. Our cup overflows. He is beyond our asking or thinking. He is more than enough. He has all our bases covered.*

*He is our Bodyguard. He is always watching us and cares for our cares. He will let no bad thing happen to us, except that it is necessary for our sanctification, our holiness.*

*He is not a weak or imperfect God. He is stronger than the ocean torrent or the raging wind, stronger than cancer or AIDS, stronger than hate and ignorance.*

*Our God is stronger than any occurrence that may rattle our lives. He is stronger than a person's pride.*

*So we ask,*

*"Father, overcome these ones for whom we pray.*

*"Overcome them with Your love, compassion, and mercy."*

\*\*\*

*"But You, O Lord, are a God full of compassion, and gracious, longsuffering, and plenteous in mercy and truth." Psalm 86:14*

## APRIL 11

### THIS IS THE DAY THAT THE LORD HAS MADE. I WILL REJOICE AND BE GLAD IN IT.

*That is never Me which seems to stir anxiety within your chest.*

*Never do I try to guide you through worry or fretting. Whenever you feel anxiety—a fearful urging within—that is not Me and should be resisted.*

*My guidance is restful, peaceful, and still.*

*Gentle is My Spirit. Peaceful is My Spirit and that is what you feel with My guidance.*

*Never do anything in anxiety. It only feeds that ugly thing within that needs to be starved. Don't give Satan his way.*

*Be still and My Spirit will make a way and you shall see, physically experience, My deliverance.*

*Resist the enemy and relax in Me.*

\*\*\*

"But the wisdom that is from above is first pure, then peaceable, gentle, and easy to be entreated, full of mercy and good fruits, without partiality, and without hypocrisy." James 3:17

"Rest in the LORD, and wait patiently for Him: fret not yourself because of him who prospers in his way, because of the man who brings wicked devices to pass." Psalm 37:7

**THIS IS THE DAY THAT THE LORD HAS MADE. I WILL REJOICE AND BE GLAD IN IT.**

*Let us make a joyful noise unto the Lord. He has done all things to bring us health and happiness. He saved us from sin and sickness AND NOW we do not have to sin and we do not have to be sick. He has a way for us to be free from sin's bondages and sicknesses. Continue to seek Him and He will give you understanding, wisdom and knowledge concerning the trials you may be going through.*

*Trust in the Lord with all your heart. "Cast not away therefore your confidence, which has great recompense of reward. For you have need of patience, that, after you have done the will of God, you might receive the promise." (Hebrews 10:35–36) "But let patience have her perfect work, that you may be perfect and entire, wanting nothing. (5) If any of you lack wisdom, let him ask of God, that gives to all men liberally, and upbraids not; and it shall be given him. (6) But let him ask in faith, nothing wavering: for he that wavers is like a wave of the sea driven with the wind and tossed. (7) For let not that man think that he shall receive any thing of the Lord." (James 1:4–7)*

*He is the One Who heals and has already healed. God has a way for you to live in love, joy and peace. His healing may not look like what you are believing for. He knows best. Do not put our Father God into a box. His ways are above ours. Get His wisdom, understanding and knowledge about your situation and trust Him.*

\*\*\*

*"Make a joyful noise unto God, all you lands: (2) Sing forth the honor of His name: make His praise glorious." Psalm 66:1–2*

## THIS IS THE DAY THAT THE LORD HAS MADE. I WILL REJOICE AND BE GLAD IN IT.

*Have I not said; will I not do?*

*The answer is Yea and Amen. The answer is Jesus.*

*He never fussed or fumed. He never hurried and scurried. He was always on time, late to some and early for others.*

*Never doing it the way established religion desired.*

*So why worry when things do not go the way you feel they should. Sometimes I call you to be still, but the churning inside of you says to get up and do something.*

*There is always something to do. I never lead by a "churning."*

*My Spirit is of love, peace, and joy, patience, gentleness, faithfulness, kindness, meekness and self-control.*

*If you are in a thither or scurrying around, My Spirit is not behind that. So be it.*

\*\*\*

*"For all the promises of God in Him are yea, and in Him Amen, unto the glory of God by us." I Corinthians 1:20*

*"But the fruit of the Spirit is love, joy, peace, longsuffering, gentleness, goodness, faith, (23) Meekness, temperance: against such there is no law." Galatians 5:22–23*

> **THIS IS THE DAY THAT THE LORD HAS MADE. I WILL REJOICE AND BE GLAD IN IT.**

*Hallelujah!*

*He is risen and since He is, I am.*

*Whatever He is, I am.*

*Come and celebrate His power to transform lives, set the captives free—make differences in ordinary lives so they become the redeemed of the Lord.*

*Come and seek His face, since that is the only place from which we gain knowledge and understanding of His will for us.*

\*\*\*

*"Herein is our love made perfect, that we may have boldness in the day of judgment: because as He is, so are we in this world." I John 4:17*

*"The Spirit of the Lord GOD is upon me; because the LORD has anointed me to preach good tidings unto the meek; He has sent me to bind up the brokenhearted, to proclaim liberty to the captives, and the opening of the prison to them that are bound;" Isaiah 61:1*

*"O give thanks unto the LORD, for He is good: for His mercy endures for ever. (2) Let the redeemed of the LORD say so, whom He has redeemed from the hand of the enemy;" Psalm 107:1–2*

*"O Lord, You have pleaded the causes of my soul; You have redeemed my life." Lamentations 3:58*

## APRIL 15
### THIS IS THE DAY THAT THE LORD HAS MADE. I WILL REJOICE AND BE GLAD IN IT.

*I have provided for all your needs today. Every incident that occurs, I have prepared for. There is nothing that will happen today that I did not already know about and have not already prepared you for.*

*There is nothing that can happen—no thing— that you will not be thoroughly prepared for.*

*So go out in confidence—never thinking about what you should do, but ONLY following the leading of the Holy Spirit within your chest.*

\*\*\*

*"Then said Jesus unto His disciples, If any man will come after Me, let him deny himself, and take up his cross, and follow Me." Matthew 16:24*

*"LORD, You have heard the desire of the humble: You will prepare their heart, You will cause Your ear to hear: (18) To judge the fatherless and the oppressed, that the man of the earth may no more oppress." Psalm 10:17–18*

*"Let not your heart be troubled: you believe in God, believe also in Me. (2) In My Father's house are many mansions: if it were not so, I would have told you. I go to prepare a place for you. (3) And if I go and prepare a place for you, I will come again, and receive you unto Myself; that where I am there you may be also." John 14:1–3*

*"You prepare a table before me in the presence of my enemies: You anoint my head with oil; my cup runs over. (6) Surely goodness and mercy shall follow me all the days of my life: and I will dwell in the house of the LORD for ever." Psalm 23:5–6*

## APRIL 16
### THIS IS THE DAY THAT THE LORD HAS MADE. I WILL REJOICE AND BE GLAD IN IT.

*For this is the day to begin and end those things for which you've waited and believed.*

*There are things you've waited and believed for and today is the day to receive them. You can say, "I have received healing for my eyes. I have received the job. I have received that car. I have received success in my company.*

*"And most of all...I have received the gift of peace.*

*"Freedom from worry, disturbing thoughts and feelings, pangs of fear.*

*"Today I have received peace."*

*"Peace I leave with you, My peace I give to you: not as the world gives do I give to you. Let not your heart be troubled, neither let it be afraid." John 14:27*

*"Now faith is the substance of things hoped for, the evidence of things not seen." Hebrews 11:1*

*It is by faith that we receive the promises of God. It is not by what we see physically. Develop your spiritual eyes...spend time with the invisible God!*

\*\*\*

*"That you be not slothful, but followers of them who through faith and patience inherit the promises." Hebrews 6:12*

## APRIL 17

## THIS IS THE DAY THAT THE LORD HAS MADE. I WILL REJOICE AND BE GLAD IN IT.

*For we are the ones He has delivered out of the mouth of the devourer.*

*He is the One that brings us into the promised land of freedom…freedom from the cares of this world.*

*For what care could arise that He could not handle?*

*So why not laugh in the face of concern—concern for children, husband, jobs, home, health.*

*If He cares for the lilies and the sparrows, surely He cares for your children, husband, job, home, and on and on.*

*So why let the enemy perch on your back?*

*Would it not be better to wear His robe of righteousness?*

\*\*\*

*"These things I have spoken unto you, that in Me you might have peace. In the world you shall have tribulation: but be of good cheer; I have overcome the world." John 16:33*

*"I will greatly rejoice in the LORD, my soul shall be joyful in my God; for He has clothed me with the garments of salvation, He has covered me with the robe of righteousness, as a bridegroom decks himself with ornaments, and as a bride adorns herself with her jewels." Isaiah 61:10*

## THIS IS THE DAY THAT THE LORD HAS MADE. I WILL REJOICE AND BE GLAD IN IT.

*Can you rejoice today?*

*Can you live with a smile on your face?*

*What a difference you could make to those around you, if you could maintain that smile. It is hard to worry when your mouth is turned up, and there's a twinkle in your eye!*

*You can never tell what mighty things the Lord may perform for you today.*

*He is looking for a way to bless you. Doesn't any good father desire to bring pleasure to his children? Blessings that make their heart swell with love, knowing how much they are loved.*

**Well... My child, I, the Creator of the worlds loves you. Let Me show you today! Be looking for that special act of love toward you, My love.**

\*\*\*

*"He brought me to the banqueting house, and His banner over me was love. (5) Stay me with flagons, comfort me with apples: for I am sick of love. (6) His left hand is under my head, and His right hand does embrace me." Song of Solomon 2:4–6*

## THIS IS THE DAY THAT THE LORD HAS MADE. I WILL REJOICE AND BE GLAD IN IT.

*Come unto Me all ye who labor and are heavy laden and I will give you rest.*

*Rest for your weary soul.*

*Weary from worry, weary from hurt and pain, weary from no love.*

*Come unto Me, let Me love you with an everlasting love, with a love that pours out life's blood, life's reputation.*

*I had no reputation so you could have one, and yours is the inheritance of Jacob. And what is the inheritance of Jacob?*

*Look it up for yourself! It's the same blessings I gave to and promised to Abraham—life forevermore.*

*Begin to look beyond your daily circumstances.*

*I have something greater on the horizon.*

\*\*\*

*"Verily, verily, I say unto you, He that believes on Me has everlasting life." John 6:47*

## THIS IS THE DAY THAT THE LORD HAS MADE. I WILL REJOICE AND BE GLAD IN IT.

*Let us rejoice. What does that mean, My child? Let us rejoice!*

*Rejoicing is more than a happy face or a good feeling inside.*

*Rejoicing is exuberant. It's overflowing. It's overcoming!*

*Overcoming bad news with the good news of Jesus Christ.*

*Did He die for nothing?*

*Did He shed His blood for nothing? Did He suffer ill repute, stripes, shame, reviling for nothing? Say,*

*"No! I will confess and profess the truth of Jesus Christ. I will bring every thought captive. I will deny Satan and take up my cross of truth today."*

*Let not fear and trembling overtake you. Let the love of Christ overtake you. Read My Word and I'll speak words of tenderness to you to quiet your restless soul.*

\*\*\*

*"The LORD your God in the midst of you is mighty: He will save, He will rejoice over you with joy; He will rest in His love, He will joy over you with singing." Zephaniah 3:17*

## APRIL 21

### THIS IS THE DAY THAT THE LORD HAS MADE. I WILL REJOICE AND BE GLAD IN IT.

*The sun is shining!*

*It is always shining.*

*Sometimes you have to get above the clouds to see it shining, but it is always shining.*

*What clouds are blocking your view of the Son? Ask yourself, "What is it that looms larger than the sacrifice of God? What problem seems to annul the death of Jesus?"*

*Come now; wait upon the Lord for revelation. He will give it.*

*He will unravel the mess and bring sense from the circumstances.*

*Is anything too hard for the Lord?*

*Is My hand shortened by your clouds?*

*No, My hand is always outreaching.*

*Tell those problems to move.*

*You're looking to God for a solution and not at the problems.*

*Lift up your eyes from whence thou help cometh.*

\*\*\*

*"Behold, the LORD'S hand is not shortened, that it cannot save; neither His ear heavy, that it cannot hear." Isaiah 59:1*

*"I will lift up my eyes unto the hills, from whence comes my help. (2) My help comes from the LORD, which made heaven and earth." Psalm 121:1–2*

## APRIL 22
### THIS IS THE DAY THAT THE LORD HAS MADE. I WILL REJOICE AND BE GLAD IN IT.

*"Holy Father, how is it that our eye looks in triumph on our enemies? How is it that we overcome them?"*

*Oh, My child, it is not thee that overcometh, but Me in thee.*

*Draw close to Me and I will draw close to you, and as I draw close, your enemies flee.*

*They cannot stand in the presence of a Holy God.*

*So be thou holy as I am holy. That does not mean be God, but it means to stand in My Holiness.*

*Stand with Me. Stand with Me, and as you stand with Me My presence will overtake you, and your enemies will flee. Outside of Me there is no holiness. So stand with Me.*

*How Lord? How do we stand with You?*

*You know, My child. Draw close. Just as You would draw close to someone on earth.*

\*\*\*

"Deliver me, O LORD, from mine enemies: I flee unto You to hide me. (10) Teach me to do Your will; for You are my God: Your Spirit is good; lead me into the land of uprightness. (11) Quicken me, O LORD, for Your name's sake: for Your righteousness' sake bring my soul out of trouble. (12) And of Your mercy cut off mine enemies, and destroy all them that afflict my soul: for I am Your servant." Psalm 143:9–12

## THIS IS THE DAY THAT THE LORD HAS MADE. I WILL REJOICE AND BE GLAD IN IT.

*... Glad for God has defeated our enemies. He has routed the despicable spirits of Satan. Say,*

*"Blessed be the God of Israel, for He has fought for us and has gained the victory crown for His children."*

*Shout aloud, oh you children of God! Shout aloud with a mighty shout! For our God has gone before us. He has cleared the way for our entrance into the kingdom.*

*Shout aloud! And bring your friends and loved ones in with you, for He has carved out a place for them too.*

*Be not hesitant in your march forward, but be courageous!*

*Be not leery of the magnificent bounty He has purchased for you, but only be courageous and bold as you grasp the mighty things He has awaiting you!*

\*\*\*

*"Only be strong and very courageous, that you may observe to do according to all the law, which Moses My servant commanded you: turn not from it to the right hand or to the left, that you may prosper whithersoever you go." Joshua 1:7*

## THIS IS THE DAY THAT THE LORD HAS MADE. I WILL REJOICE AND BE GLAD IN IT.

*It is not said that perhaps we should rejoice, but that we will rejoice.*

*Make a free-will offering of rejoicing today, for His steadfast love endures forever.*

*Grasp hold of His Body. Hang onto Him. Lay hold of Him. Embrace Him. He will not ask anything of you. He will not push you away. He will respond to your affection with His own yearning for you.*

*Has man disappointed you? Jesus will not. Has man asked and taken from you without your permission? Jesus will not. Jesus gives.*

*He places in your life choices that are not forced upon you. He does not take unwillingly. He gives without asking anything in return. He gives and expects nothing. He simply wants to love you, take care of you, lie with you, embrace you, hold you until His love permeates you. Receive Him today.*

\*\*\*

*"I sleep, but my heart wakes: it is the voice of my Beloved that knocks, saying, Open to Me, My sister, My love, My dove, My undefiled: for My head is filled with dew, and My locks with the drops of the night." Song of Solomon 5:2*

## APRIL 25
## THIS IS THE DAY THAT THE LORD HAS MADE. I WILL REJOICE AND BE GLAD IN IT.

*He says over and over again to rejoice. But oh, it is hard when life seems to make no sense! But He still says, "Rejoice in the Lord always." (Philippians 4:4)*

*What should we rejoice in?*

*Rejoice in the fact that I AM is in control. See answers come when you least expect them. Answers do come. Now look not at the way things are, but look at the way things will be. I will bring sense to the things that are bothering you. Trust in Me.*

*Let not the things of life bring to naught the reality of I AM.*

*Think on these things: I AM is in control. I AM moves mountains and brings up the valleys.*

*I AM has nothing that is impossible for Him.*

*I AM makes the weak knees strong and lifts up the limp hands.*

*I AM creates something from nothing, and I AM works on your behalf to turn all things to your good!*

*Forget your problems and think on the God that works for thee!*

\*\*\*

"Strengthen the weak hands, and confirm the feeble knees. (4) Say to them that are of a fearful heart, Be strong, fear not: behold, your God will come with vengeance, even God with a recompense; He will come and save you." Isaiah 35:4–5

## THIS IS THE DAY THAT THE LORD HAS MADE. I WILL REJOICE AND BE GLAD IN IT.

*Let us rejoice!*

*Rejoice with the birds and grass, with the sun and moon, with the air!*

*Babies wake up with no thoughts of worry. They live from moment to moment never worrying. They are totally dependent upon others for their continued existence. As we grow older, we think we can take care of ourselves, not realizing we are still dependent creatures—dependent upon the grace and mercy of Almighty God.*

*He is here to take care of those things we cannot. We only hurt ourselves when we fret (Psalm 37:8). He is always taking care of us. Always has us on His mind (I Peter 5:7).*

*Let us rejoice for His love endures forever!*

*He will make a way where there seems to be no way. Isn't that comforting? He will make a way over, around or through that mountain of concern.*

*Whatever it is, He will make a way.*

*Let us allow Him to show Himself mighty on our behalf. Trust Him!*

\*\*\*

*"For who is God, save the LORD? And who is a rock, save our God? (33) God is my strength and power: and He makes my way perfect." II Samuel 22:32–33*

## APRIL 27

### THIS IS THE DAY THAT THE LORD HAS MADE. I WILL REJOICE AND BE GLAD IN IT.

*Forget the past, and remember the exploits of the Lord.*

*Think not of the future, and hope in the Lord.*

*Live in the present, and rejoice.*

*When the day has ended, you will be proud you decided to rejoice in Jesus rather than give in to the "down times" of the day.*

*When discouragement comes during the day, stop and sit for a while to put your mind back on Jesus. After all He is the Way, the Truth, and the Life.*

*If after reading something about our Father, you do not feel better, continue to read, pray, or sing praises.*

*Sometimes the mind likes to have its own way and desires not to give reign to Jesus. Don't worry; the Spirit will overcome the soul, for greater is He Who is in you than he who is in the world.*

**Oh, My child, let your requests be known unto Me with thanksgiving, and I will give you peace. Isn't that one of My names?**

**Fear not, My little flock, it is My good pleasure to bless you.**

\*\*\*

*"Fear not, little flock; for it is your Father's good pleasure to give you the kingdom." Luke 12:32*

*"Be careful for nothing; but in every thing by prayer and supplication with thanksgiving let your requests be made known unto God. (7) And the peace of God, which passes all understanding, shall keep your hearts and minds through Christ Jesus." Philippians 4:6–7*

## APRIL 28

### THIS IS THE DAY THAT THE LORD HAS MADE. I WILL REJOICE AND BE GLAD IN IT.

*Rejoice for we know not the wonderful things He has in store for us today!*

*… A wonderful thing—forgiveness given to someone else. Even though their words hurt, Jesus is right there to apply the soothing ointment so you can forgive. It is truly an act of His grace.*

*It cannot come from our evil heart, but from the heart He has given and prepared for us.*

*Oh! our spirit grows every day! It gets stronger every day.*

*But those that seek Me, find Me and those that knock and continue to knock, I will come into them and sup and share and love and embrace.*

*Oh, come unto Me! I yearn and cry out for you! Oh, why is the time so long in you coming to Me? Why linger on the outside when I desire your presence inside with Me.*

*Quiet…Hush…Listen. You will hear Me calling you.*

*Hush, you must hush. Only then will you hear Me. Hush…*

\*\*\*

*"And after the earthquake a fire; but the LORD was not in the fire: and after the fire a still small voice." I Kings 19:12*

## APRIL 29
### THIS IS THE DAY THAT THE LORD HAS MADE. I WILL REJOICE AND BE GLAD IN IT.

*When you're glad about something, do you usually smile? Smile with your face, and smile inside? Yes. Think of something that makes you happy... See the smile. Maybe you don't have anything to be happy about. Is that really true? Say aloud, "Okay, God, if there's something I could be happy about, show me today."*

*Don't forget to record it in your journal. Then you can look back at it in a few days to remind yourself of God's provisions.*

*I'm glad of the fact that I have been brought out of a life of destruction into a life that gets better and better. That is the way life with Christ is. Although it may not appear that way sometimes, you are advancing! You are not spiraling downward as you once were.*

*Listen to Me, My children. The time has come to rejoice. Do not give Satan a second of complaining, regretting, discouraging thoughts, or despondent feelings. Think on these things—the purity of an infant, the redemption of My Son, the love that yearns for you. The love that yearns and yearns for you until finally I have your face turned to Me. Seeking Me, receiving My love and tenderness for you. Oh! that you would linger a while in My Presence. I promise everlasting blessings.*

\*\*\*

*"Happy is that people, that is in such a case: yea, happy is that people, whose God is the LORD." Psalm 144:15*

## APRIL 30
## THIS IS THE DAY THAT THE LORD HAS MADE. I WILL REJOICE AND BE GLAD IN IT.

*Oh hallelujah! Jesus is my Healer. For years I have sought Him for a physical healing, and it is today in the early hours that He manifested His healing through tenacious reliance of faith in the Blood of Jesus.*

*Oh, the Blood of Jesus that washes white as snow! The Blood that redeems what the enemy has done. Heals what the enemy has made weak. Restores what the enemy has destroyed.*

*Oh, do not let go of your hope; for in due time you will rejoice!*

*You will reap the blessings of Abraham, Isaac, and Jacob—your due inheritance.*

*God's ways are good all the time, even when we temporarily doubt His goodness, because the circumstances look so bad! Yes, healing came this morning, but healing can leave just as quickly, for sometimes our healing is by faith. Each of our lives is in His hand. If we are His, He wields them whichever way He desires. Give thanks that He is a good God and Father.*

**Look not to the right nor the left! Keep your eyes on the Shepherd. I provided Him for you. Neglect not My sacrifice of love. He is the only way.**

\*\*\*

*"Jesus says unto him, I am the Way, the Truth, and the Life: no man comes unto the Father, but by Me." John 14:6*

# MAY

"Who, when he had found one pearl
of great price, went and sold all that
he had, and bought it."

MATTHEW 13:46

## MAY 1
## THIS IS THE DAY THAT THE LORD HAS MADE. I WILL REJOICE AND BE GLAD IN IT.

*How is it that Love can go so far to relieve the pain of life?*

*Because Love never fails. It looks like Love has turned Its back on you. Perhaps sent you to a lonely place. It is only to find you.*

*Love does not always appear kind and loving. But It is.*

*Can you walk close enough to Me to trust Me when life does not make sense? Can you obey when it is so hard?*

*Do people turn on you? Does the one you love reject you, because of your obedience to Me?*

*Get use to it. That was My life. The ones I came for rejected Me—even My own brothers and sisters. Did that stop My obedience to My Father? No. I continued to love them, but they did not see it as love. And the one you are making angry will not see your actions as love. Is that going to negate My Father's directions for you? Read Psalm 22 and 35. Look not at the people you are disappointing.*

*Look to Me, My child. Stay focused on your Shepherd. I will lead you through the valley of the shadow of death, for the other side is LIFE!*

\*\*\*

"Jesus said unto her, I am the resurrection, and the life: he that believes in Me, though He were dead, yet shall he live: (26) And whosoever lives and believes in Me shall never die. Do you believe this?" John 11:25–26

## MAY 2

### THIS IS THE DAY THAT THE LORD HAS MADE. I WILL REJOICE AND BE GLAD IN IT.

*Let us rejoice and be glad! Oh hallelujah! Sing for joy! He has delivered us from sin and sickness! He has given us life for death. And He will vindicate us in the congregation of evildoers. God's light will shine forth!*

*Look to Me and I AM will lead you into all righteousness. The battle has just begun! But whose battle is it? "The battle is Mine," says the Lord of Host. A mighty host is on your side.*

"Open our eyes, Lord, so we may see this mighty host."

*Let us encourage ourselves in the Lord. Read of His mighty deeds on our behalf. Will He fail us now? Only do not doubt! The enemy wants us to doubt His lead. With doubt, we cannot go forward 100 percent. For this battle, we must be strong and courageous. Banish fear and doubt.*

*Stay close, My child! Stay close! Do not be swayed by outward appearances. I am working and will bring about the changes. I will bring about the changes. I will bring about the changes.*

*Only DO NOT DOUBT.*

\*\*\*

"And he answered, Fear not: for they that be with us are more than they that be with them. (17) And Elisha prayed, and said, LORD, I pray You, open his eyes, that he may see. And the LORD opened the eyes of the young man; and he saw: and, behold, the mountain was full of horses and chariots of fire round about Elisha." II Kings 6:16–17

## MAY 3

## THIS IS THE DAY THAT THE LORD HAS MADE. I WILL REJOICE AND BE GLAD IN IT.

*You see He has made this day to show forth His glory.*

*At the end of each day, you can recount what He has done for you that day. Record these blessings, because in so doing you bless the Lord.*

*Yes, that's what He means in Psalm 103, "Bless the Lord, O my soul and all that is within me. Bless His Holy name."*

*You bless Him as you remember what He has done for you and tell (witness to) others what He has done.*

*Recall His many, many blessings. He does so much for us. Can we not do something for Him?*

*Bless Him, my child; recall His mighty deeds for the children of Israel, our ancestors.*

*What He did for them He did for us, and will do for us again.*

*Hallelujah!*

\*\*\*

*"And I will bring the blind by a way that they knew not; I will lead them in paths that they have not known: I will make darkness light before them, and crooked things straight. These things will I do unto them, and not forsake them." Isaiah 42:16*

## THIS IS THE DAY THAT THE LORD HAS MADE. I WILL REJOICE AND BE GLAD IN IT.

*What a declaration, "I will rejoice."*

*Well, there will be times during the day that you will need to remember your statement of faith. When people are upset, think in your heart, "Oh, God, help them!" and then smile with assurance God can and will help them.*

*Just because others are upset doesn't mean you must become downcast. Hope in God! (Psalm 42:5)*

*Remember His provisions for you in the past. He will provide again. Give Him a chance, and you'll glorify Him. Remember not the former things. He is doing something new. New truths He is giving you. Uncovering lies and deceptions you've walked in for years.*

*The truth sets you free, and it will set others free around you.*

*When you're having a problem with another person, look in the mirror. It is that person that God is trying to clean up and set free! He loves you and wants you to walk in freedom alongside of others as irritating as they may be.*

*Ask Him what your problem is. He'll tell you and give you the solution. Hallelujah!*

\*\*\*

*"But I say unto you, Love your enemies, bless them that curse you, do good to them that hate you, and pray for them which despitefully use you, and persecute you;" Matthew 5:44*

**THIS IS THE DAY THAT THE LORD HAS MADE. I WILL REJOICE AND BE GLAD IN IT.**

*Let us consider the Blood of Jesus. If the blood of a lamb protected His children from the death angel, how much more will the Blood of His Son protect us? His Blood has healing power.*

*"Who His own self bore our sins in His own body on the tree that we, being dead to sins, should live unto righteousness: by whose stripes ye were healed." I Peter 2:24*

*"Oh, Father, give us wisdom and understanding of Your Son's Blood. Let us not neglect His Blood. Let us know what it is that You have done for us. So that we receive all the blessings You have provided for us. Forgive us and have mercy on us! We repent of our ignorance and plead for Your mercy."*

Come unto Me all ye who are weary and heavy laden and I will give you rest. Learn of Me. For I am meek and lowly in heart and you will find rest for your soul. Look not to the right nor left, and I will lead you forward. All your needs were provided for when I shed My Blood. Now come to Me, acknowledging the accomplishments of My Blood and you will see miracles occur. Except they are not really miracles, but simply the result of My Blood properly applied to your life. Think this not strange. The truth may seem strange, but it will set you free.

\*\*\*

*"Then Jesus said unto them, Verily, verily, I say unto you, Except you eat the flesh of the Son of man, and drink His blood, you have no life in you. (54) Whoso eats My flesh, and drinks My blood, has eternal life; and I will raise him up at the last day." John 6:53–54*

## MADE. I WILL REJOICE AND BE GLAD IN IT.

*Is anything too hard for God?*

*No.*

*We believe nothing is too hard for God, don't we? Then why don't we bring to Him the things in life that are causing disorder in our home? The small things like attitudes, unkind remarks, impatience, and on and on...*

*What are those character qualities in your children that need correcting? Ask your Father what the problem is with you, what the problem is with your child, and what the solution is. He will answer.*

*He will lead you each day.*

*This is serious stuff—the training of God's children. Are we being good stewards of His possessions?*

*We are not our own, but we have been bought and paid for with a great price—Jesus' Blood.*

*The Blood, the precious Blood—it has cleared the way through all problems.*

*So carry forth the Word of God with boldness and love!*

\*\*\*

*"Ah Lord GOD! Behold, You have made the heaven and the earth by Your great power and stretched out arm, and there is nothing too hard for You:" Jeremiah 32:17*

Ye shall reap if ye faint not (Galatians 6:9). Do not grow weary in well doing (II Thessalonians 3:13). Don't lose your confidence in the hope placed before you! (Hebrews 10:35) Hang on! Persevere.

Be encouraged for He Who promised is faithful (Hebrews 10:23). He is faithful even when our faith grows dim.

He is working even when we are not. He never slumbers nor sleeps (Psalm 121:4). He is ever watchful and mindful of us (Psalm 139:17–18).

He Who keeps Israel never slumbers nor sleeps (Psalm 121:4). Rest. He calls us to rest in Him (Hebrews 4:10).

When having done all, stand (Ephesians 6:13). Stand strong. Be not weary. He shall bring it to pass, only believe.

He is able; nothing is too hard for Him (Jeremiah 32:27).

We can do all things through Christ (Philippians 4:13). Stand close to Christ. Keep in touch. Do not wander out on your own. And having received from Him,

DO NOT DOUBT! (James 1:6–8)

\*\*\*

"Who is among you that fears the LORD, that obeys the voice of His servant, that walks in darkness, and has no light? Let him trust in the name of the LORD, and stay upon his God." Isaiah 50:10

## MAY 8

## THIS IS THE DAY THAT THE LORD HAS MADE. I WILL REJOICE AND BE GLAD IN IT.

*Stand back and see the glory of the Lord (Exodus 14:13).*

*Ask Him for all things, and He will give. Nothing is too small.*

*As a matter of fact, until you can trust Him to supply your smallest of needs, you'll not be able to trust Him to supply your larger ones. He who is faithful in small things will receive larger things.*

*Think it not strange that these sources of irritation have come upon you. It is in the small things that you must learn to trust Me.*

*It is the small things that spoil and defeat the mighty.*

*Be an overcomer in the smallest of things, and see your victory spread to the mountain tops.*

*Seek not those things you have been taught. But seek Me and I'll supply all the minutest of things.*

*You'll see. I AM is able!*

*Hallelujah!*

\*\*\*

"And he said unto him, Well, you good servant: because you have been faithful in a very little, have you authority over ten cities." Luke 19:17

"He that is faithful in that which is least is faithful also in much: and he that is unjust in the least is unjust also in much." Luke 16:10

## MAY 9
## THIS IS THE DAY THAT THE LORD HAS MADE. I WILL REJOICE AND BE GLAD IN IT.

*Oh hallelujah! Let us sing unto the Lord, for He has triumphed mightily; the horse and rider He has thrown into the sea (Exodus 15:1).*

*Come unto Me all ye who labor and are heavy laden and I will give you rest. Rest for that weary soul. That soul that tends to take on more than is called for. Why do you humans always take on more than is necessary? Because you know no better. That is why I say, "Come unto Me."*

*I have a way out of the rat race. But how can I show you, unless you come aside and listen to Me? How can you receive knowledge unless you come to the Teacher for instruction? Do you not realize I AM created you and therefore I can instruct you in the ways of motherhood, fatherhood, businesshood, childhood, wifehood, husbandhood, auto mechanichood....*

*Do you not know I have the answer and answers for your hectic life?*

*Come unto Me and I will instruct you in the ways of a simple life—a life without hurry, a life without pressure, a life without worry, a life without fear. Come! Come! Come unto Me!*

*Hallelujah!*

\*\*\*

*"And the Spirit and the bride say, Come. And let him that hears say, Come. And let him that is athirst come. And whosoever will, let him take the water of life freely." Revelation 22:17*

*There is a day of reckoning in each of our lives. Oh yes, there is a final day of reckoning, but there are also many days in our lives on earth that are days of reckoning.*

*These are days when final decisions are made—decisions that have long awaited closure. Oh, we decided before, but we've fallen back, compromised, doubted, wavered. That's okay. Make that decision again. The Lord will help and continue to help until we experience solid victory in that area of our life.*

*Well, this is the day of reckoning. Come to a firm decision about that problem that's bugged you, off and on for a long, long time. Make a statement of finality and go on with life. With all of your heart determine to never go back, knowing that only God's grace, His power, can keep you from falling again and keep you going forward!*

*Put your confidence in Him and His great love for you. He is working on your behalf, just like any good parent does for their children.*

*Lean hard into Him. He is strong, stable, and compassionate.*

*Hallelujah!*

\*\*\*

*"Multitudes, multitudes in the valley of decision: for the day of the LORD is near in the valley of decision." Joel 3:14*

*I will. Let others be as they are, but make the confession that, "I will rejoice." I will rejoice.*

*Oh yes, it is easy to rejoice when things are going smoothly, but how about the times your body aches with pain and all around you seems out of joint... when your energy is not there and hope is dim.*

*He said to rejoice in the Lord at all times (I Thessalonians 5:16) (Philippians 4:4). Rejoice wherever you are.*

*You may think there's nothing to rejoice over, but rejoice anyway. Offer a sacrifice of praise. Just sing, "Hallelujah."*

*Fight! You must fight the enemy and not give in. How do you fight?*

*By falling back into the loving arms of your Father. His Spirit dwells within you. Help comes from within.*

**Lift up your eyes. Go! Be mean! Be tough! This life is in enemy territory. So take your stand and don't back down! Go forward! Do what you can, and I'll do the rest!**

*Hallelujah!*

\*\*\*

*"Neither shall they say, Lo here! Or lo there! For, behold, the kingdom of God is within you." Luke 17:21*

*"Rejoice evermore. (17) Pray without ceasing. (18) In every thing give thanks: for this is the will of God in Christ Jesus concerning you." I Thessalonians 5:16–18*

## MAY 12
## THIS IS THE DAY THAT THE LORD HAS MADE. I WILL REJOICE AND BE GLAD IN IT.

*How about you? Will you rejoice or will you follow the people around you who moan and groan? Do not listen to their murmuring. Listen to Me.*

*Listen to the voice of the Lord. And that voice is the Holy Spirit—the Spirit of Jesus who says, "I have come to do My Father's will." Are you doing His will or are you being tossed back and forth trying to do the will of those around you?*

*Seek ye first the kingdom of God.*

*Seek His face. Seek His will. Seek His voice.*

*Strain to hear His voice above the maddening crowd. Seek His voice above the clamoring voices in your life. And once you've heard Him—follow it. Follow what He has said.*

*Obey! Be ye doers of the word and not hearers only (James 1:22). Faith without works is dead (James 1:20). Don't see in a mirror and then go away and do nothing (James 1:23).*

*Don't crucify the Christ all over again. Seek to do His will—not only to know His will, but to do it.*

**If you love Me, you will keep My commandments.**

\*\*\*

*"He that says, I know Him, and keeps not His commandments, is a liar, and the truth is not in him." I John 2:4*

## THIS IS THE DAY THAT THE LORD HAS MADE. I WILL REJOICE AND BE GLAD IN IT.

*This is the day of salvation. If you hear His voice today, harden not your heart. There are new mercies every day (Lamentations 3:23). Today is the day of rest. Rest in Him, knowing He does everything well, and what He allows is in His ultimate plan for good! Do not put off the will of the Lord today. You know not when the Master comes. Our Father speaks much of the importance of today.*

**Forget the things of the past, for I am doing a new thing. Don't miss it. Today is new. Never written on before.**

*Let us see how we can rejoice in the Lord today. Praise Him for we have a new day every 24 hours. Praise Him for we have another chance to be better at praising Him today! You may have had a terrible yesterday, but here we are starting a new day. Recall His Words to you. Rejoice in the Lord. And again I say, Rejoice. Let all men know your patience, perseverance. The Lord is at hand (Philippians 4:5). He is here. He is here to help! Oh, hallelujah! His name is Helper. Do you need help in anything today? Well, rejoice you have the greatest carpenter, physician, mind, psychologist, counselor at your side. Not only at your side, but as close as inside you! Plus He always has time for you. No waiting for an appointment. As a matter of fact, He is waiting for you now! Just look in His direction. He is smiling at you and pleased with you. There is no condemnation, only love! (Romans 8:1) You are the apple of His eye! (Deuteronomy 32:10)*

\*\*\*

*"Keep me as the apple of the eye, hide me under the shadow of Your wings, (9) From the wicked that oppress me, from my deadly enemies, who compass me about." Psalm 17:8–9*

## MAY 14
## THIS IS THE DAY THAT THE LORD HAS MADE. I WILL REJOICE AND BE GLAD IN IT.

*Be glad! We will be glad! Let us together be glad. Not standing alone, but together. Rejoice with those who rejoice.*

*Help each other through the times of hardship, for we all go through them. We all go through times of testing, and it isn't cheating to get help from a brother or sister.*

*Leaning on your Big Brother, Jesus, you'll find the help you need wherever that may come from. He has the answer to your cry. He has the piece that is missing.*

*He fits right into that problem perfectly. Let Him minister life to you. Let Him minister truth.*

*Oh, how He sets you free, and then He sets others free around you! Just as a ripple in water vibrates outward, the truth will ripple out to others who are surrounding you to also set them free.*

**Oh, look not to the right nor the left, only forward. That's where I'll be for no other holds that position of head-on. Seek to know Me. Seek to hear Me and seek to trust Me. It is only in trusting and not doubting that I can work in your life. So hang on and don't give up. Don't lose your confidence of which has a great reward.**

\*\*\*

*"Cast not away therefore your confidence, which has great recompense of reward. (36) For you have need of patience, that, after you have done the will of God, you might receive the promise." Hebrews 10:35–36*

*"Turn not to the right hand nor to the left: remove your foot from evil." "Proverbs 4:27*

## ✝
## MAY 15
## THIS IS THE DAY THAT THE LORD HAS MADE. I WILL REJOICE AND BE GLAD IN IT.

*This day was made by God.*

*He made it for me. Yes, He did!*

*Did He make it for you? Are you His child?*
*Then He made it for you too.*

*I wonder what wonders God wants to show us today. Let's open our mind and heart to receive something new from Him.*

*I know He would love to give His child something special today, because He made it just for you!*

*Write down in your journal that special wonder He showed you today.*

\*\*\*

*"I am my Beloved's, and His desire is toward me." Song of Solomon 7:10*

*"Henceforth I call you not servants; for the servant knows not what his lord does: but I have called you friends; for all things that I have heard of My Father I have made known unto you." John 15:15*

## THIS IS THE DAY THAT THE LORD HAS MADE. I WILL REJOICE AND BE GLAD IN IT.

*Oh hallelujah! He is prepared to give you knowledge and truth—knowledge to know the way. What a better Provider can we have?*

*He knows the way, and He'll show you the way. No matter where you are in your walk with God, He'll have a way for you. Years down the road, the way may be different in the same circumstance, simply because of your maturity in Him.*

*You are growing in freedom, being set free from bondages. As you are set free, the way changes because you're able to handle things in a more Christ-like manner. Years before you were limited in your actions and what He could advise you to do. But now because of hours…years of sanctification, you've come to a place in Christ of strength and courage like Joshua.*

*So go forth in courage!*

*Do not doubt! Stay close to your Source.*

*He said your days would be prosperous, if you did not let His Words out of your mouth, but spoke them day and night (Joshua 1:8).*

*Keep your eyes in a heavenly posture so your orders are received from above and not from those around you.*

*Keep the Boss the Boss and others your neighbor.*

\*\*\*

*"Hear, O Israel: The LORD our God is one LORD: (5) And you shall love the LORD your God with all your heart, and with all your soul, and with all your might." Deuteronomy 6:4–5*

## THIS IS THE DAY THAT THE LORD HAS MADE. I WILL REJOICE AND BE GLAD IN IT.

*Oh, how we will rejoice and be glad!*

*Rejoice by trusting Me. How can a child show his love more for a parent than by trusting—not worrying? Trusting that the parent will let him know what he should do. Trusting the parent will not let him veer off course too much before bringing him back. Oh, just trust Me to take care of the smallest things—like what's for supper and what to give in tithes and offerings.*

*Trust Me to speak clearly to you. If I can't get you to understand, I'll speak to a donkey to get your attention.*

*My hand is not shortened by your deficiencies. I can make a way to lead you. You think you're too messed-up to receive accurate direction from Me. Well, no matter your deficiencies I can overcome them. Nothing is impossible for Me. All I need is a yielded heart to know and do My will. I can take care of the rest.*

*Trust and don't doubt!*

*Trust and go forward.*

*Don't fear error. That's why I'm here with grace and mercy.*

*Hallelujah! He is here for me—for you!*

\*\*\*

*"And the LORD opened the mouth of the ass, and she said unto Balaam, What have I done unto you, that you have smitten me these three times?" Numbers 22:28*

## THIS IS THE DAY THAT THE LORD HAS MADE. I WILL REJOICE AND BE GLAD IN IT.

*What more can be said about rejoicing? Oh, there is much!*

*Bless the Lord, Oh my soul; and all that is within me, bless His Holy name! (Psalms 103:1) Oh, He is worthy of praise—worthy of honor, glory, majesty, exaltation, fear, time, money, energy, thought.*

*Love the Lord your God with all your heart, mind, soul and strength. Meditate on those words today.*

*How can you love Him with all your heart? What is most precious to you? Give it to Him, just as Abraham did. Give it to Him. Trust Him. Don't receive it back just as Hannah did (Samuel 1), and Mary the mother of Jesus. Sever those ties, cut the strings that hinder your whole heart from loving God.*

*Oh, cry out for His revelation that shows you your heart so you may surrender those things that keep you less than whole-hearted for God! Our hearts are deceiving above all things (Jeremiah 17:9). That is why we need His revelation.*

*"Search us, oh Father, and see if there be any wicked thing in us and lead us in the path of righteousness.*

*"Search us! Search us! Cleanse us!"*

\*\*\*

*"Search me, O God, and know my heart: try me, and know my thoughts: (24) And see if there be any wicked way in me, and lead me in the way everlasting." Psalm 139:23–24*

## THIS IS THE DAY THAT THE LORD HAS MADE. I WILL REJOICE AND BE GLAD IN IT.

*Who knows the mind of Christ, except the Spirit of the Lord, and He has shown this mind to you (I Corinthians 2:16).*

**Look not to the right nor left, but look unto Me the Author and Finisher of your faith.**

*It is faith that pleases God (Hebrews 11:6). Do not deceive yourself into thinking that your will and desires are acceptable as sacrifices. For without faith it is impossible to please Him. And faith without works is dead (James 2:20).*

*So what is hindering you from marching forward? It is fear. Fear of failure. Fear of what? Failure of missing the Spirit. This fear is not pleasing to God. Failure to hear Him correctly is no sin, but to walk in fear of hearing Him correctly is sin.*

**So go forward, My child, and do as your spirit leads you; and if you're in error, why do you think My Son came and died for you? He is your Redeemer!**

**There is nothing you can do in faith that is not pleasing to Me. But to hold back in fear is least of all pleasing.**

\*\*\*

*"...for whatsoever is not of faith is sin." Romans 14:23b*

*"But without faith it is impossible to please Him: for he that comes to God must believe that He is, and that He is a rewarder of them that diligently seek Him." Hebrews 11:6*

## MAY 20

### THIS IS THE DAY THAT THE LORD HAS MADE. I WILL REJOICE AND BE GLAD IN IT.

*Hold not back in your rejoicing. Your will will not be thwarted. For any hand that raises itself against you shall be rebuked. (Isaiah 54:15 & 17) Again I say look not to the right nor left. It is I that leads you. Do not question and ponder your leading. This is a hazardous place to dwell—doubt. Yes, you shall be tossed back and forth like the waves in the sea only to be disappointed at your lack of accomplishments.*

*Oh, works are not everything, but what if My Son came to earth and accomplished nothing? That's right, not a pretty thought. He did and said only what I did and said. That is your mission. Will you fail? Yes, there will be times of failure, but to fail is far and above fear—for fear paralyzes.*

*Who came to kill, steal, and destroy? Nowhere in his mission is said anything of accomplishments, success, and advancement. Of course not, for his mission is to hinder, slow down, halt, stop anything contributing to My kingdom. Look not to the right nor left, but keep your eye on the high calling of Jesus Christ as to walking by faith and not by sight!*

\*\*\*

"I can of Mine own self do nothing: as I hear, I judge: and My judgment is just; because I seek not Mine own will, but the will of the Father which has sent Me." John 5:30

"Turn not to the right hand nor to the left: remove your foot from evil." Proverbs 4:27

## MAY 21

## THIS IS THE DAY THAT THE LORD HAS MADE. I WILL REJOICE AND BE GLAD IN IT.

*It is a decision to rejoice or not. What will you do today? What did you do today? Was there rejoicing? Will there be rejoicing?*

*He says to rejoice in the Lord always; let your requests be made known to God and the peace that passes understanding will be yours (Philippians 4:6–7). Let your requests be made known to Him. Ask Him. He'll be delighted to answer and give you what you need.*

*Seek first His kingdom (Matthew 6:22). Be single minded. Have a single eye (Matthew 6:22). Walk on the water with Him (Matthew 14:29). He is sufficient to support you. Lean on Him. Hang onto Him. Neglect not to think on Him. Love Him. Yearn for Him. Desire Him. He is the Lover of your soul. He is the Rock of your salvation, the Rock upon which you are growing; the Rock upon which you are established.*

*He is your foundation. Every house has a foundation and you have a foundation too, for you are the temple of the Holy Spirit.*

***So seek not what I can do for you, but seek ye first the kingdom of God. REJOICE ALWAYS!***

\*\*\*

*"Whosoever comes to Me, and hears My sayings, and does them, I will show you to whom he is like: (48) He is like a man which built a house, and dug deep, and laid the foundation on a rock: and when the flood arose, the stream beat vehemently upon that house, and could not shake it: for it was founded upon a rock." Luke 6:47–48*

## THIS IS THE DAY THAT THE LORD HAS MADE. I WILL REJOICE AND BE GLAD IN IT.

*In rejoicing, the answer will come. Those that sow in tears will reap in joy. Joy cometh in the morning (Psalm 30:5). Morning could be night, but when His light comes, it is morning and it is a time of joy.*

*Forget not those things He has spoken unto you. Be not like a child that hears, but doesn't put into effect the words having spoken unto him (James 1:24).*

*We need to be like that child who follows his mother. He tries to do exactly as she does. It may not look like what she is doing, but his heart is to follow. God knows our heart. And He will help us just as a mother helps her child.*

*What is it He has said to you, and you have let it linger too long?*

*Do it today. Make some movement in accomplishing that of which He has spoken. Do not let it die.*

*Act in faith believing for a completion to your endeavors!*

\*\*\*

*"But be you doers of the word, and not hearers only, deceiving your own selves. (23) For if any be a hearer of the word, and not a doer, he is like unto a man beholding his natural face in a glass: (24) For he beholds himself, and goes his way, and straightway forgets what manner of man he was." James 1:22–24*

> **THIS IS THE DAY THAT THE LORD HAS MADE. I WILL REJOICE AND BE GLAD IN IT.**

"Oh God, manifest Yourself in us today! Let us see what You would do today if You had a body available to You. You do have a body. It is the body of believers in Your Son Jesus. May it be wholly submitted to You today. Let my body be Yours.

"Show me Your actions today.

"Show me Your thoughts, words, visions.

"Show me who You would see today.

"Oh God! let my body and soul be Your habitation today. You can do it. You say, 'Ask and ye shall receive.' We are asking for You to manifest today in our lives."

We say, "Be gone with the old life. Be filled with the life of Christ and see new and wonderful things accomplished for Him today."

Hallelujah!

\*\*\*

"What? Know not that your body is the temple of the Holy Ghost which is in you, which you have of God, and you are not your own? (20) For you are bought with a price: therefore glorify God in your body, and in your spirit, which are God's." I Corinthians 6:19–20

## THIS IS THE DAY THAT THE LORD HAS MADE. I WILL REJOICE AND BE GLAD IN IT.

*Oh, that we could rejoice!*

"I know You have made it available to us and possible for us. How do we get this joy to manifest in our lives? This is the day. This…not that. Here…not there."

*TODAY is the day of salvation.*

*Read of the mighty acts of faith I have brought My children through. I will bring you too. This you can rejoice in. I will bring you through.*

*If you can believe, you can rejoice. But if you doubt this, your rejoicing will be minimal and intermittent.*

*Why not believe what your Father says? Don't you desire that your children believe you?*

*Go just for today and believe I will carry you through.*

*I carried the three Israelite children through the fire and they did not even smell of smoke.* (Daniel 3:27)

*Don't you think I am able to carry you?*

"Yes, Lord. I believe; help my unbelief!"

\*\*\*

"And straightway the father of the child cried out, and said with tears, Lord, I believe; help thou mine unbelief." Mark 9:24

## THIS IS THE DAY THAT THE LORD HAS MADE. I WILL REJOICE AND BE GLAD IN IT.

*We will rejoice! Take time to rejoice.*

*In the busyness of the day, take time to rejoice.*

*Hallelujah for His care!*

*He takes care of us.*

*If we trust Him, we can live in peace. If we are busy taking care of ourselves, then we cannot know His peace.*

*Give yourself over to His care. When you're preoccupied with concern for yourself, it inhibits the Holy Spirit from manifesting His peace within and around you.*

*If you center your attention on pleasing Him, you will know the care that He is always giving you.*

*You have not been able to receive, because of the worry and fear having blocked it.*

**Oh, for a person to look to Me for their sustenance!**

**Look to Me for your love. Lay down your concerns and come away with Me. I will comfort you. I do love you.**

\*\*\*

*"My Beloved spoke, and said unto me, Rise up, My love, My fair one, and come away. (11) For, lo, the winter is past, the rain is over and gone; … (13c) Arise, My love, My fair one, and come away." Song of Solomon 2:10–11, and 13c*

† 

## MAY 26

### THIS IS THE DAY THAT THE LORD HAS MADE. I WILL REJOICE AND BE GLAD IN IT.

*Oh hallelujah! What a mighty God we serve. We serve a Mighty God. All hail to the King! He is our Father. Oh! He is our Daddy and our Husband! He looks over us with love—with love and attention (Song of Solomon 2:4). What are His thoughts? His thoughts are to do us good in the end (Jeremiah 29:11). His thoughts are always toward us, guarding us in the rear and all sides.*

*Who or what can penetrate the protection of the mightiest God? Heaven, hell, or earth does not contain anything or anyone that can separate God's love from us. Let us rejoice in our resting place! For this is the place our Husband and Father has provided for us. Let us seek to rest in His place of immunity. A place that is guarded from all evil for the work is finished. It was finished when Jesus said, "It is finished." He never spoke an untruth.*

*We must believe Him and not doubt. Let us not leave Him on the cross. Let us not crucify Him all over. Let us not hold our Savior's work up in contempt. Do not walk devoid of His accomplishments for you. Do not let life and all its circumstances nullify Christ's love for you. Abide under the shadow of the Almighty (Psalm 91:1). Abide.*

\*\*\*

*"For I know the thoughts that I think toward you, says the LORD, thoughts of peace, and not of evil, to give you an expected end." Jeremiah 29:11*

*"Abide in Me, and I in you. As the branch cannot bear fruit of itself, except it abide in the vine; no more can you, except you abide in Me." John 15:4*

## MAY 27

### THIS IS THE DAY THAT THE LORD HAS MADE. I WILL REJOICE AND BE GLAD IN IT.

*"What have we, but You?*

*"Oh, yes there are many people around. But who have we, but You?*

*"You, the stable force in our life.*

*"You, the strength of our life.*

*"Oh, Father, make us to know You! That was Your Son's prayer so it must be that we are getting to know You (John 17:3).*

*"Stir our hearts to seek You, and not just answers to our problems. Yes, You do have the answers, and desire to give us the answers, but lop-sided relationships are bad.*

*"We want to love You and spend time with You as a friend and a lover. We want to do something for You."*

**Oh, My child, lend Me your heart today. I will show you what I desire from you—what you can do for Me.**

**I've been waiting for you to ask Me what you could do for Me.**

**I will make you cognizant of My Spirit all day today, and you'll know what it is you can do for Me!**

**Write it down. It will be new revelation for you and many.**

\*\*\*

*"And now, Lord, what wait I for? My hope is in thee." Psalm 39:7*

## THIS IS THE DAY THAT THE LORD HAS MADE. I WILL REJOICE AND BE GLAD IN IT.

*Oh hallelujah! He has made and given us this day to show His glory on this earth.*

*The revelation shown me yesterday was "Joy." He wants us to be joyful—joyful and relaxed.*

*Is this not different from what the world offers? Yes. And does it not bring Him glory, when His children are joyful and relaxed?*

*I never thought of being joyful as something I could do for my Father. But doesn't it make you feel good when you see your earthly children walking in joy, and not moping in complaints, fears, and worries?*

*I've long desired joy, but didn't realize it was something I could actually do for my Father. I guess we have a choice to be joyful versus fearful—to have joy versus worry.*

*"Oh, Father, show us today where we can be joyful to Your glory rather than moping and groaning to Your disgrace. We do not want to bring a reproach upon Your name. We want to give You a sacrifice of joy. We want to walk in joy today! This is what we can do for You!"*

\*\*\*

*"And now shall mine head be lifted up above mine enemies round about me: therefore will I offer in His tabernacle sacrifices of joy; I will sing, yea, I will sing praises unto the LORD." Psalm 27:6*

## THIS IS THE DAY THAT THE LORD HAS MADE. I WILL REJOICE AND BE GLAD IN IT.

*What is it we should rejoice in?*

*We should rejoice in the day that He has made. The day that He has given us to know Him, experience Him, share Him, love Him, and minister to Him. The day that we can make a decision to rejoice whether circumstances yield to rejoicing or not.*

**Oh, that they would praise Me.**

**Come unto Me all ye who labor and are heavy laden. I will give you rest. My yoke is easy and so is yours if you're carrying My yoke.**

**Let go of all things except your love of Me. Desire Me above all. Set your mind on Me, not your children, mate, home, job.**

**Set your mind on knowing Me. That should fill up your time for eternity. Seek Me, and all things will be added unto You.**

**Are these words familiar? They should be. I've spoken them many years prior. Oh, come to Me, My beloved. Let Me give you rest for your soul and body. I desire to wash your feet and cleanse your mind. Oh, that you would seek Me!**

\*\*\*

"Rejoice evermore… (18) In everything give thanks: for this is the will of God in Christ Jesus concerning you." I Thessalonians 5:16 & 18

"But seek ye first the kingdom of God, and His righteousness; and all these things shall be added unto you." Matthew 6:33

## MAY 30

### THIS IS THE DAY THAT THE LORD HAS MADE. I WILL REJOICE AND BE GLAD IN IT.

*Oh, that we would rejoice!*

*Let's rejoice that we are His children and that when we mess up He forgives, He redeems, and He gives a clean conscience!*

*Oh, He is our Father! One like we've never known, but One that Jesus and the Holy Spirit are revealing to us!*

*He cares.*

*He loves.*

*Each day is new.*

*New to try His ways and not ours.*

*"Oh, Father, open our ears and then our mouths to speak Your words. What does this summer hold in store for us? What does this day?*

*"Be in us today even as You were in Your Son. Let us know Your acting in us as You would act on earth. For You are on earth in each of us, as we surrender our ways to You."*

**Remember to do for Me what I have revealed. Walk in joy—bubbling joy, unexplainable joy, indescribable joy. Look for My joy in each moment of the day!**

\*\*\*

*"But let all those that put their trust in You rejoice: let them ever shout for joy, because You defend them: let them also that love Your name be joyful in You." Psalm 5:11*

## MAY 31
## THIS IS THE DAY THAT THE LORD HAS MADE. I WILL REJOICE AND BE GLAD IN IT.

*You see the Lord is also our Father—our Daddy—the One on whom we nestle in His lap—lie at His feet—hug and lie our head on His shoulder—walk beside in trust and security.*

*Imagine walking along the beach with Jesus…*

*He will show you many wonderful things. Write these down, for you know He is the fountain of knowledge.*

*Oh, the many new things He will show you today!*

*Be ready!*

*Be ready to receive—like the baby bird in his nest with his mouth open ready to receive that food from his mother.*

*Have your ears open!*

*You'll hear new and you'll speak new— wondering where that came from.*

*Oh, He wants to fill your ears and mouth with good things.*

*Be ready. Be ready—for He is coming with good things!*

\*\*\*

*"I am the LORD your God, which brought you out of the land of Egypt: open your mouth wide and I will fill it." Psalm 81:10*

# JUNE

"Can two walk together, except they be agreed?"

AMOS 3:3

## JUNE 1

## THIS IS THE DAY THAT THE LORD HAS MADE. I WILL REJOICE AND BE GLAD IN IT.

*Do we find it hard to rejoice? This is because we have much of the world occupying our mind and body.*

*Come unto Me all ye who labor and are heavy laden. I will give you rest. I will give you My yoke which is easy and My burden which is light. Oh, come unto Me.*

*I have many things to tell you that you know not of.*

*Lie down with a gentle ear. An ear resting in assurance your Father has something to say to you and assurance that He will say something.*

*Rest in assurance.*

*Reject any doubts!*

*Come and rest! And as your heart stills, I will come! I have promised, "Be still and know that I AM God."*

*"To know Me is eternal life," My Son said.*

*Come and know Me. Come and know Me. I do not desire to keep Myself a secret.*

\*\*\*

*"And this is life eternal, that they might know You the only true God, and Jesus Christ, whom You have sent." John 17:3*

## THIS IS THE DAY THAT THE LORD HAS MADE. I WILL REJOICE AND BE GLAD IN IT.

*Oh hallelujah! He is King! Lord over everything.*

*In your weakness, He is shown to be strong. So rejoice when you've come to your end. Stop and thank Him.*

*Enter His gates with thanksgiving and go into His courts with praise (Psalm 100:4a).*

*What better time to praise Him than when it is not easy. Your soul does not feel like praising Him. Just try saying, "Hallelujah," over and over and clapping your hands! Yes, clap your hands in victory over your infirmity, sickness, weariness.*

*Clap your hands and shout, "Praise the Lord; for His mercy endures forever." (II Chronicles 20:21b)*

*Yes, shout with a sound of trumpets. Play worship music loudly! Drowned out the negative thoughts and emotions; replace them with praise and thanksgiving to the God who watches over you.*

*Give glory to your God for everything—past, present, and future.*

*Oh, hallelujah!*

\*\*\*

*"So the people shouted when the priests blew with the trumpets: and it came to pass, when the people heard the sound of the trumpet, and the people shouted with a great shout, that the wall fell down flat, so that the people went up into the city, every man straight before him, and they took the city." Joshua 6:20*

## THIS IS THE DAY THAT THE LORD HAS MADE. I WILL REJOICE AND BE GLAD IN IT.

*It's a choice. The Lord always gives us a choice. We can obey His Word or disobey. We can follow His lead or not follow. Jesus defeated Satan on the cross and gave us the ability to defeat him in our life also!*

*Isn't that wonderful? We can follow His lead. We can. We are able to follow His lead. Though we may be hard of hearing, seeing, discerning, He is not hindered by our deficiencies.*

*"Behold, the LORD's hand is not shortened, that it cannot save; neither His ear heavy, that it cannot hear." (Isaiah 59:1)*

*He does not try to trick us. If we desire to do His will, He is able to make known His will.*

*He has grace and mercy to accompany us. He has redemption, when we fail. He is our Shepherd. We are His sheep. He is the One with the responsibility to lead. We are the sheep. Let us get that into our head and heart.*

*You are My sheep. I AM cares for you. Looks after you. Leads you. Protects you. Trains you. Forgave you. Prepares you for every good work. It is I who waits for you.*

\*\*\*

*"And therefore will the LORD wait, that He may be gracious unto you, and therefore will He be exalted, that He may have mercy upon you: for the LORD is a God of judgment: blessed are all they that wait for Him." Isaiah 30:18*

## THIS IS THE DAY THAT THE LORD HAS MADE. I WILL REJOICE AND BE GLAD IN IT.

*Rejoice in your weakness. That is when the Lord can be shown strong in your life. Do not mope in your infirmities. Rejoice, because He who is in you is greater than he who is in the world (I John 4:4).*

*Be made strong in your weakness. Look to Him and He will make you strong in Him, not in your strength, not in your ability, not in your accomplishments! That is why we can rejoice. But in our weakness we look to Him, and He makes a way where there is no way.*

**Listen to My voice today. You will hear a word behind you saying, "Walk ye this way when you turn to the left and the right." *(Isaiah 30:21)***

*Go with what you get.*

*Don't doubt.*

*Don't hesitate.*

*Don't back down.*

*Don't retreat. Go with determination and courage!*

*Hallelujah!*

\*\*\*

*"Therefore I take pleasure in infirmities, in reproaches, in necessities, in persecutions, in distresses for Christ's sake: for when I am weak, then am I strong." II Corinthians 12:10*

**THIS IS THE DAY THAT THE LORD HAS MADE. I WILL REJOICE AND BE GLAD IN IT.**

*Yes, we will.*

*We will rejoice!*

*In all things, we will rejoice.*

*We will let all men know our forbearance.*

*For the Lord is at hand.*

*We will not worry about anything.*

*We will tell the Lord our requests and with thanksgiving we will receive His peace.*

*Oh, hallelujah!*

\*\*\*

"Rejoice in the Lord always: and again I say, Rejoice. (5) Let your moderation be known unto all men. The Lord is at hand. (6) Be careful for nothing; but in every thing by prayer and supplication with thanksgiving let your requests be made known unto God. (7) And the peace of God, which passes all understanding, shall keep your hearts and minds through Christ Jesus." Philippians 4:4–7

## JUNE 6

### THIS IS THE DAY THAT THE LORD HAS MADE. I WILL REJOICE AND BE GLAD IN IT.

*Will we not rejoice?*

*Has He not done great things for you? Has He not rebuked the devourer? He has called forth a host of angels on your account. He has called heaven and earth to proclaim His glory just for you. Oh, why not rejoice in such a love expended for you!*

*Rejoice and kiss the Son lest He be angry (Psalm 2:12).*

*He awaits your embrace. Write. Write out your love letters to Him.*

*He awaits your embrace. Your words will be life and healing for they spring from your love for Him.*

*Linger not in the things of this world, but meditate on His love for you.*

*"Oh, Father, we want to love You! We want to gladden your heart! Show us the way. We want to know how much You love us. We are Your sheep, Your children that desperately need You! Amen."*

\*\*\*

*"Kiss the Son, lest He be angry, and you perish from the way, when His wrath is kindled but a little. Blessed are all they that put their trust in Him." Psalm 2:12*

*"Set your affection on things above, not on things on the earth. (3) For you are dead, and your life is hid with Christ in God. (4) When Christ, who is our life, shall appear, then shall you also appear with Him in glory." Colossians 3:2–4*

## JUNE 7
## THIS IS THE DAY THAT THE LORD HAS MADE. I WILL REJOICE AND BE GLAD IN IT.

*You are so beautiful to Me.*

*(Song of Solomon 6:4a)*

*That is what our God says to each of us.
We are so beautiful to Him.*

*Today, ask Him to live His life in you. You have done this before, many times, but today remind yourself who you are. Observe the difference in this day as He is free to express Himself in your body and soul.*

*Your spirit is already under His control and total influence. Let Him have your body and soul. This is His desire and from this you'll see who you really are—who you were created to be. Not hindered by the past or future, but walking in freedom.*

*It is in Him that we find freedom to be who He created us to be, and rest from the world's expectations and influence.*

*Our prayer: "Oh Father, You created me for something. Yes, it is to give You pleasure (Revelation 4:11). To follow You. To be Your child. Father, cut through all the superficial things in my life. Bring me to the simplicity of my life in You on this earth, in this world. Amen."*

\*\*\*

*"I am crucified with Christ: nevertheless I live; yet not I, but Christ lives in me: and the life which I now live in the flesh I live by the faith of the Son of God, who loved me, and gave Himself for me." Galatians 2:20*

## THIS IS THE DAY THAT THE LORD HAS MADE. I WILL REJOICE AND BE GLAD IN IT.

We must rejoice before others can rejoice with us.

Why not be the person spreading the joy? Let's not allow the circumstances to dictate our mood.

Rejoice always. He tells us over and over again.

There will not always be circumstances that yield themselves to rejoicing. Do not let yourself be downcast in threatening situations. God is always there ready to give expert advice or help.

He is never too busy or overextended. He has the time, ability, and love that are necessary to solve your problem and get you out of a mess. Hallelujah!

With each problem, look to Him. It is not automatic, because we've been taught to handle our own problems. But He wants us to ask Him, to lean on Him, to trust Him, to fall back in His arms.

His wisdom is higher than ours, and He'll get all the glory as we see His ways coming to earth as they are in heaven.

**It is I who has said, "Be still and know that I AM God."**

\*\*\*

"Be still, and know that I am God: I will be exalted among the heathen, I will be exalted in the earth." Psalm 46:10

## THIS IS THE DAY THAT THE LORD HAS MADE. I WILL REJOICE AND BE GLAD IN IT.

*Have I not said it? Will I not perform it?*

"God is not a man, that He should lie; neither the son of man, that He should repent: has He said, and shall He not do it? Or has He spoken, and shall He not make it good?" Numbers 23:19

**You were healed with My Son's stripes. He was bruised for your iniquities and with His stripes you were healed.** *(Isaiah 53:5)*

*So rejoice in your healing. Don't question any more, but maintain your confidence, hoping against hope, not doubting, but being patient and faithful.*

*The Son will come to you with healing in His wings (Malachi 4:2). He has come, but you have need of patience that when you have patiently endured you will receive the promises of God. You will receive. Do not lose hope, but persist in your faith in Him as your Healer. Your healing will come. Let Him decide when and what that healing looks like. He is a good Daddy!*

**Do not shrink back, but persist in your faith in My Word. Satan is a liar and a deceiver.** *(John 8:44)*

\*\*\*

"Cast not away therefore your confidence, which has great recompense of reward. (36) For you have need of patience, that, after you have done the will of God, you might receive the promise." Hebrews 10:35–36

"And we desire that every one of you do show the same diligence to the full assurance of hope unto the end: (12) That you be not slothful, but followers of them who through faith and patience inherit the promises." Hebrews 6:11–12

## JUNE 10
## THIS IS THE DAY THAT THE LORD HAS MADE. I WILL REJOICE AND BE GLAD IN IT.

*Oh, hallelujah! Rejoice!*

*Sing praises! Shout for joy! Sing a new song!*

*Sing praises to your King! For He is Lord. His mercy never ends! It is new every morning! New every moment! Oh, give thanks to the Lord for He is good. His mercy endures forever!*

*Sing praises to His name. The name above every name—above depression, disease, death, hopelessness, suffering, sin, impotence, false piety, false religion, every evil word, thought and action.*

*Oh, that we would praise His name! Praise Him for His love, His healing care, tenderness, abiding grace, mercy, faithfulness, salvation, redemption, justification, righteousness, endurance, strength, courage, gentleness, peace, rest, protection, provision, joy, counsel, knowledge, wisdom, understanding, beauty, mightiness, power, glory, light, truth, patience, self-control, meekness, goodness, holiness, worthiness, servanthood, humility, passion, vision, and plans.*

*Oh praise Him for what He has done in your life! Make a record in your journal. This may be something you can refer to often—as often as the enemy brings distressing thoughts and situations to you.*

\*\*\*

*"Let every thing that has breath praise the LORD. Praise ye the LORD." Psalm 150:6*

## THIS IS THE DAY THAT THE LORD HAS MADE. I WILL REJOICE AND BE GLAD IN IT.

*Oh give thanks to the Lord, for His love endures forever.*

*Endures—isn't that a comforting word when it is the other person enduring on your account? But who likes to endure for themselves or for someone else?*

*Endure denotes patience—waiting. Also pain. If we endure something, it is usually not something we want to continue, but something that we want to come to an end—a happy end.*

*God's love endures forever, and I know He sometimes tires of waiting on His love being reciprocated.*

*No matter the wait, He is still there waiting with love—waiting for us to receive His blessings of peace and joy. When will we receive? Oh, we are in the process now, and when that joyful day comes for us to go to Heaven, our peace and joy will be complete!*

\*\*\*

*"Be patient therefore, brethren, unto the coming of the Lord. Behold, the Husbandman waits for the precious fruit of the earth, and has long patience for it, until He receives the early and latter rain." James 5:7*

*"The Lord is not slack concerning His promise, as some men count slackness; but is longsuffering to us-ward, not willing that any should perish, but that all should come to repentance." II Peter 3:9*

# JUNE 12

## THIS IS THE DAY THAT THE LORD HAS MADE. I WILL REJOICE AND BE GLAD IN IT.

*...For this is the day that we have. Now is the time of salvation.*

*What will this day bring? Looking always to Him, for your help is from the Lord. His truth is forever. It is the same yesterday, today, and tomorrow.*

*What He has said today will be good for tomorrow. Build on it. Don't neglect it. Don't be like the parable of the seeds where the Word of God gets eaten by the birds, doesn't take deep roots, or gets overcome by the cares of the world (Matthew 13:3ff & Luke 8:5ff). Meditate on the seeds He plants within you. Do not allow the enemy to steal them due to lack of attention. Keep them in the forefront of your mind.*

*Oh, that you would sit and listen. I long to converse readily with you—as readily as your own thoughts. I want to be as close as your own thoughts. Communion is what I desire. Intimate communion so close one cannot recognize the separation between us, because there is no separation.*

*You in Me and I in you. Just as it was and is with My Son, it shall be with you. Look not unto the right nor left. Continue your gaze upon Me. Looking to the Son of Righteousness to come with healing in His Wings.*

\*\*\*

*"I in them, and You in Me, that they may be made perfect in one; and that the world may know that You have sent Me, and have loved them, as You have loved Me." John 17:23*

*"Who is among you that fears the LORD, that obeys the voice of His servant, that walks in darkness, and has no light? Let him trust in the name of the LORD, and stay upon his God." Isaiah 50:10*

## JUNE 13
### THIS IS THE DAY THAT THE LORD HAS MADE. I WILL REJOICE AND BE GLAD IN IT.

*Oh, that you would rejoice! Would I ever leave you out in the cold with no one to turn to? Would I leave you with no advice, no counsel, no guidance, no wisdom?*

*No! My Spirit is forever brooding to create in you My Life, My Truth. Oh, listen My child and you will hear. Be not afraid to speak from the rooftops what you hear in private. I shall speak to you more and more readily as you speak in assurance those things you hear Me say. Look not to the right nor left. Keep your concentrated gaze upon Me, for I long to reveal Myself to you as you learn more and more about My Son.*

*Oh, how He loves you too, and has given His life for you. Listen to His words to you. Write them down. Read them again and again. Read His Words in the New Testament. Believe His words to you and doubt not. For those who doubt do not receive anything, but are tossed back and forth.*

*Are you tossed back and forth concerning something? Settle on the answer and waver not.*

*Do not consider again and be done with it. Now is the time—not later—now. Speak forth My word and be done with it.*

\*\*\*

"For let not that man think that he shall receive any thing of the Lord. (8) A double minded man is unstable in all his ways." James 1:7–8

## THIS IS THE DAY THAT THE LORD HAS MADE. I WILL REJOICE AND BE GLAD IN IT.

*Oh, hallelujah and give thanks to the Lord for His mercy endures forever, and so may your mercy toward others endure.*

*Love is patient. Love is kind. Love endures all things.*

*So give thanks and keep on loving and giving; and the Lord that sees in secret will reward you openly.*

*Do not lose your confidence, but continue to hope in the Lord for His mercy will extend to you, and you in turn will extend your mercy to those you love!*

\*\*\*

*"For I desired mercy, and not sacrifice; and the knowledge of God more than burnt offerings." Hosea 6:6*

*"But go and learn what that means, I will have mercy, and not sacrifice: for I am not come to call the righteous, but sinners to repentance." Matthew 9:13*

*"Blessed are the merciful: for they shall obtain mercy." Matthew 5:7*

*"Charity suffers long, and is kind; charity envies not; charity vaunts not itself, is not puffed up, (5) Does not behave itself unseemly, seeks not her own, is not easily provoked, thinks no evil; (6) Rejoices not in iniquity, but rejoices in the truth; (7) Bears all things, believes all things, hopes all things, endures all things. (8) Charity never fails…" I Corinthians 13:4–8a*

*"That your alms may be in secret: and your Father which sees in secret Himself shall reward you openly." Matthew 6:4*

*"Cast not away therefore your confidence, which has great recompense of reward. (36) For you have need of patience, that, after you have done the will of God, you might receive the promise." Hebrews 10:35–36*

> **THIS IS THE DAY THAT THE LORD HAS MADE. I WILL REJOICE AND BE GLAD IN IT.**

*What more can we say, if God is for us who can be against us? When God is for us, it does not matter who is against us. Let God be true and every man a liar.*

*Are there dreams that haven't come true yet? They will. Nothing is impossible with God. It is He that has made us and not we ourselves (Psalm 100:3).*

*It is He Who will bring to pass those things He has planted in our hearts. Did we think those were our ideas? Or maybe we knew they were His, but can't think of a way for those dreams to come true.*

*Keep your gaze on Him for it is He Who shall bring it to pass. Oh, give thanks to the Lord for He is good and His mercy endures forever.*

*Keep a forward stance and do not look back, for He is doing a new thing.*

\*\*\*

*"Commit your way unto the LORD; trust also in Him; and He shall bring it to pass." Psalm 37:5*

*"Behold, I will do a new thing; now it shall spring forth; shall you not know it? I will even make a way in the wilderness, and rivers in the desert." Isaiah 43:19*

*"Brethren, I count not myself to have apprehended: but this one thing I do, forgetting those things which are behind, and reaching forth unto those things which are before, (14) I press toward the mark for the prize of the high calling of God in Christ Jesus." Philippians 3:13–14*

**THIS IS THE DAY THAT THE LORD HAS MADE. I WILL REJOICE AND BE GLAD IN IT.**

*Speak and My words will be your words.*

*My wisdom, your wisdom.*

*Oh! that man would search for God with all his heart.*

***There is an unfathomable amount of riches awaiting you as you seek Me. Seek and ye shall find.***

*Is that not a glorious assurance of treasure?*

*Does God lie?*

*He cannot!*

*So let us seek, and we shall find!*

\*\*\*

*"Which things also we speak, not in the words which man's wisdom teaches, but which the Holy Ghost teaches; comparing spiritual things with spiritual." I Corinthians 2:13*

*"In hope of eternal life, which God, that cannot lie, promised before the world began:" Titus 1:2*

*"God is not a man, that He should lie; neither the Son of man, that He should repent: has He said, and shall He not do it? Or has He spoken, and shall He not make it good?" Numbers 23:19*

*"Call unto Me, and I will answer you, and show you great and mighty things, which you know not." Jeremiah 33:3*

*"And I say unto you, Ask, and it shall be given you; seek, and you shall find; knock, and it shall be opened unto you." Luke 11:9*

> **THIS IS THE DAY THAT THE LORD HAS MADE. I WILL REJOICE AND BE GLAD IN IT.**

*Isn't it wonderful to rejoice in the Lord, disregarding the hectic life around you?*

*Try it. You'll like it!*

*He is worthy of our attention. He is jealous for our attention.*

*What thoughts occupy your mind?*

\*\*\*

*"For you shall worship no other god: for the LORD, whose name is Jealous, is a jealous God:" Exodus 34:14*

*"Speaking to yourselves in psalms and hymns and spiritual songs, singing and making melody in your heart to the Lord; (20) Giving thanks always for all things unto God and the Father in the name of our Lord Jesus Christ;" Ephesians 5:19–20*

*"Rejoice evermore. (17) Pray without ceasing. (18) In every thing give thanks: for this is the will of God in Christ Jesus concerning you." I Thessalonians 5:16–18*

*"Finally, brethren, whatsoever things are true, whatsoever things are honest, whatsoever things are just, whatsoever things are pure, whatsoever things are lovely, whatsoever things are of good report; if there be any virtue, and if there be any praise, think on these things." Philippians 4:8*

## JUNE 18

### THIS IS THE DAY THAT THE LORD HAS MADE. I WILL REJOICE AND BE GLAD IN IT.

*Oh, let us rejoice. Rejoice! And again I say rejoice. He is in control, whether we are or not. So rejoice and look not at the circumstances, for they will change as we praise the Lord. And even if the circumstances do not seem to change, our perspective of them does.*

*With that change will come wisdom—His wisdom, understanding and knowledge. As long as our mind is on the circumstances, we have little hope of receiving God's perspective. And that is really what we need!*

*Did He not open the prison doors for Paul and Silas? Read and listen to those stories of God's deliverance; Esther, Ruth, Gideon, Deborah, Samson, Jehoshaphat, David, Lot, and on and on.*

*He will deliver you. The battle may be injurious, but freedom and truth are worth it. And the injuries do heal, for He came to heal the brokenhearted.*

\*\*\*

*"And at midnight Paul and Silas prayed, and sang praises unto God… (26) And suddenly there was a great earthquake, so that the foundations of the prison were shaken: and immediately all the doors were opened, and every one's bands were loosed." Acts 16:25a–26*

*"Then sang Deborah and Barak… (2) Praise ye the LORD for the avenging of Israel, when the people willingly offered themselves." Judges 5:1a–2*

*"And when they began to sing and praise, the LORD set ambushments against the children of Ammon, Moab, and mount Seir, which were come against Judah; and they were smitten." II Chronicles 20:22*

## JUNE 19
## THIS IS THE DAY THAT THE LORD HAS MADE. I WILL REJOICE AND BE GLAD IN IT.

*"I was glad when they said unto me, Let us go into the house of the Lord." (Psalm 122:1)*

*Oh, that we would praise the mighty Creator!*

*He has created just for you. Oh yes, think of it and take it personally. He has created this day just for you. He has created the sky and air just for you, and the sea with its majestic surf that continues day after day.*

*Our God is a personal God.*

*That is the only way you can truly receive Him.*

*He is not a god of the masses or of a group or a church.*

*No, He is one on one.*

*He is individual and yes, then He can be received as a group. But always first privately.*

*Oh, worship Him! And give Him praise!*

\*\*\*

*"O clap your hands, all you people, shout unto God with the voice of triumph... (6) Sing praises to God, sing praises: sing praises unto our King, sing praises." Psalm 47:2 & 6*

*"For the Son of man is come to seek and to save that which was lost." Luke 19:10*

## JUNE 20
## THIS IS THE DAY THAT THE LORD HAS MADE. I WILL REJOICE AND BE GLAD IN IT.

*We will rejoice!*

*We will keep our mind stayed on Jesus. He is the Author and the Finisher of our faith. He has the wisdom bound up in Himself. He is Wisdom. From whence will we receive wisdom, if not from Him?*

*So keeping our mind on Him should solve all our problems. So why go around mourning? He is our peace. It is from our position in Him that we'll make it out of the current situation that we may find ourselves.*

*Oh, sing praises to His name! Think on His names—Counselor, Mighty God, Prince of Peace, Rose of Sharon, Bright Morning Star, Husband, Father, Daddy, Healer, Redeemer, Provider, Lover and Shepherd. Add you own names for Jesus:*

_____, _____, _____, _____,

_____, _____, _____, _____.

\*\*\*

*"For the LORD gives wisdom: out of His mouth comes knowledge and understanding." Proverbs 2:6*

*"Looking unto Jesus the Author and Finisher of our faith; who for the joy that was set before Him endured the cross, despising the shame, and is set down at the right hand of the throne of God." Hebrews 12:2*

*"Why are you cast down, O my soul? And why are you disquieted within me? Hope in God: for I shall yet praise Him, who is the health of my countenance, and my God." Psalm 42:11*

## THIS IS THE DAY THAT THE LORD HAS MADE. I WILL REJOICE AND BE GLAD IN IT.

*Oh rejoice! Rejoice in the Lord for He is good!*

*He is looking for ways to bless His children and that includes you!*

*Seek Him for who He is and not just for your relief from pain.*

*Seek Him to satisfy His heart's yearning for you. He wants you. He wants you like a lover wants his beloved.*

*God is a lover and He loves you and wants you and needs you. Yes, God needs you. Does God need anything? Yes, He needs you.*

*When He decided to create someone in His image, He set in motion a need in His heart. And that need is you receiving His love, and you giving your love to Him in return.*

*Jesus came to earth to provide the way for His Father to have children to love. It is all about love. Pure and simple.*

*For God is love (I John 4:16).*

*Spend some of your time with God saying and asking for nothing. Simply looking to Him and admiring His beauty.*

*Reading about Him in the Psalms is a good place to get acquainted with your Lover.*

\*\*\*

*"Seek ye first the kingdom of God, and His righteousness; and all these things shall be added unto you." Matthew 6:33*

## JUNE 22

## THIS IS THE DAY THAT THE LORD HAS MADE. I WILL REJOICE AND BE GLAD IN IT.

*Oh, give thanks to the Lord for His mercy endures forever.*

*Forever is hard to comprehend, but forever does include this day and the rest of my life and my children's lives and their children's lives, and on and on.*

*His mercy never ends. I guess it's like love, but mercy implies a sympathy for the person's situation. Knowing that the person has done wrong, but mercy finds a way to forgive and continue blessing.*

*God seeks over and over to bless us. We are too ignorant to know what to do, and in His mercy He orchestrates things to our benefit.*

*Oh, that we would know Him, for He is good and His mercy endures forever.*

\*\*\*

*"O give thanks unto the LORD; for He is good; for His mercy endures for ever." I Chronicles 16:34*

*"These things have I written unto you that believe on the name of the Son of God; that you may know that you have eternal life, and that you may believe on the name of the Son of God." I John 5:13*

*"The blessing of the LORD, it makes rich, and He adds no sorrow with it." Proverbs 10:22*

*"Blessed be the LORD, who daily loads us with benefits, even the God of our salvation. Selah." Psalm 68:19*

*"Praise ye the LORD, O give thanks unto the LORD; for He is good: for His mercy endures for ever." Psalm 106:1*

## THIS IS THE DAY THAT THE LORD HAS MADE. I WILL REJOICE AND BE GLAD IN IT.

*We will rejoice for He has made us glad (Psalm 9:2).*

*Rejoice and doubt not. This questioning back and forth is not of God. Seek Him, the Lover of your soul. Go forth and do good.*

*Many questionings will come. Many doubts will bombard your mind. But stand firm and rejoice.*

*Let your requests be known to your Father and give thanks (Philippians 4:6). Everything is in His control. He is in charge, because you are His child and you have given yourself to Him.*

*Would He forsake you? No! (Hebrews 13:5) He could not, for He cannot lie. He knows your sitting down and rising up (Psalm 139:2).*

*He knows your thoughts and words before they are even spoken (Psalm 139:4). He knows you and He loves you! Isn't that wonderful?*

*He knows you like no one else knows you, even yourself. He loves you and thinks about you. You are always on His mind.*

*Grace and mercy, peace and love be with you this day and forever.*

\*\*\*

*"How precious also are Your thoughts unto me, O God! How great is the sum of them! (18) If I should count them, they are more in number than the sand: when I awake, I am still with You." Psalm 139:17–18*

*"Let your conversation be without covetousness; and be content with such things as you have: for He has said, I will never leave you, nor forsake you." Hebrews 13:5*

## JUNE 24

## THIS IS THE DAY THAT THE LORD HAS MADE. I WILL REJOICE AND BE GLAD IN IT.

*Oh, that we would rest! He has called us to rest with Him. He has rested from His work. He said, "It is finished." Can we not rest in His accomplishments?*

*Did Jesus fret? He did not. Why? Because His Father has said many times, "Fret not," and Jesus always obeyed His Father. He may have been tempted to fret, but He sinned not.*

*What does He say in Hebrews? He rested from His work, and those that believe will rest from their work (Hebrews 4:10). When will we believe the Lord? When will we walk in His ways?*

*"Father, help our unbelief. We want to believe! Forgive us for our unbelief. We do not want to be pushed around by fears and doubts! Help us to resist them with the assurance that You are in charge—in charge of our lives. Fill us with Your perfect love so we are not tormented with fear. Lead us, Almighty Father, to dwell in Your shadow and rest under Your wings! Amen."*

\*\*\*

*"He that dwells in the secret place of the most High shall abide under the shadow of the Almighty. (2) I will say of the LORD, He is my refuge and my fortress: my God; in Him will I trust." Psalm 91:1–2*

*"There is no fear in love; but perfect love casts out fear: because fear has torment. He that fears is not made perfect in love." I John 4:18*

## JUNE 25
### THIS IS THE DAY THAT THE LORD HAS MADE. I WILL REJOICE AND BE GLAD IN IT.

*Look not back, but set your gaze upon the Lord. He is faithful to forgive and forget. He has forgiven you in Christ. Jesus received the punishment for your sins. See yourself in Christ and know that your sins are forgiven and remembered no more.*

*When you have gone wrong and done wrong, it is Jesus Who has prepared the way back. He has made the way to repair the wrong. He is your Redeemer. He is the Way. Confess and renounce your wayward ways. He is faithful to forgive and cleanse you from all unrighteousness (I John 1:9).*

**Your sins are forgiven My child even before you commit them. Your repentance is for your sanctification, not for My forgiveness or even to bring us into relationship. We are always in relationship as far as I am concerned, but your repentance puts you on the right track.**

\*\*\*

"Or do you despise the riches of His goodness and forbearance and longsuffering; not knowing that the goodness of God leads you to repentance?" Romans 2:4

"As far as the east is from the west, so far has He removed our transgressions from us. (13) Like as a father pities his children, so the LORD pities them that fear Him. (14) For He knows our frame; He remembers that we are dust." Psalm 103:12–14

## JUNE 26

### THIS IS THE DAY THAT THE LORD HAS MADE. I WILL REJOICE AND BE GLAD IN IT.

*Sing unto the Lord a new song. Make praises unto His name, for He has done great things for you.*

*He has destroyed the destroyer for your sake.*

*Now receive His victory and deny the lies of the enemy. Satan wants you to worry, but that is not the Father's way.*

*Remember His Word to us, "Rest. Come unto Me, all ye who labor and are heavy laden and I will give you rest."*

*They entered not into the Promised Land because of their unbelief (Hebrews 3:19). God calls unbelief, disobedience. If it is disobedience, then we have a choice whether to obey or disobey. We have a choice to believe or not.*

*Let us believe our Father and rest today.*

***Today, do not harden your heart, but believe. I have rest for you.***

\*\*\*

*"And the LORD gave them rest round about, according to all that He swore unto their fathers: and there stood not a man of all their enemies before them; the LORD delivered all their enemies into their hand. (45) There failed not ought of any good thing which the LORD had spoken unto the house of Israel; all came to pass." Joshua 21:44–45*

*"So we see that they could not enter in because of unbelief. (1) Let us therefore fear, lest, a promise being left us of entering into His rest, any of you should seem to come short of it." Hebrews 3:19–4:1*

> ## THIS IS THE DAY THAT THE LORD HAS MADE. I WILL REJOICE AND BE GLAD IN IT.

*Oh hallelujah! He is risen. He is not dead. He is alive. Alive to walk with us and talk with us.*

*He had to leave for a while, but He returned in glory and sent His Spirit to us.*

*Commune with Him upon your bed (Psalm 4:4), in your closet, on your way to work, during your work. Oh give thanks to the Lord for He is good, His mercy endures forever!*

*He will never leave you. Are you worried about something? Sit down right now. Tell Him your worries. List them on paper and leave them there with God, your Father. Then give thanks to Him. When those worries come to your mind again just say, "They're God's worries now. They belong to God. I don't have them anymore."*

*Let us see how God handles our worries and record His way. This record will bless Him as we witness His care for us. It will strengthen our faith. Oh, Hallelujah to our Lord for He is good! He loves and even adores us.*

*"Oh, Father, let us see Jesus. Let us experience Your love for us. Oh, let us know You! Amen."*

***

*"Tell me, O You whom my soul loves, where You feed, where You make Your flock to rest at noon: for why should I be as one that turns aside by the flocks of Your companions?" Song of Solomon 1:7*

*"And there were certain Greeks among them…(21) The same came therefore to Philip, which was of Bethsaida of Galilee, and desired him, saying, Sir, we would see Jesus." John 12:20a–21*

## JUNE 28
## THIS IS THE DAY THAT THE LORD HAS MADE. I WILL REJOICE AND BE GLAD IN IT.

*Be glad in this day. What has this day brought? What will this day bring? The Lord says, "Be glad in it."*

*Oh, to rejoice in all things (Ephesians 5:20). That is our goal. If He is in charge, should we not then rejoice in all things? Love all things. Love never ends. It doesn't tire of loving the unlovable.*

*Rejoice in your suffering. Perhaps He will open the prison doors, and free you just as He did for Paul and Silas and Peter (Acts 16:24–26; Acts 12:7).*

*Rejoice in your sickness, and He may come your way as He did with the woman with the issue of blood (Luke 8:44). Perhaps He is in your way, and perhaps your faith and perseverance will touch the hem of His garment, and you shall be made whole.*

*Love never fails. God is love. So He never fails. Faith, hope and love—the greatest of these is love (I Corinthians 13:13).*

*"Lord, teach us what love is."*

\*\*\*

*"Behold, what manner of love the Father has bestowed upon us, that we should be called the sons of God: therefore the world knows us not, because it knew Him not. (2) Beloved, now are we the sons of God, and it does not yet appear what we shall be: but we know that, when He shall appear, we shall be like Him; for we shall see Him as He is." I John 3:1–2*

**THIS IS THE DAY THAT THE LORD HAS MADE. I WILL REJOICE AND BE GLAD IN IT.**

*Oh, hallelujah! The Lord is good. His mercy endures forever. It is He who cares for our every need. He, it is who, has supplied His blood for our healing, protection, provision, preparation, sanctification. His Blood has cleared the path for our glory and His glory.*

*Oh, yes, glory is for you too. I died for your glory also. If a man's children do well, is it not a reflection of the father's excellent training? Am I not training you?*

*Before you chose Me, My eyes were upon thee to bless and keep thee. Have no fear for I AM is with thee. Why do you fret and wonder? Is it not I who has His hands upon thee to bless and keep thee? Wonder not at the good fortune or bad fortune that comes your way, because I AM is in charge of your life.*

\*\*\*

*"Can a woman forget her sucking child, that she should not have compassion on the son of her womb? Yea, they may forget, yet will I not forget thee." Isaiah 49:15*

*"Neither pray I for these alone, but for them also which shall believe on Me through their word; (21) That they all may be one; as You, Father are in Me, and I in You, that they also may be one in Us: that the world may believe that You have sent Me. (22) And the glory which You gave Me I have given them; that they may be one, even as We are One: (23) I in them, and You in Me, that they may be made perfect in one; and that the world may know that You have sent Me, and have loved them, as You have loved Me." John 17:20–23*

## JUNE 30

## THIS IS THE DAY THAT THE LORD HAS MADE. I WILL REJOICE AND BE GLAD IN IT.

*Be glad for the Lord is on your side to bless you and give you hope. Faith, hope and love—and the greatest of these is love (I Corinthians 13:13). What is love? It is patient. Waiting, waiting, waiting.*

*Can you wait on the Lord? He has and is waiting on you. So rejoice in His patience. Those that wait on the Lord shall receive manifold blessings—blessings of honor and glory (Psalm 37:34).*

*Repent and wait on the Lord. He is desirous to bestow manifold blessings upon you (Ephesians 1:3).*

*Be ready as you wait. Be poised for blessings. Let your heart rejoice and be hopeful.*

*He has come and will come with healing in His wings (Malachi 4:2).*

\*\*\*

*"The LORD bless you, and keep you: (25) The LORD make His face shine upon you, and be gracious unto you: (26) The LORD lift up His countenance upon you, and give you peace." Numbers 6:24–26*

*"And now, Lord, what wait I for? My hope is in Thee." Psalm 39:7*

*"But I will hope continually, and will yet praise You more and more." Psalm 71:14*

*"Blessed be the LORD, who daily loads us with benefits, even the God of our salvation. Selah." Psalms 68:19*

*"Bless the LORD, O my soul, and forget not all His benefits: (3) Who forgives all your iniquities; who heals all your diseases; (4) Who redeems your life from destruction; who crowns you with lovingkindness and tender mercies; (5) Who satisfies your mouth with good things; so that your youth is renewed like the eagle's." Psalm 103:2–5*

# JULY

*"Jesus answered and said unto her, If you knew the gift of God, and who it is that says to you, Give Me to drink; you would have asked of Him, and He would have given you living water."*

JOHN 4:10

## THIS IS THE DAY THAT THE LORD HAS MADE. I WILL REJOICE AND BE GLAD IN IT.

*Oh, give thanks to the Lord!*

*"Thank You, Lord, for this day, for air and sun, for love of a child and the pain of one too."*

*Oh, give thanks to the Lord for His love for us. He gives us all good things. Even when life seems to deal out bad, our Father turns them into good.*

*We cannot lose. But we can hurt. Life is full of pain. Pain of loss, separation, rejection, misunderstanding. I could go on and on.*

*But Jesus says, like the lyrics of this song, "Turn your eyes upon Me and the things of this world will grow strangely dim in the light of My glory and grace." ("Turn Your Eyes Upon Jesus", Helen H. Lemmel, 1922)*

*There's so much for us to experience of God—His glory, His grace, His goodness, His love, His mercy, His forgiveness...*

*"Open our hearts to know You—to receive Your love."*

\*\*\*

*"That Christ may dwell in your hearts by faith; that you, being rooted and grounded in love, (18) May be able to comprehend with all saints what is the breadth, and length, and depth, and height; (19) And to know the love of Christ, which passes knowledge, that you might be filled with all the fullness of God." Ephesians 3:17–19*

*"There is no fear in love; but perfect love casts out fear: because fear has torment. He that fears is not made perfect in love." I John 4:18*

## JULY 2
## THIS IS THE DAY THAT THE LORD HAS MADE. I WILL REJOICE AND BE GLAD IN IT.

*Oh, give thanks to the Lord for He is good! His mercy endures forever! His kindness to the ends of the earth.*

*What is kindness?*

*Doing for others and not expecting a return. Doing for others when they do not expect it to be done. Doing for another when they have done nothing to deserve it.*

*Kindness has to do with one's actions. Kindness cannot be shown unless there is action.*

*Kindness is a fruit of the Spirit, and it can only come from those walking in God's Spirit.*

*"Oh, Father, let us experience kindness. We know it is a part of Your love. We so yearn to experience Your love that will wash away our pain."*

**You have called upon Me, and you will find rest for your soul.**

\*\*\*

*"And call upon Me in the day of trouble: I will deliver you, and you shall glorify Me." Psalms 50:15*

*"The LORD is good, a strong hold in the day of trouble; and He knows them that trust in Him." Nahum 1:7*

> **THIS IS THE DAY THAT THE LORD HAS MADE. I WILL REJOICE AND BE GLAD IN IT.**

*Oh, give thanks to the Lord for He is good! His mercy endures forever!*

*Oh, how we need His mercy! He has suffered long with us and how He wants us to suffer with Him. Suffer with Him through intercession for those who do not know Him, those who know Him slightly yet are so cold toward Him, and those that are His children yet do not love Him.*

*"God, we need You to reveal Yourself to us!"*

**I have, My child, in the form of a man named, Jesus.**

*"Oh, Father open our cold, cold hearts so we can know Jesus and see Him. So we can love Him as He so deserves. Father, our sins are so deep only You can open the hurts and reveal the truths that our hearts so desperately need.*

*"Open our hearts and give us hearts of flesh to know You. If we could only see Jesus, we would have to love Him!"*

**No. My children saw Him on earth and did not love Him. Pray for your hearts to be seared with His Love and then you will know Him, and then you will love Him.**

\*\*\*

*"And when they had lifted up their eyes, they saw no man, save Jesus only." Matthew 17:8*

*"I indeed baptize you with water unto repentance: but He that cometh after me is mightier than I, whose shoes I am not worthy to bear: He shall baptize you with the Holy Ghost, and with fire:" Matthew 3:10–12*

† 

## JULY 4
## THIS IS THE DAY THAT THE LORD HAS MADE. I WILL REJOICE AND BE GLAD IN IT.

*"Oh, Father, lead us into Your path not ours! Lead us into life, everlasting life that is overflowing with wisdom and understanding.*

*"Oh, Father, that our lives would reflect You on earth. Teach us Your statutes that we can walk in Your ways. It is from You that we have eternal life and abundant life.*

*"Oh, that we would spread the gospel. But do we have enough of the gospel to spread? Our hearts are cold, and we need heat. We need the fire of the Holy Spirit to sear our hearts as You told us to pray.*

*"Oh God, sear our hearts so we can know Jesus."*

**There is that prayer in Ephesians that is perfect for you to pray. Now pray it with all your heart and never give up praying it.**

\*\*\*

*"That He would grant you, according to the riches of His glory, to be strengthened with might by His Spirit in the inner man; (17) That Christ may dwell in your hearts by faith; that you, being rooted and grounded in love, (18) May be able to comprehend with all saints what is the breadth, and length, and depth, and height; (19) And to know the love of Christ, which passes knowledge, that you might be filled with all the fullness of God. (20) Now unto Him that is able to do exceeding abundantly above all that we ask or think, according to the power that works in us, (21) Unto Him be glory in the church by Christ Jesus throughout all ages, world without end. Amen." Ephesians 3:16–21*

## JULY 5
## THIS IS THE DAY THAT THE LORD HAS MADE. I WILL REJOICE AND BE GLAD IN IT.

*Let us rejoice! That is an invitation from our Father. Invitations are always accepted when they come from someone with much authority and majesty. If we received an invitation from the President of the United States, we would be sure to make arrangements to accept his invitation.*

*Let us rejoice! Our Father and our God invites His children. Listen to Him. What is He saying to you today? Don't go day to day without knowing what your Father is saying. He seeks those who will listen. He does have an agenda He wants to share with you.*

*Listen…*

*What is He saying?*

*Find out and then rejoice as His Words come to pass. Rejoice as you experience your life changing, because of your obedience to His Words.*

*Listen…*

*God is waiting to speak. The Creator of all waits upon His creatures to listen!*

\*\*\*

*"…Speak for Your servant hears." I Samuel 3:10b*

*"For thus says the Lord GOD, the Holy One of Israel; In returning and rest shall you be saved; in quietness and in confidence shall be your strength: and you would not." Isaiah 30:15*

## THIS IS THE DAY THAT THE LORD HAS MADE. I WILL REJOICE AND BE GLAD IN IT.

*Oh! how we need to rejoice instead of belabor our plot in life. For our plot can change in a twinkling of an eye.*

*Let us not be found bemoaning our position. When the Bridegroom comes, let us be rejoicing at His coming. Rejoicing in anticipation. After all, does He not come many times in our life—not just at our physical death or the second coming?*

*He comes with deliverance, healing, hope, comfort, love, provision, answers to prayer, a voice in the dark! Oh, let Him find us rejoicing in anticipation of His coming—coming to our rescue. For He has promised, He would open the eyes of the blind and are we not blind? So let us rejoice. He will open our eyes.*

*He promised He would come with healing in His wings. Do we not need healing? Repent for the kingdom of God is at hand. Do not let the Bridegroom find His bride not ready! Repent and return to your God. Repent in sackcloth and ashes. Repent with a broken and contrite heart. Repent with wailing and tears. Repent and rend your heart for the lost souls in your presence! Repent and He will come and bless you with His knowledge! Repent!*

\*\*\*

*"And at midnight there was a cry made, Behold, the bridegroom cometh; go ye out to meet him... (10) And while they went to buy, the bridegroom came; and they that were ready went in with Him to the marriage: and the door was shut." Matthew 25:6 & 10*

*"From that time Jesus began to preach, and to say, Repent..." Matthew 4:17a*

> **THIS IS THE DAY THAT THE LORD HAS MADE. I WILL REJOICE AND BE GLAD IN IT.**

*Rejoice in the Lord always! And again I say rejoice! He has called us out of darkness into His marvelous light (I Peter 2:9). Let us take off our heavy grave clothes and rejoice in the light. He has spoken and can we not obey? Must we continue to side step His directions? Must we continue to put His requests behind the requests of our family and ourselves?*

*Seek Him early, seek Him late and seek Him at the midday. He desires a people who will be after Him in all things—at all times. Many times we do things when, yes, it is time to sit and be with Him.*

**When will you give in to My unrelenting desire for you? When will you get organized and have a place set aside just for you and Me? Do not scatter your life with Me all around the house. Have a place for Me. I have given you a home. Can you not find a corner for Me? I not only want a tithe of your finances. I want a tithe of your time, emotions, mind, body and home. Give unto Me and I will return to you pressed down, shaken together and running over will I pour into your lap!**

\*\*\*

*"And He said unto them, Come ye yourselves apart into a desert place, and rest a while: for there were many coming and going, and they had no leisure so much as to eat." Mark 6:31*

*"Give, and it shall be given unto you; good measure, pressed down, and shaken together, and running over, shall men give into your bosom. For with the same measure that you mete withal it shall be measured to you again." Luke 6:38*

## JULY 8
## THIS IS THE DAY THAT THE LORD HAS MADE. I WILL REJOICE AND BE GLAD IN IT.

*Though it tarry, wait on it (Habakkuk 2:3).*

*Do not faint, but hope against hope for that which the Lord has promised (Romans 4:18).*

*Do not grow weary in well doing, for it is He Who rewards the faithful and sustains the persistent (Hebrews 11:6).*

**Oh, do not faint for the battle is Mine, not yours.**

**Do not look to the right nor the left, but stay on the straight path.**

*Why do you linger so long in the things of this world?*

**Seek ye first the kingdom of God and all these things shall be added unto you, but you linger so long in the things of this world.**

"Oh, Father, have mercy on us. Show us where it is that we can seek You better. Show us where we turn to the right and the left.

"Thank You, Father. Amen.

"We desire to know Your voice."

\*\*\*

"Who against hope believed in hope, that he might become the father of many nations; according to that which was spoken, So shall your seed be." Romans 4:18

"My sheep hear My voice, and I know them, and they follow Me: (28) And I give unto them eternal life; and they shall never perish, neither shall any man pluck them out of My hand." John 10:27–28

> **THIS IS THE DAY THAT THE LORD HAS MADE. I WILL REJOICE AND BE GLAD IN IT.**

*He does things of which we do not know.*

*He works and we do not know.*

*But His work always comes to pass.*

*Will it come to pass in your lifetime?*

*I do not know, but it will come to pass.*

*Simply follow Him, walk with Him, and listen to Him every day.*

*Every day is that which years and centuries are made.*

*You cannot erase a day.*

*Each day is important in itself. That is why it is important to hear Him every day.*

*Now listen, for He is always eager to reveal His plans to you, His friend.*

\*\*\*

*"Henceforth I call you not servants; for the servant knows not what his lord does: but I have called you friends; for all things that I have heard of My father I have made known unto you." John 15:15*

*"For He is our God; and we are the people of His pasture, and the sheep of His hand. Today if you will hear His voice, (8) Harden not your heart, as in the provocation, and as in the day of temptation in the wilderness: (9) When your fathers tempted Me, proved Me, and saw My work," Psalm 95:7–9*

## JULY 10
### THIS IS THE DAY THAT THE LORD HAS MADE. I WILL REJOICE AND BE GLAD IN IT.

*Rejoice in the God that saves His children!*

*We are all like sheep that have gone astray, but God saves us.*

*Even as His children, we still go astray and He saves us. He never stops saving us.*

*Rejoice in this if you see one of your loved ones going astray. Be assured that He will save him.*

*Oh, pray for My lost sheep, saints. I need you to stand in the gap like Abraham did.*

*My Son has given His all for the lost sheep. Now you must give your all for the lost.*

*Can you not pray and fast concerning those who walk without Me. You know the danger in which they are. I need you to pray!*

*I still need intercessors. Someone prayed for you. Someone gave their life for you. Oh, maybe not their life blood, but they gave their time to pray for you. Pray. Pray. Pray. They need you.*

*Don't give up.*

*Don't give up for in due time you shall reap. Just don't give up.*

\*\*\*

*"What man of you, having a hundred sheep, if he loses one of them, does not leave the ninety and nine in the wilderness, and goes after that which is lost, until he finds it?" Luke 15:4*

## JULY 11
### THIS IS THE DAY THAT THE LORD HAS MADE. I WILL REJOICE AND BE GLAD IN IT.

*Oh, how is it that we get so consumed with daily life that we forget our Lord and Savior?*

*It is that our eyes are yet physical, and our spiritual eyes have not grown to full stature.*

*Oh, that we would lay down the cares of the world and come away with our Lover—the Lover of our soul, Jesus.*

\*\*\*

*"Has a nation changed their gods, which are yet no gods? But My people have changed their glory for that which does not profit. Be astonished, O heavens, at this, and be horribly afraid, be very desolate, says the LORD. (13) For My people have committed two evils; they have forsaken Me the fountain of living waters, and hewed them out cisterns, broken cisterns, that can hold no water." Jeremiah 2:11–13*

*"Set your affection on things above, not on things on the earth." Colossians 3:2*

*"My Beloved spoke, and said unto me, Rise up, My love, My fair one, and come away." Song of Solomon 2:10*

*"Therefore take no thought, saying, What shall we eat? Or, What shall we drink? Or Wherewithal shall we be clothed? (32) (For after all these things do the Gentiles seek;) for your heavenly Father knows that you have need of all these things. (33) But seek you first the kingdom of God, and His righteousness; and all these things shall be added unto you." Matthew 6:31–33*

*"Let Him kiss me with the kisses of His mouth: for Your love is better than wine. (3) Because of the savor of Your good ointments Your name is as ointment poured forth, therefore do the virgins love Thee. (4) Draw me, we will run after Thee…" Song of Solomon 1:2–4a*

## JULY 12
## THIS IS THE DAY THAT THE LORD HAS MADE. I WILL REJOICE AND BE GLAD IN IT.

*Come unto Me all ye who labor and are heavy laden and I will give you rest.*

*We've talked about this before, but what is rest and how do we get it?*

*Rest is calm in the storm, knowledge in the confusion, courage in the fight, wisdom in the ignorance, and most of all love in the anger. I see—rest is the Spirit of God ruling in my life. The Spirit of the Lord, the Spirit of wisdom, the Spirit of understanding, the Spirit of counsel and strength, the Spirit of knowledge and the fear of the Lord (Isaiah 11:2).*

*How is it that we can obtain the Spirit of God? It is a gift, but you have to be in the presence of the Gift Giver in order to receive the gift. Seek not to please man, but to please your Father.*

*Is that not how it should be with our children? How often we find them pleasing their friends or themselves versus trying to please their father. Oh, how obvious God has shown us how to be parents. The relationship between God and us is just as the relationship should be between parents and children. Are you experiencing trouble in training your children? Look to the Word and how God expects us to live with Him, and you will discover how children should live with you. And it has been said, "There's no training for parenthood!"*

*But there is. God has not left us without a witness.*

\*\*\*

*"Nevertheless he left not Himself without witness, in that He did good, and gave us rain from heaven, and fruitful seasons, filling our hearts with food and gladness." Acts 14:17*

## JULY 13
## THIS IS THE DAY THAT THE LORD HAS MADE. I WILL REJOICE AND BE GLAD IN IT.

*"Come Lord Jesus and make us whole. Come and restore our soul. We search for You in a dry and thirsty land. We yearn for You in a cold and disintegrating world—a world with many voices calling for our attention."*

*To whose voice will we respond? Do we know the voice of God our Father? We can recognize our husband's voice, each of our children's, our friend's. Can we recognize the voice of our Father? That's the first prerequisite for doing the Father's will. How can we do His will when we can't recognize His voice?*

**Oh, that you would know My voice, to seek My face and throw yourself on the mercy of God. Seek not your own agenda. Seek to know My agenda, do My will and follow in My path.**

**Let those that linger back fall into the trap laid for them. They will no longer hear My voice as they continue to choose opposing sides and methods to do My work. I do not seek workers as much as I seek followers. Those submitted to My way.**

**Seek to know Me and these things shall be added to you.**

\*\*\*

*"My sheep hear My voice, and I know them, and they follow Me: (28) And I give unto them eternal life; and they shall never perish, neither shall any man pluck them out of My hand." John 10:27–28*

## MADE. I WILL REJOICE AND BE GLAD IN IT.

*Lord God, heavenly King, Almighty God is He. He created the wind and waves, and He created you.*

*Do you not know He knows you and your problems?*

*Go to Him.*

*Simply say,*

*"Father, today You hold the reigns of my life. Be to me as a gentle horseman with his horse. Ride as ruler over my thoughts, mouth, eyes, ears, actions. Train me today as a horseman trains his horse.*

*"Make me KNOW your guidance. Amen."*

\*\*\*

*"For to be carnally minded is death; but to be spiritually minded is life and peace. (7) Because the carnal mind is enmity against God: for it is not subject to the law of God, neither indeed can be. (8) So then they that are in the flesh cannot please God. (9) But you are not in the flesh, but in the Spirit, if so be that the Spirit of God dwell in you. Now if any man have not the Spirit of Christ, he is none of His. (10) And if Christ be in you, the body is dead because of sin; but the Spirit is life because of righteousness." Romans 8:6–10*

*"But now, O LORD, You are our Father; we are the clay, and You our potter; and we all are the work of Your hand." Isaiah 64:8*

*"Nay but, O man, who are you that replies against God? Shall the thing formed say to Him that formed it, Why have You made me thus? (21) Has not the potter power over the clay, of the same lump to make one vessel unto honor, and another unto dishonor?" Romans 9:20–21*

*Let us declare:*

*"I will do all that the Lord has said. I will be a blessing to others. He said Abraham and his children would be blessed, and they would bless others. I am a child of Abraham."*

*We are the children of the promise with the inheritance of Jacob. In Isaiah 51, God tells us to look to Abraham. Look to the life of Abraham, and you will see your life.*

*We walk by faith and not by sight just like Abraham. He went out not knowing where he was going (Hebrews 11:8). Our everyday should be going out not knowing where we are going, except that we know the voice of our Daddy and we obey!*

*How can we obey a voice we cannot hear? Oh, please let us make it our objective to know His voice. Without knowing His voice, how can we obey? God says, "Those that love Me follow My commandments." (John 14:21)*

*How can we follow His commandments when we can't hear His voice? Obedience is better than sacrifice (I Samuel 15:22). And Jesus learned obedience through the things He suffered (Hebrews 5:8).*

\*\*\*

*"And Samuel said, Has the Lord as great delight in burnt offerings and sacrifices, as in obeying the voice of the LORD? Behold, to obey is better than sacrifice, and to hearken than the fat of rams." I Samuel 15:22*

## JULY 16

### THIS IS THE DAY THAT THE LORD HAS MADE. I WILL REJOICE AND BE GLAD IN IT.

*"Oh, Lord our God how awesome is Your Name above every name. Oh, that we could know and believe Your Name is above every name. It is too wonderful for me, this knowledge of You."*

*We shall see clearly His face as we seek Him. We shall see Him in all His glory. We shall know Him of Whom our heart desires. Oh, to know Him!*

*"Woo us until we can no longer resist Your pleasure. Oh, Father, we cry out to You for Your anointing. For Your love is better than all the glory this world has to offer.*

*"How can we neglect You? How can we wander from one thing to another? When all the while You wait for us. In Your mercy, You wait and have waited.*

*"Come Lord Jesus and pierce our hearts with the love that You have for each one of us individually. Father, do whatever it takes with our lives for us to hunger and thirst after You, for there is life nowhere else.*

*"Only come, Lord Jesus. Come. Amen."*

\*\*\*

*"Blessed are they which do hunger and thirst after righteousness: for they shall be filled." Matthew 5:6*

*"For the kingdom of God is not meat and drink; but righteousness, and peace, and joy in the Holy Ghost." Romans 14:17*

## JULY 17

## THIS IS THE DAY THAT THE LORD HAS MADE. I WILL REJOICE AND BE GLAD IN IT.

*Give thanks to the Lord. Set your eyes and ears to see and hear Him. Yes, living in this physical body in this physical world, God wants us to see and hear in the spirit world. Jesus said He only did what He saw His Father doing. He lived in a physical body in this physical world, but He walked in the spirit world. And that is what He calls us to do!*

*How do we do that? By ever seeking to know Him. And as we live with Him more and more in our daily lives, Jesus becomes our barometer or plumb line. Then we see and hear things according to Him.*

*It is hard to quiet the sounds around you in order to hear your Father.*

*When they came to Jesus about Lazarus, He could not leave for days, because His Father was calling for that (John 11). Do you think it was hard for Him? Do you think He received criticism for that? Nevertheless, He knew His Father's voice.*

*You may think, "Yes, but He was God's Son, of course, He knew what God wanted Him to do." However if Jesus is not man as fully as He is God, He is not a high priest tempted in all ways like we (Hebrews 4:15).*

*Jesus had to learn His Father's voice just as we do. And once we know His voice, obedience of necessity follows!*

\*\*\*

"Then answered Jesus and said unto them, Verily, verily, I say unto you, The Son can do nothing of Himself, but what He sees the Father do: for what things soever He does, these also does the Son likewise. John 5:19

## JULY 18
## THIS IS THE DAY THAT THE LORD HAS MADE. I WILL REJOICE AND BE GLAD IN IT.

*How can we rejoice except that we trust that God is in control? He is the One in Psalm 37 that says, "Evildoers will perish, but the righteous will see the desires of their heart come to pass." Yes, rejoice, that God is your Father and His delight is in His children. He has spared nothing in bringing you to Himself, and He will spare nothing in keeping you and blessing you. Oh, there will be trials, but those only strengthen you for the battle! Yes, the battle—there is one large battle and it is life. With Him, nothing is lost. Everything is used.*

*He delights to see His children reveling in His provisions. Give unto Him His due reward—your life surrendered to His service. In that only, will you rest and be at peace. He has created you that way. You will be restless until you rest in Him (St. Augustine).*

*Oh, give thanks to Him for He is good and His mercy endures forever. Cry out for His mercy to be on America, the President and all in authority, the policemen and firemen, churches and priests, your family and friends. Oh, cry out for His mercy!*

\*\*\*

*"Be merciful unto me, O God, be merciful unto me: for my soul trusts in You: yes, in the shadow of Your wings will I make my refuge, until these calamities be overpast. (2) I will cry unto God Most High; unto God that performs all things for me." Psalm 57:1–2*

*"O give thanks unto the LORD; for He is good: for His mercy endures for ever. (2) O give thanks unto the God of gods: for His mercy endures for ever. (3) O give thanks to the Lord of lords: for His mercy endures for ever." Psalms 136:1–3*

## THIS IS THE DAY THAT THE LORD HAS MADE. I WILL REJOICE AND BE GLAD IN IT.

*This is the day to listen and believe. Our
Father is always ready to speak to us.*

*Like our children that go about their way and never come
to us unless there are problems, let us not be like that.*

*Let us refer to Him often during the day—
seeking His lead, wondering what He would be
doing if He had a body here on earth.*

*Let us declare, "My body is His. My mind, emotions are
His—His to live through, His to see with, His to hear with,
His to go and do with. Oh, that He would inhabit my body
and soul that His will would be accomplished this day."*

*He does not walk with those that desire their own way. He
walks with those whose bodies and souls are surrendered to
Him. He walks with humble souls—souls that desire Him
above all—above sickness, poverty and any care of the day.*

\*\*\*

*"And He said unto them, When you pray, say, Our Father
which art in heaven, Hallowed be Thy name. Thy kingdom come.
Thy will be done, as in heaven, so in earth." Luke 11:2*

*"And what agreement has the temple of God with idols? For you are
the temple of the living God" as God has said, I will dwell in them, and
walk in them; and I will be their God, and they shall be My people.
(17) Wherefore come out from among them, and be you separate,
says the Lord, and touch not the unclean thing; and I will receive
you, (18) And will be a Father unto you, and you shall be My sons
and daughters, says the Lord Almighty." II Corinthians 6:16–18*

> "Hear O Israel: the LORD our God is one LORD: (5) And you shall love the LORD your God with all your heart, and with all your soul, and with all your might." (Deuteronomy 6:4–5)

"Oh God, how can we do this? Teach us, Father. Gather us under Your wings. Do not listen to our complaining or resistance. Make us come to You. Our desire is ever for You, but our flesh is weak and likes comfort and ease."

**Oh, deny your flesh and come follow Me. I will give you the desires of your heart, only follow Me.**

**Turn not to the right nor left. You look for approval and the only approval you need is Mine.**

So desire the higher gift—the gift of love. Love is not understood by the mind nor gained by intelligence. Love is a gift from God and returned to Him and then turned toward others. Love is not earned by acts. No, love is God. Seek God and you shall find love and be loved.

\*\*\*

> "And we have known and believed the love that God has to us. God is love; and he that dwells in love dwells in God, and God in him:" I John 4:16

"Then said Jesus unto His disciples, If any man will come after Me, let him deny himself, and take up his cross, and follow Me. (25) For whosoever will save his life shall lose it: and whosoever will lose his life for My sake shall find it." Matthew 16:24–25

*Oh, that you would seek Me, the One Whose heart cries out for you. The One Who humbled Himself for you. The One Who disgraced Himself for you. The One Who suffered all the torments that Satan had to offer human beings.*

*Seek Me, the One Whose love has never waned but is always waxing in strength for you. Oh, yes My love does grow and grow. It is not a stationery emotion.*

*Cry out to Me in a dry and thirsty, very thirsty land. You know the things I have said to you will come to pass—now praise Me for their manifestation and go on from here seeking Me. Seeking to know My plans, My will, My vision, My wisdom, My knowledge.*

*Oh, child, I AM is infinite and you have boxed Me into a small place.*

*Get excited for I AM has eternity on His mind not just the present moment! And you too can have eternity on your mind.*

*Seek Me!*

\*\*\*

*"O God, You are my God; early will I seek You: my soul thirsts for You, my flesh longs for You in a dry and thirsty land, where no water is... (3) Because Your lovingkindness is better than life, my lips shall praise You." Psalm 63:1 & 3*

*"He has made every thing beautiful in His time: also He has set the world in their heart, so that no man can find out the work that God makes from the beginning to the end." Ecclesiastes 3:11*

## JULY 22
### THIS IS THE DAY THAT THE LORD HAS MADE. I WILL REJOICE AND BE GLAD IN IT.

*This is the day to apply the Blood of Jesus just as the Israelites applied the blood of the sacrificial lamb in Egypt the night before their exodus.*

*Let us not neglect the Blood.*

*His Blood is sufficient to ward off all evil. As well, it restores what the locusts have eaten.*

*Give thanks to God for Jesus' Blood.*

*Give thanks to Jesus for His Blood poured out for us.*

*And give thanks to the Holy Spirit Who empowers the Blood today still.*

**It is an eternal salvation, for before the worlds were made My Blood was spilled. My Blood is eternal; always was and ever will be.**

\*\*\*

*"Now the God of peace, that brought again from the dead our Lord Jesus, that great Shepherd of the sheep, through the blood of the everlasting covenant, (21) Make you perfect in every good work to do His will, working in you that which is well pleasing in His sight, through Jesus Christ; to whom be gory for ever and ever. Amen." Hebrews 13:20–21*

*"And all that dwell upon the earth shall worship Him, whose names are not written in the book of life of the Lamb slain from the foundation of the world." Revelation 13:8*

*"And they sang a new song saying, You are worthy to take the book, and to open the seals thereof: for You were slain, and have redeemed us to God by Your blood out of every kindred and tongue, and people, and nation;" Revelation 5:9*

## JULY 23
### THIS IS THE DAY THAT THE LORD HAS MADE. I WILL REJOICE AND BE GLAD IN IT.

*Let us, you and I, rejoice!*

*Let Almighty God and you, a single human being, rejoice! Isn't that a novel thought, God and you rejoicing? Is that what God meant when He said that He rejoices over us with joy? (Zephaniah 3:17)*

"Oh glory, Father! You rejoice and we rejoice. We rejoice together."

*I am pleased with My creation and I've called all things into submission to you. My Son, purchased all things for you! All things! The air, food, love, communion with Me. By His Blood your air has been sanctified. By His Blood, your food has been sanctified.*

*By His Blood you have been enabled to love Me and your brothers. By His Blood you have been brought close.*

*Rejoice in His Blood as I rejoice in His obedience that brought the shedding of Blood which brought relief from the imprisonment of sin.*

\*\*\*

"And they sang a new song, saying, You are worthy to take the book, and to open the seals thereof: for You were slain, and have redeemed us to God by Your blood out of every kindred, and tongue, and people, and nation; (10) And have made us unto our God kings and priests: and we shall reign on the earth...(12) Saying with a loud voice, Worthy is the Lamb that was slain to receive power, and riches, and wisdom, and strength, and honor, and glory, and blessing. (13) And every creature which is in heaven, and on the earth, and under the earth, and such as are in the sea, and all that are in them, heard I saying, Blessing, and honor, and glory, and power, be unto Him that sits upon the throne, and unto the Lamb for ever and ever." Revelation 5:9–10; 12–13

## THIS IS THE DAY THAT THE LORD HAS MADE. I WILL REJOICE AND BE GLAD IN IT.

*Be glad that you have been called, and you accepted the call. Now go forth seeking this Man that called you. Spend today and eternity getting to know Him. He has yet many lessons to teach you, much training to do with you.*

*Would you deny the Master access to your life? Hold not back your life which includes many things—thoughts, words, actions, desires, hopes, visions.*

*Oh, that you would surrender and cry out to Him for mercy!*

*Our hearts have languished in a cold place—satisfied with little glimpses of Him, brief touches of Him.*

*"Stir our hearts, Lord, to repentance. Turn us to You that we may be on fire, burning with desire for You. Your first and great commandment was to love the Lord with all our heart, mind, and strength. Forgive our coldness. Turn us to You that we may fear You. Fear You above all people and things. That our heart, mind, and body would groan for communion with You. Amen and amen."*

\*\*\*

*"Jesus said unto him, You shall love the Lord your God with all your heart, and with all your soul, and with all your mind." Matthew 22:37*

*"I am come to send fire on the earth; and what will I, if it be already kindled? (50) But I have a baptism to be baptized with; and how am I straitened till it be accomplished!" Luke 12:49–50*

## THIS IS THE DAY THAT THE LORD HAS MADE. I WILL REJOICE AND BE GLAD IN IT.

*Let no one steal your joy and peace. He has said every tongue that rises against you; you shall show to be in the wrong (Isaiah 54:17).*

*Those voices that said, "Hurry, Hurry!" or "You're not doing right," etc., you can tell them that they are wrong. God does not speak thus to us. He does not condemn His children. He gently leads us, not with fear but with kindness. "Thy rod and thy staff they comfort me." (Psalm 23:4d)*

*As He leads and corrects us, it is a comfort. He does not cause anxiety within when He is leading. We should not and cannot and will not listen to the judgment of our enemy.*

*We have been set free by the Blood of Jesus. Do not fall back into slavery (Galatians 5:1). Do not crucify Christ over again. Do not tread underfoot the freedom He has purchased for you.*

*Resist the enemy in whatever unrestful way he attacks you. Resist any unrest, anxiety, hurry, fear. Resist whatever comes to disturb your peace within. It is not from God. Amen.*

\*\*\*

*"In righteousness shall you be established: you shall be far from oppression; for you shall not fear: and from terror; for it shall not come near you. (15) Behold, they shall surely gather together, but not by Me: whosoever shall gather together against you shall fall for your sake... (17) No weapon that is formed against you shall prosper; and every tongue that shall rise against you in judgment you shall condemn. This is the heritage of the servants of the LORD, and their righteousness is of Me, says the LORD." Isaiah 54:14–15, 17*

## THIS IS THE DAY THAT THE LORD HAS MADE. I WILL REJOICE AND BE GLAD IN IT.

*The Lord says, "Rejoice in the Lord always: and again I say, Rejoice!" (Philippians 4:4) "In every thing give thanks: for this is the will of God in Christ Jesus concerning you." (I Thessalonians 5:18)*

*"Oh, Father, forgive us for dwelling on what we have not, instead of rejoicing in what we have!" We have eternal life through Jesus Christ.*

*We have all wisdom. God has told us, "If any man lacks wisdom, ask of God and He'll give abundantly—not doubting." (James 1:5) Now ask for wisdom concerning that which is bothering you, and then rejoice that you'll have wisdom to handle the situation. Sometimes you have to ask and seek and knock. Asking is using your tongue (praying). Seeking is using your eyes (studying/ researching) and knocking is using your body (watching/ fasting). All these parts have physical and spiritual attributes.*

*Prayer needs to be vocalized, and empowered by the Spirit of God. Studying and researching to find the wisdom is done through your intellect, but led by the Spirit of God. Knocking is the final effort to receive that for which you are yearning from the Lord. Knocking is a full thrust of all bodily and spiritual parts through watchings (denying the body sleep) and fasting (denying the body food) so as to become more receptive to what God is saying and doing. Jeremiah says, "And you shall seek Me, and find Me, when you shall search for Me with all your heart." (Jeremiah 29:13)*

\*\*\*

*"And I say unto you, Ask, and it shall be given you; seek, and you shall find; knock, and it shall be opened unto you. (10) For every one that asks receives; and he that seeks finds; and to him that knocks it shall be opened." Luke 11:9–10*

## THIS IS THE DAY THAT THE LORD HAS MADE. I WILL REJOICE AND BE GLAD IN IT.

*Oh, hallelujah for our God reigns!*

*We may find ourselves in a hard place. A place we do not know what is going on, but our God knows. So cast your cares upon Him and in due time He shall deliver you (I Peter 5:7–10).*

*In the meantime, rejoice in His deliverance and do not be overcome with worry for it only leads to evil (Psalm 37:1). Overcome evil with good (Romans 12:21); and that good can be rejoicing and giving thanks for His provision even before it manifests!*

*Why fret? The God Who spoke a word and the worlds were created is your Daddy, and there's nothing a Daddy won't do to protect and provide for His children.*

*Love the Lord with all your heart, and you'll see the recompense of the wicked come to pass (Proverbs 20:22). Those spirits of darkness which have caused sickness and a sadness to overcome you shall whither and fade as the grass (Psalm 37:1–2).*

*Doubt not the Word of God for it shall never fade away (Isaiah 40:8). It accomplishes that for which it was sent (Isaiah 55:11). And the wickedness in your life shall whither and fade and all men shall know your righteousness—ONLY BELIEVE!*

*\*\*\**

*"Fret not yourself because of evildoers, neither be envious against the workers of iniquity. (2) For they shall soon be cut down like the grass, and wither as the green herb. (3) Trust in the LORD, and do good; so shall you dwell in the land, and verily you shall be fed." Psalm 37:1–3*

## JULY 28
### THIS IS THE DAY THAT THE LORD HAS MADE. I WILL REJOICE AND BE GLAD IN IT.

*Come unto Me all ye who are weary and heavy laden and I will give you rest. Rest from your cares, because in coming to Me you'll learn to trust Me; and when you trust Me, you'll have no cares.*

*Those cares can make you weary! So don't carry any cares, commit them to Me. Roll them over on My shoulders and trust Me. I will come through, if you continue and faint not.*

*All is Mine and I give it to you. Seek not to understand, just accept and understanding will come. First there has to be trust, and then all will follow.*

*Those that worship Me must worship Me in spirit and in truth. It is a worship by faith. So relax and stick your neck out one more time. You'll not be put to shame. You'll not be disappointed. Follow Me, My child.*

*I gave My life, and then I received it back. Give yours again. I promise, you'll not be disappointed. Seek not those things that the world offers, but seek ye the kingdom of God.*

*Ask not what I can do for you. I have already done it. Find out what I have done.*

\*\*\*

*"He that spared not His own Son, but delivered Him up for us all, how shall He not with Him also freely give us all things?" Romans 8:32*

## JULY 29
### THIS IS THE DAY THAT THE LORD HAS MADE. I WILL REJOICE AND BE GLAD IN IT.

*"Oh Father, melt us, then mold us into Your image.*

*"What Adam surrendered, You have recaptured for us. Let us trust You to fulfill Your best for us.*

*"You have given Your all. Now, let us receive Your gift and go on to greatness—the greatness You planned for us from the beginning.*

*"Now we know we can't be great outside of Christ. So capture our hearts and make them beat after Your Son—Your Son Who died for us, rose from the dead and now lives forever."*

*Because He lives, we can be an overcomer of self and the world. We are no longer pawns of the devil.*

*God has given to us victorious living.*

*Now believe He wants to live through you, and give Him permission to do just that!*

\*\*\*

*"O house of Israel, cannot I do with you as this potter? says the LORD. Behold, as the clay is in the potter's hand, so are you in My hand, O house of Israel." Jeremiah 18:6*

*"I am crucified with Christ: nevertheless I live; yet not I, but Christ lives in me: and the life which I now live in the flesh I live by the faith of the Son of God, who loved me, and gave Himself for me." Galatians 2:20*

## THIS IS THE DAY THAT THE LORD HAS MADE. I WILL REJOICE AND BE GLAD IN IT.

*It is now made available to us, the love of God. The love of God is Christ. He has made known His love for us by the life and death of Jesus. Oh, that we could know the love of God for His Son, Jesus! And in knowing it our hearts cannot contain lust, hate, jealousy, complaining, etc. The love God has for Christ will overcome our fleshly emotions and bring us to a realization of who we are.*

*How can you think little of yourself knowing what Jesus and the Father did for you? They did this for you—not me or anyone else—only you. This is the way God looks at us—each one of us individually.*

*God is an individual God. He humbled Himself for you! He lived on earth for you! He suffered physical pain and humiliation for you. If He, the ultimate living creature, ultimate eternal Spirit, thinks this much of you, can you not realize some of your great worth?*

*Rejoice! The Creator loves you!*

\*\*\*

*"In this was manifested the love of God toward us, because that God sent His only begotten Son into the world, that we might live through Him. (10) Herein is love, not that we loved God, but that He loved us, and sent His Son to be the propitiation for our sins." I John 4:9–10*

*"Jesus answered and said unto her, If you knew the gift of God, and who it is that says to you, Give Me to drink; you would have asked of Him, and He would have given you living water." John 4:10*

> THIS IS THE DAY THAT THE LORD HAS MADE. I WILL REJOICE AND BE GLAD IN IT.

"Holy Jesus, Faithful Father and Loving Spirit, keep our thoughts on You today.

"Lead us not into temptation, but deliver us from all the evil we would walk in lest we offend Your Holy Spirit."

Think not of the former things, today is a new day and I will give you new revelation into the ways of the Spirit.

Keep your thoughts on Me today.

Ask yourself, "What is God doing now?" Then go for it! Don't hold back.

Today is the day of salvation.

It is not the day of shrinking back in timidity.

Today is the day of boldness.

Hold not back, but go forth.

Do not linger in doubt.

Go!

\*\*\*

"For we are made partakers of Christ, if we hold the beginning of our confidence steadfast unto the end; (15) While it is said, Today if you will hear His voice, harden not your hearts as in the provocation...(19) So we see that they could not enter in because of unbelief." Hebrews 3:14–15, & 19

# AUGUST

"In His hand are the deep places of the earth: the strength of the hills is His also. ⁵ The sea is His, and He made it: and His hands formed the dry land. ⁶ O come, let us worship and bow down: let us kneel before the LORD our maker."

PSALM 95:4-6

> MADE. I WILL REJOICE AND BE GLAD IN IT.

*Hallelujah, He has broken through our hollow wall of faith!*

*We believe we have faith until He says, Let go and Let Me.*

*When the battle has been long, there comes a time for supernatural exposure. Exposure of activity only God can manifest.*

*Yes, you have been under His direction and you have done all He's instructed, but now is the time to stand for the battle is His. Read about it in II Chronicles 20.*

*Those that are for us are more than those that are against us (II Kings 6:16). Supernatural intervention is what you need. Only when you stand back and wait on Him will you see the glory of the Lord.*

*Some battles He allows His children to participate in and some battles are His only.*

\*\*\*

*"Moses said unto the people, Fear not, stand still, and see the salvation of the LORD, which He will show to you today: for the Egyptians whom you have seen today, you shall see them again no more for ever." Exodus 14:13*

*"And when he had consulted with the people, he appointed singers unto the LORD, and that should praise the Beauty of Holiness, as they went out before the army, and to say, Praise the LORD; for His mercy endures for ever." II Chronicles 20:21*

*"Wherefore take unto you the whole armor of God, that you may be able to withstand in the evil day, and having done all, to stand." Ephesians 6:13*

## AUGUST 2
### THIS IS THE DAY THAT THE LORD HAS MADE. I WILL REJOICE AND BE GLAD IN IT.

*Think it not strange when diverse trials come your way, for the testing of your faith is more precious than gold (I Peter 1:7).*

*"Oh, give thanks unto the Lord for His steadfast love endures forever. Oh, give thanks unto the Lord for His steadfast love endures forever!" This is the song that the people sang in Jehoshaphat's army (II Chronicles 20).*

*And when they sang it, the Lord set an ambush against their enemies. When Jehoshaphat's army got to the enemy, they were already destroyed!*

*Have you prayed and fasted concerning a burden in your life? You may have to fall down hard before the Lord for His counsel on the matter. Pray! Fast! Don't let go of Him until you know His counsel. When He gives it (and He will), look for confirmation of His words to you. He'll confirm His word, too. Then set your heart to trust Him and obey, for truly there is no other way!*

*His counsel to Jehoshaphat was to praise Him. Could the answer to your burden be that simple? Praise opened the prison doors for Paul and Silas. Perhaps they can open your prison doors also!*

\*\*\*

*"And at midnight Paul and Silas prayed, and sang praises unto God: and the prisoners heard them. (26) And suddenly there was a great earthquake, so that the foundations of the prison were shaken: and immediately all the doors were opened, and every one's bands were loosed." Acts 16: 25–26*

## AUGUST 3
### THIS IS THE DAY THAT THE LORD HAS MADE. I WILL REJOICE AND BE GLAD IN IT.

*It is good to give thanks to the Lord (Psalm 92:1). He is worthy of our praise. And since we have no idea how worthy, let your imagination go as far as you can in worshiping Him, and still we are nowhere near His worthiness.*

*Our God is a great God and a great King above all the earth (Psalm 95:3). Let us neither slumber nor sleep in our worship of Him. Sing praises to Him, sing praises! (Psalm 47:6) Let your voice be heard over all the earth at least in your home, neighborhood and workplace!*

*Sing a new song to Him. We can always think of new songs! He is the One that inspires them. If you find yourself unable to sing new songs to the Lord, ask Him for help. He is the One and only One that initiates praise.*

*We cannot praise Him without He first gives us the praise to give back to Him. He is the creator of everything, and in all things He begins and ends.*

\*\*\*

*"O come, let us sing unto the LORD: let us make a joyful noise to the rock of our salvation. (2) Let us come before His presence with thanksgiving, and make a joyful noise unto Him with psalms. (3) For the LORD is a great God, and a great King above all gods." Psalm 95:1–3*

*"O sing unto the LORD a new song; for He has done marvelous things: His right hand, and His holy arm has gotten Him the victory." Psalms 98:1*

*"O praise the LORD, all ye nations: praise Him all ye people. (2) For His merciful kindness is great toward us: and the truth of the LORD endures for ever. Praise ye the LORD." Psalm 117*

## THIS IS THE DAY THAT THE LORD HAS MADE. I WILL REJOICE AND BE GLAD IN IT.

*Look not to the things of this world. Look to Me. Call things that are not as though they were. Call things that are not into things that are. Hope against hope. Look to Abraham your father and Sarah your mother. (Isaiah 51:1–2)*

*Look and keep on looking, for I have the answer. And those that seek will find. Be like the woman looking for her lost coin. (Luke 15:8–9) Do not neglect to seek Me in all things—the cries, the laughs, the hardships, the struggles, the unknowings of life. I AM in all things. Don't be afraid. It is true, I AM in all things—even the bad times. I AM in all things.*

*Try it today. In every situation that seems not of Me or from the devil, look and you'll see My hand in it.*

*Did not My hand work in Joseph's life in all the hard things the devil did to him. Now look and know My hand is in everything that happens in your life.*

\*\*\*

"Who against hope believed in hope, that he might become the father of many nations; according to that which was spoken, So shall your seed be… (20) He staggered not at the promise of God through unbelief; but was strong in faith, giving glory to God;" Romans 4:18 & 20

"But as for you, you thought evil against me; but God meant it unto good, to bring to pass, as it is this day, to save much people alive." Genesis 50:20

## THIS IS THE DAY THAT THE LORD HAS MADE. I WILL REJOICE AND BE GLAD IN IT.

*It is a day of rejoicing that the Lord calls for!*

*Rejoice for I have conquered all your enemies. Rejoice for I have set you free.*

*Was not Jesus free? Was not Adam free? You too are free! But because of Jesus, you have freedom Adam knew not. Adam did not have the power to resist temptation. You do! My Son took on human flesh and performed all the human functions to satisfy My judgment on mankind. In doing that He not only carved the way for you, He destroyed the power of the devil.*

*I said he is like a roaring lion. I did not say he is a devouring lion. No! You are the one that devours evil, destroys the work of the devil.*

*Go and set My people free! Go and spread the word! I have not made you timid, but powerful, loving, and brilliant. (II Timothy 1:7) So go, do, say, the works of My Son. They are My works. Heal the sick, raise the dead, cast out demons and cleanse the lepers. (Matthew 10:8)*

*Go! I say, "Do! And never doubt, but always believe."*

\*\*\*

*"Be sober, be vigilant; because your adversary the devil, as a roaring lion, walks about, seeking whom he may devour:" I Peter 5:8*

*"He that commits sin is of the devil; for the devil sins from the beginning. For this purpose the Son of God was manifested, that He might destroy the works of the devil." I John 3:8*

## THIS IS THE DAY THAT THE LORD HAS MADE. I WILL REJOICE AND BE GLAD IN IT.

*I have given you this day to proclaim the good news to the suffering and dying. People are dying in more ways than just physical. Take, for instance, your neighbor.*

"But what can I do, Lord?"

*Go and do. I'll lead you in all things.*

"Here I am, Lord, send me. I have no idea what to say or do. Here I am. I'm available. Do with me as You please! I would like to see You work here on earth. We've been too long without You. So here's a body to use.

"Empty me.

"Mold me.

"Fill me.

"Here I am!

"Go for it!"

\*\*\*

"Also I heard the voice of the Lord, saying. Whom shall I send, and who will go for us? Then said I, Here am I; send me." Isaiah 6:8

"Go ye therefore, and teach all nations, baptizing them in the name of the Father, and of the Son, and of the Holy Ghost: (20) Teaching them to observe all things whatsoever I have commanded you: and, lo, I am with you always, even unto the end of the world. Amen." Matthew 28:19–20

> **THIS IS THE DAY THAT THE LORD HAS MADE. I WILL REJOICE AND BE GLAD IN IT.**

*Be glad for Jesus is the Victor. He has captured our victory for us.*

*Look in His Word!*

*There are promises for you to believe, if you'll look.*

*He has already solved your problem. He has and knows the solution. Why not go to Him?*

*You are hesitating. You don't believe you'll get an answer. Jesus turns no one away. He said, "Ask, believing and you'll receive." (Matthew 7:7–8) The problem sometimes is that we don't keep asking, seeking, and knocking.*

*Why give up? There is no answer other than Jesus and that which proceeds from His mouth.*

\*\*\*

*"For the LORD gives wisdom: out of His mouth comes knowledge and understanding." Proverbs 2:6*

*"I am Alpha and Omega, the beginning and the ending, says the Lord, which is, and which was, and which is to come, the Almighty." Revelation 1:8*

*"Ask, and it shall be given you; seek, and you shall find; knock, and it shall be opened unto you: (8) For every one that asks receives; and he that seeks finds; and to him that knocks it shall be opened." Matthew 7:7–8*

*"These things I have spoken unto you, that in Me you might have peace. In the world you shall have tribulation: but be of good cheer; I have overcome the world." John 16:33*

## AUGUST 8
### THIS IS THE DAY THAT THE LORD HAS MADE. I WILL REJOICE AND BE GLAD IN IT.

*When My Son was contemplating His final day—His final hour—was there anyone to comfort or understand Him? NO! Mary had anointed His feet, and she felt to a degree His death. But there was no one except His Father.*

*You do not need to look for sympathy. I AM is here! I shall sustain thee. I shall uphold you with My righteous right hand. (Psalm 118:14–16) I shall not forsake you, but you shall reign. You shall see the recompense upon your enemies, and you shall see the reward of the righteous.*

*My love has been poured out into your heart. My love shall sustain thee, and make you walk in the ways of righteousness all the days of your life.*

\*\*\*

*"Be strong and of a good courage, fear not, nor be afraid of them: for the LORD your God, He it is that does go with you; He will not fail you, nor forsake you." Deuteronomy 31:6*

*"A voice of noise from the city, a voice from the temple, a voice of the LORD that renders recompense to His enemies." Isaiah 66:6*

*"And hope makes not ashamed; because the love of God is shed abroad in our hearts by the Holy Ghost which is given unto us." Romans 5:5*

*"He restores my soul: He leads me in the paths of righteousness for His name's sake. (4) Yea, though I walk through the valley of the shadow of death, I will fear no evil: for You are with me; Your rod and Your staff they comfort me... (6) Surely goodness and mercy shall follow me all the days of my life: and I will dwell in the house of the LORD for ever." Psalm 23:3–4, 6*

## AUGUST 9
### THIS IS THE DAY THAT THE LORD HAS MADE. I WILL REJOICE AND BE GLAD IN IT.

*Be silent before the Lord, and let Him minister to you.*

*Your world has been going very fast. Try a slower life style. See what God can do in a life that is yielded to Him and not the pressures of life.*

*He gave us life so we could give it back to Him. And in giving it back, we realize true life.*

*Let us see and experience what true life is—life as Jesus experienced it. Oh, we can't be perfect as Jesus, but we reach for the goal of knowing Him (Philippians 3:10). Let us know Him today in whatever we think, whatever we do, and wherever we go.*

*"Oh, God, hear the cry of our hearts to serve You, to know You. Live Your life in our bodies and souls today.*

*"Let us know (experience) Your life on earth today. What would You do on earth today in a physical body? Do it, God. You have mine. Amen."*

\*\*\*

*"Then said I, Lo, I come: in the volume of the book it is written of Me, (8) I delight to do Your will, O My God: yea, Your law is within My heart." Psalm 40:7–8*

*"That I may know Him, and the power of His resurrection, and the fellowship of His sufferings, being made conformable unto His death; (11) If by any means I might attain unto the resurrection of the dead." Philippians 3:10–11*

## THIS IS THE DAY THAT THE LORD HAS MADE. I WILL REJOICE AND BE GLAD IN IT.

*Oh, that we would sing the praises of our God in the land of captivity (Psalms 126).*

*For surely you shall be delivered and that right soon. But do not look for deliverance. Continue to praise Me. Praise Me for Who I am and if you don't know, make it a project of yours to find out. If I never do anything for you, I AM worthy to be praised—not for what I do, but for Who I AM. Find out Who I AM.*

Read Psalm 23 and ponder Who this wonderful God is. Since He is our Shepherd, we do not want because the Shepherd has to provide. He makes us rest and leads us into peace. That is His job, not ours. He heals our wounded souls and leads us in the right way. That is His job, not ours. He is always with us so we do not have to fear; His hand and voice are there to make sure we get through safely. He makes us victorious over our enemies and empowers us with His Spirit so that our lives run over with blessings onto others. He says goodness and mercy follow us all the days of our lives so it must be…no matter the situation we find ourselves.

Let us know and hold tightly the fact that He is, and we are His.

\*\*\*

*"The LORD is my Shepherd; I shall not want."* Psalm 23:1

## THIS IS THE DAY THAT THE LORD HAS MADE. I WILL REJOICE AND BE GLAD IN IT.

*Oh, give thanks to the Lord for He is good (Psalm 107:1). Has He not prepared your day for you?*

*When a mother prepares a meal for her family, they come to the table to consume the food made ready for them. God has prepared this day for you. Begin the day by looking to Him with thanks for His preparation. "Thank You, Jesus!"*

*Each substance that you receive, receive it as from Him— the provision of morning from a safe night, the provision of health to get out of bed, provision to accomplish your duties for the day, the provision of His guidance…*

*He desires to lead you today as a shepherd leads his flock.*

*Won't you be gentle and submissive as the sheep?*

\*\*\*

*"Know that the LORD He is God: it is He that has made us, and not we ourselves; we are His people, and the sheep of His pasture. (4) Enter into His gates with thanksgiving, and into His courts with praise: be thankful unto Him, and bless His name." Psalm 100:3–4*

*"For in Him we live, and move, and have our being; as certain also of your own poets have said, For we are also His offspring." Acts 17:28*

*"But now, O LORD, You are our Father; we are the clay, and You our potter; and we all are the work of Your hand." Isaiah 64:8*

## THIS IS THE DAY THAT THE LORD HAS MADE. I WILL REJOICE AND BE GLAD IN IT.

*"Lift high the cross, the love of Christ proclaim till all the world adore His precious name." (First line of the song by George W. Kitchin and music by Sydney H. Nicholson.)*

*Lift high the name of Jesus over all your cares of today, for His name has already accomplished all. His name has prepared today for you, now walk in Him.*

*Do not permit a moment to exist that hints of worry or fear. That is not Him. It is not you. That is the enemy. Do not give him any place in your life. When the enemy comes in any form of distress (especially in your thoughts), simply say, "You were finished off at the cross. Take a hike!"*

*Christ dwells in you. Surrender your doing and going to Him. He will not overrule your will. NOW say in your heart and with all that you are,*

*"Lord, this body and soul are Yours. You have my permission to lead me in all things today. Stop me when I'm going my way and not Yours. And most of all, make me to know You."*

\*\*\*

*"And this is life eternal, that they might know You the only true God, and Jesus Christ, whom You have sent." John 17:3*

*Pray.*

*Always pray.*

*Pray for those in public ministry and their families. We know Satan desires to have them.*

*Then pray for our federal, state and local governments. Pray for our teachers and school administrators. Pray for your local church for God's presence to manifest. Pray for your home.*

*Oh, if He would manifest His presence, all knees would bow! Let us cry out for God to show Himself to us in the congregation and in our home. We need to experience His love for us.*

*Our hearts are so cold we do not know the difference between church and the real presence of God.*

*"Oh, God our Father, have mercy on us and open the door so we can see, hear, experience You—not just sing about Your presence but experience it."*

\*\*\*

*"Oh that You would rend the heavens, that You would come down, that the mountains might flow down at Your presence." Isaiah 64:1*

*"That Christ may dwell in your hearts by faith; that you, being rooted and grounded in love, (18) May be able to comprehend with all saints what is the breadth, and length, and depth, and height; (19) And to know the love of Christ, which passes knowledge, that you might be filled with all the fullness of God." Ephesians 3:17–19*

## ✝
### AUGUST 14
### THIS IS THE DAY THAT THE LORD HAS MADE. I WILL REJOICE AND BE GLAD IN IT.

*Oh, give thanks to the Lord for His mercy endures forever. And we need His mercy every day.*

*"Lord, have mercy.*

*"Christ, have mercy.*

*"Lord, have mercy."*

*It is His mercy that keeps us—keeps us safe from the wiles of the devil. Oh, he roars like a lion, but he is kept on a leash (I Peter 5:8). We do not have to get too close. Keep your thoughts captive (II Corinthians 10:5). Do not give place to the devil (Ephesians 4:27).*

*Linger not in the things of this world, but stay close to the thoughts and actions of God.*

*He is not looking for saints that are busy with worldly endeavors (II Corinthians 4:18), but saints that have their mind on pleasing Him.*

*Ask Him today to show you His will for you each moment of TODAY!*

\*\*\*

*"Submit yourselves therefore to God. Resist the devil, and he will flee from you. Draw nigh to God, and He will draw nigh to you. Cleanse your hands, ye sinners; and purify your hearts, ye double minded." James 4:7–8*

*"Casting down imaginations, and every high thing that exalts itself against the knowledge of God, and bringing into captivity every thought to the obedience of Christ;" II Corinthians 10:5*

† 

## AUGUST 15

### THIS IS THE DAY THAT THE LORD HAS MADE. I WILL REJOICE AND BE GLAD IN IT.

*Those thoughts that return and return to steal your peace, God admonishes us in His Word,*

*Humble yourselves unto God, and resist the devil and he will flee (James 4:7 & I Peter 5:6–9).*

*"Lord, how do I humble myself and resist the devil?"*

**The most humbling act My children can do is to pray, "Thy will be done." As you pray that surrendering prayer to Me, the enemy flees. He flees because he knows, one so committed to his Lord, he can find no place within. He flees as you humble and surrender to Me. And your surrender is expressed and demonstrated most purely as you pray,**

*"Your will be done, Lord, Your will be done."*

*"Oh, Lord, help us to surrender to You. Help us to humble ourselves before You. Help us to trust that You are good and You do good! Amen and amen."*

\*\*\*

*"You are good, and do good…"Psalm 119:68a*

*"He went away again the second time, and prayed, saying, O My Father, if this cup may not pass away from Me, except I drink it, Thy will be done." Matthew 26:42*

*"And He said unto them, When you pray, say, Our Father which art in heaven, Hallowed be Thy name. Thy kingdom come. Thy will be done, as in heaven so in earth." Luke 11:2*

*"Hereafter I will not talk much with you: for the prince of this world comes, and has nothing in Me." John 14:30*

## THIS IS THE DAY THAT THE LORD HAS MADE. I WILL REJOICE AND BE GLAD IN IT.

*This is the day to tell God your concerns and then… believe He'll take care of them!*

*An old priest once told me, "If you're not sure what God is saying, just go with what you get." In other words, whatever inclination you have after you have looked to the Lord for His guidance, go and do that.*

*And if you have no inclination, continue to be still until you do have peace about going forward. Don't run hither and thither. Throughout the day, look for chances to think about Him, read about Him, or do something for Him. He has many times said, "Be joyful."*

**That is something you can do for Me. Rest. I am coming, and that right soon. Do not let Me find you worrying. Let Me find you believing. Believing! Oh, that I could find a believer. Believe Me when I say, "I take care of you!"**

\*\*\*

"…Nevertheless when the Son of man comes, shall He find faith on the earth?" Luke 18:8b

"For the eyes of the LORD run to and fro throughout the whole earth, to show Himself strong in the behalf of them whose heart is perfect toward Him…" II Chronicles 16:9a

"The eyes of the LORD are upon the righteous, and His ears are open unto their cry." Psalm 34:15

"Rest in the LORD, and wait patiently for Him: fret not yourself because of him who prospers in his way, because of the man who brings wicked devices to pass." Psalm 37: 7

> **THIS IS THE DAY THAT THE LORD HAS MADE. I WILL REJOICE AND BE GLAD IN IT.**

*Oh, to be free from the burdens of life!*

*He said, "Come unto Me all ye who labor and are heavy laden, and I will give you rest. Take My yoke upon you, and learn of Me; for I am meek and lowly in heart: and you shall find rest for your souls. For My yoke is easy, and My burden is light." (Matthew 11:28–30)*

*Be obedient and go to Him now.*

*Today is the day of salvation.*

\*\*\*

*"And I said, Oh that I had wings like a dove! For then would I fly away, and be at rest… (22) Cast your burden upon the LORD, and He shall sustain you: He shall never suffer the righteous to be moved." Psalm 55:6 & 22*

*"Yes, let none that wait on You be ashamed… (4) Show me Your ways, O LORD; teach me Your paths. (5) Lead me in Your truth, and teach me: for You are the God of my salvation; on You do I wait all the day…(15) My eyes are ever toward the LORD; for He shall pluck my feet out of the net." Psalm 25:3a–5 & 15*

*"Be careful for nothing; but in every thing by prayer and supplication with thanksgiving let your requests be made known unto God. (7) And the peace of God, which passes all understanding, shall keep your hearts and minds through Christ Jesus." Philippians 4:6–7*

*"Humble yourselves therefore under the mighty hand of God, that He may exalt you in due time: (7) Casting all your care upon Him; for He cares for you… (10) But the God of all grace, who has called us unto His eternal glory by Christ Jesus, after that you have suffered a while, make you perfect, stablish, strengthen, settle you. (11) To Him be glory and dominion for ever and ever. Amen." I Peter 5:6–7, 10–11*

## THIS IS THE DAY THAT THE LORD HAS MADE. I WILL REJOICE AND BE GLAD IN IT.

*Oh, hallelujah, for the day has come to rejoice and be glad!*

*How hard it is to rejoice when we're in a storm. The disciples said, "Wake up, Jesus. Don't you care that we're about to drown?" (Mark 4:35–41)*

*Jesus cares. He says, "Don't you know I am here to save and protect. Why are you afraid?"*

*Why do we fear? Because we do not believe His Word. We believe our circumstances.*

*When the storm is present, do not be downcast, just go to God. He is your refuge and strength (Psalm 46:1).*

*He will make wars to cease (Psalm 46:9). Is there trouble between you and someone? Go to Him! He will make the war cease. He will not let you fall.*

*Psalm 46 will give you the truth about the storm and make it to cease.*

*Only expect... listen... hear... and follow Him.*

\*\*\*

*"God is our refuge and strength, a very present help in trouble. (2) Therefore will not we fear, though the earth be removed, and though the mountains be carried into the midst of the sea; (3) Though the waters thereof roar and be troubled, though the mountains shake with the swelling thereof. Selah... (10) Be still, and know that I am God..." Psalm 46:1–3, 10a*

*Those who seek Me with all their heart will find Me. All those who come to Me will not be ashamed. I have the solution to your problems, and I desire to reveal them to you. But you must come and come and not give up. For I will answer the cry of your heart, just do not give up.*

> *Do not think it is a waste of time to linger in My courts. I will lead you to the Holy of Holies. I will not disappoint you.*

*Do not give up hope and do not stop seeking Me. Seek and you shall find. My Word does not return void.*

**Find My Word for you. Listen and obey. Do not stop until you have My Word. Then obey!**

*Psalm 46:1 says, "God is our refuge and strength." He is our refuge. When the storm is raging, go into your prayer closet and do not let go of God until He has you walking on water with Him, instead of running around in confusion and fear.*

\*\*\*

"If any of you lack wisdom, let him ask of God, that gives to all men liberally, and upbraids not; and it shall be given him. (6) But let him ask in faith, nothing wavering. For he that wavers is like a wave of the sea driven with the wind and tossed." James 1:5–6

> "Submit yourselves therefore to God. Resist the devil, and he will flee from you. (8) Draw nigh to God, and He will draw nigh to you. Cleanse your hands, you sinners; and purify your hearts, you double minded." James 4:7–8

> "And He arose, and rebuked the wind, and said unto the sea, Peace, be still…" Mark 4:39a

## AUGUST 20
### THIS IS THE DAY THAT THE LORD HAS MADE. I WILL REJOICE AND BE GLAD IN IT.

*Rejoice and again I say rejoice. Let all men know your forbearance.*

*Are you patiently waiting for your Father to reveal His will to you? Patiently waiting for His deliverance and justification in the matters that are so weighing upon your soul?*

*These matters weigh upon your soul and in turn weigh upon your spirit, as well as your body. Think it not strange when diverse temptations come upon you such as you're experiencing now. The brethren throughout the generations have stumbled over the same tactics of the devil (I Peter 5:9).*

*Read My Word and you shall discover your problems have already been taken care of. Yes, they are already solved, but you are ignorant of My provisions for you.*

*So when a problem arises, go first to My Word. Find the solution already provided, and stand on My Word instead of moaning and groaning as one left without hope and provision. Do not make the Word of God void by your tradition of worry!*

\*\*\*

*"Therefore take no thought, saying, What shall we eat? Or, What shall we drink? Or, Wherewithal shall we be clothed? (32) (For after all these things do the Gentiles seek:) for your heavenly Father knows that you have need of all these things. (33) But seek ye first the kingdom of God, and His righteousness; and all these things shall be added unto you." Matthew 6:31–33*

*"I sought the LORD, and He heard me, and delivered me from all my fears." Psalm 34:4*

## AUGUST 21

### THIS IS THE DAY THAT THE LORD HAS MADE. I WILL REJOICE AND BE GLAD IN IT.

*Oh, let us say, "This is the day that the LORD has made for me. I will rejoice and be glad in it."*

*Look for His blessings at every turn. Sometimes this means even at seemingly bad turns.*

*Joseph did not know being sold as a slave by his brothers would be cause to rejoice, but he nevertheless rejoiced in his dreams he knew to be true.*

*God has given us many dreams in His Word. Read it and discover the dreams and hold tight. Wax strong in faith as your father, Abraham. Think it not strange the happenings, but wax strong in faith, hoping against hope and believing that which is not, will come into that which is.*

*Yes, it is already in the spirit realm as Isaac was already in Abraham's bosom before manifesting in the physical.*

*So look not at the things that are, but look at the things that are not and call them into being.*

\*\*\*

*"Therefore it is of faith, that it might be by grace; to the end the promise might be sure to all the seed; not to that only which is of the law, but to that also which is of the faith of Abraham; who is the father of us all, (17) (As it is written, I have made you a father of many nations,) before Him whom he believed, even God, who quickens the dead, and calls those things which be not as though they were. (18) Who against hope believed in hope, that he might become the father of many nations, according to that which was spoken, So shall your seed be." Romans 4:16–18*

## THIS IS THE DAY THAT THE LORD HAS MADE. I WILL REJOICE AND BE GLAD IN IT.

*Have you ever heard the Lord say, "Let go!"? This is a hard thing to hear, for it sounds like you are to give up.*

*But this is the calm before the storm—the storm coming against your enemies. The battle is now the Lord's. You have done all; now it is time to stand.*

*Yes, just stand, for the battle is the Lord's.*

*What has He done that He cannot do again? Did He not use a whale to capture Jonah and a pigpen to capture the prodigal son?*

*He has not expended His methods for delivering a troubled soul. God is not brought low or made to be empty by our lowliness and emptiness.*

*As a matter of fact, stand back and see what He can and will do on behalf of His righteous ones. You are righteous, because of Jesus. He will answer their heart's cry. He will answer your heart's cry!*

\*\*\*

*"The eyes of the LORD are upon the righteous, and His ears are open unto their cry… (17) The righteous cry, and the LORD hears, and delivers them out of all their troubles." Psalm 34:15 & 17*

*"And Moses said unto the people, Fear you not, stand still, and see the salvation of the LORD, which He will show to you today: for the Egyptians whom you have seen today, you shall see them again no more for ever. (14) The LORD shall fight for you, and you shall hold your peace." Exodus 14:13–14*

## THIS IS THE DAY THAT THE LORD HAS MADE. I WILL REJOICE AND BE GLAD IN IT.

*Rejoice! Rejoice! Let your mouth smile. This is the day He has made for you.*

*O come and see that the Lord is good! (Psalm 34:8) Taste and enjoy His fruits of love, joy, and peace!*

*Peace for a weary soul, joy for a heavy heart, and love for a hungry body.*

*Yes, your body does need love. Do not neglect to care for the physical. God created it too. He did not say all flesh is bad. He said all fleshly desires meaning Adamic desires have to be put under the cross. Christ provided for victory over carnal desires, like pride, anxiety, greed, lust…*

*Take not the burden of this life upon your shoulders. When you find that you can no longer go on (and this is a place hard to get to), then the Lord says, "Stand, and having done all, stand." (Ephesians 6:13)*

*And you will see the glory of the Lord in your stead.*

*The Lord has said to me, "Keep walking." We can walk and stand at the same time. We stand in assurance and confidence in Him as we keep walking forward.*

\*\*\*

*"But He knows the way that I take: when He has tried me, I shall come forth as gold." Job 23:10*

## THIS IS THE DAY THAT THE LORD HAS MADE. I WILL REJOICE AND BE GLAD IN IT.

*Oh, that we would praise the Lord! We are fearfully and wonderfully made (Psalm 139:14).*

*Oh, come and see that the Lord is good (Psalm 34:8). His mercy endures forever.*

*The horse and rider He has thrown into the sea (Exodus 15:1). What is your horse and rider? And how do we get the Lord to throw them into the sea? He said to Moses,*

*"... Wherefore do you cry unto me? Speak unto the children of Israel that they go forward: (16) But lift up your rod, and stretch out your hand over the sea, and divide it: and the children of Israel shall go on dry ground through the midst of the sea." (Exodus 14:15–16)*

*What has this story to do with us? We are the Israelites and Jesus is Moses. Jesus has His staff raised and His hand stretched out. We are to move on in faith—faith in the accomplished work of our Lord. We are also Moses when God says, "Why are you complaining?"*

*Why ARE we complaining? Jesus says, "Say unto the mountain, 'Move,' and it will move." Why do we doubt? Let's confess our unbelief, and ask God to cleanse and wash us in Jesus' Blood. He has and He will. Oh, give thanks unto the Lord for His Blood! Remember, "Move on."*

\*\*\*

*"Being confident of this very thing, that He which has begun a good work in you will perform it until the day of Jesus Christ:" Philippians 1:6*

> MADE. I WILL REJOICE AND BE GLAD IN IT.

*Has the Lord lifted the burden for a while? Give thanks.*

*Has He increased your faith to believe despite the obvious? His Word is above the obvious. His Word is true and everlasting. It does not return void (Isaiah 55:11). Only believe, only believe—nothing is impossible, only believe His Word to you today! (Luke 8:50)*

*Ask God to reveal your gravest sin.*

*He will, and it will set you free.*

*Don't be afraid.*

*There's no hurt when He uncovers your sin. It is so good and refreshing. It is like getting rid of a splinter that's been causing irritation.*

*Oh, faithful one, go to Him in the quiet and ask Him to reveal to you your sin. Then your sin will become your greatest strength. Instead of unbelief there will be trust.*

*Go to Him as you would a loving, tender, gentle father—He is, so go. He is waiting.*

\*\*\*

*"And he arose, and came to his father. But when he was yet a great way off, his father saw him, and had compassion, and ran, and fell on his neck, and kissed him." Luke 15:20*

## AUGUST 26
### THIS IS THE DAY THAT THE LORD HAS MADE. I WILL REJOICE AND BE GLAD IN IT.

*Where is your faith?*

*Is it in the harrowing circumstances in which you find yourself?*

*Abraham's circumstances for having an heir didn't look too good for a long time. Did that change God's Word? NO!*

*What has God said to you recently? Rehearse it. Review it. Meditate on it.*

*In other words don't let it leave your mouth or eyes (Joshua 1:8). His Word must be fertilized. His Word is a seed, and just like the parable, His Word can get eaten by Satan, or not given enough place in your heart, or choked out by the cares of the world (Matthew 13).*

*But then there's good soil, and the seed is held fast and brings forth fruit with patience (Hebrews 10:36). Patience is a definite part of faith. Belief is the foundation. First you have to believe, and then faith comes. Believe!*

*Believe what I say, and I'll give you the faith to hang on. The belief is your part. You have to decide in your heart to believe.*

\*\*\*

*"Jesus said unto him, If you can believe, all things are possible to him that believes." Mark 9:23*

*"But with whom was He grieved forty years? Was it not with them that had sinned, whose carcasses fell in the wilderness? (18) And to whom swore He that they should not enter into His rest, but to them that believed not? (19) So we see that they could not enter in because of unbelief." Hebrews 3:17–19*

## AUGUST 27
## THIS IS THE DAY THAT THE LORD HAS MADE. I WILL REJOICE AND BE GLAD IN IT.

*Oh, give thanks unto the Lord for His mercy endures forever! Forever—that means even the place in which you now find yourself. Hallelujah!*

*His mercy extends to the far off places of our lives—where no one else has gone or can go. We are never beyond His reach.*

*He is never made to linger away from us any longer than is necessary for our maximum benefit. He is not like earthly parents who cannot wait to bless their children, so they short circuit the process in order to get to the finish line. They subsequently reduce the blessings their children receive.*

*He knows beginning to end, and He is patient and faithful to His children.*

*Are you a child of His? Then rest assured that for which you are waiting will come at the time for you to receive maximum blessings.*

\*\*\*

"The Lord is not slack concerning His promise, as some men count slackness; but is longsuffering to us-ward, not willing that any should perish, but that all should come to repentance." II Peter 3:9

"And therefore will the LORD wait, that He may be gracious unto you, and therefore will He be exalted, that He may have mercy upon you: for the LORD is a God of judgment: blessed are all they that wait for Him." Isaiah 30:19

## THIS IS THE DAY THAT THE LORD HAS MADE. I WILL REJOICE AND BE GLAD IN IT.

*Jehoshaphat sang,*

*"Praise the Lord, for His mercy endures forever." (II Chronicles 20:21)*

*As he sang, God defeated his enemies for him. Let us sing today as a sacrifice—as a statement of belief in God's Word when He said,*

*"The battle is not yours, but Mine." (II Chronicles 20:15)*

*Let us pray:*

*"Oh, God, I will sing today, because You are cleansing my heart!*

*"You are changing me from glory to glory (II Corinthians 3:18). You are delighted in me (Proverbs 8:30). I am the apple of Your eye (Zechariah 2:8). You will finish what You began (Philippians 1:6).*

*"Oh, Father, You say You will keep me in the way for You are the Good Shepherd that cares for His sheep. This is a comfort when I feel so lost—to know that You are my Shepherd, and You are responsible for me (Psalm 23).*

*"Let me be forever in Your care Who seeks and saves that which is lost. I humble myself today to rejoice always, and I give to You these prayers with thanksgiving. Amen."*

\*\*\*

*"Give thanks unto the LORD, call upon His name, make known His deeds among the people. (9) Sing unto Him, sing psalms unto Him, talk of all His wondrous works. (10) Glory in His holy name: let the heart of them rejoice that seek the LORD." I Chronicles 16:8–10*

## THIS IS THE DAY THAT THE LORD HAS MADE. I WILL REJOICE AND BE GLAD IN IT.

*His mercy endures forever. His mercy did not seem so evident as Jesus was hanging on the cross, but jump ahead three days, and His mercy reigns in victory over death.*

*If you feel like you're dying, then you probably are; and Jesus probably wants you to die so you can be resurrected.*

*Resurrection life is much more glorious than life before death. We die many deaths in this life, and each resurrection life is worth the death.*

*Seek not life for yourself, but seek life found in Jesus Christ. It is abundant and full of joy.*

*Where is your joy? Has it faded from whence it was?*

*There is abundance of peace and joy in Christ. Seek Him and all the rest will follow.*

*What does Proverb 4:7 say? "Wisdom is the principal thing; therefore get wisdom: and with all your getting get understanding."*

*The Spirit of Jesus is wisdom and understanding; counsel and strength; knowledge and the fear of God (Isaiah 11:1).*

*Seek to know Jesus. He is eternal life.*

\*\*\*

*"But of Him are you in Christ Jesus, Who of God is made unto us wisdom, and righteousness, and sanctification, and redemption:" I Corinthians 1:30*

## THIS IS THE DAY THAT THE LORD HAS MADE. I WILL REJOICE AND BE GLAD IN IT.

*"You are in control, Father. You have the worlds in Your hands and You have us in Your hands. You have our children and spouses in Your hands."*

*How can we be downcast when so great a God is taking care of us?*

*Seek not answers, but rejoice in His holiness and His ways. They are greater than our ways.*

*In time you shall rejoice, if you faint not.*

*He who has started a good work in you, shall continue it until the day of the Lord.*

*This day is the day that He has made.*

*Rejoice and be glad in it!*

\*\*\*

*"For My thoughts are not your thoughts, neither are your ways My ways, says the LORD? (9) For as the heavens are higher than the earth, so are My ways higher than your ways, and My thoughts than your thoughts." Isaiah 55:8–9*

*"And let us not be weary in well doing: for in due season we shall reap, if we faint not." Galatians 6:9*

*"Being confident of this very thing, that He which has begun a good work in you will perform it until the day of Jesus Christ:" Philippians 1:6*

*"Why are you cast down, O my soul? And why are you disquieted within me? Hope in God: for I shall yet praise Him, who is the health of my countenance, and my God." Psalm 42:11*

## THIS IS THE DAY THAT THE LORD HAS MADE. I WILL REJOICE AND BE GLAD IN IT.

He said in our weakness He is made strong (II Corinthians 12:10). So if and when you are weak, lean heavily into the chest of Jesus. He will sustain you. He will make the weak strong and the sick well.

So rejoice in Whom you have so great a possession.

Yes, to think you possess Christ! But we do. He gave Himself to us and we receive Him and possess Him as our own. He is our all.

"My Beloved is mine, and I am His: He feeds among the lilies." (Song of Solomon 2:16)

What is it you need?

It is supplied in Him, because He is the Beginning and the End (Revelation 1:8).

All things originate in Him, proceed from Him and in fact were made for His pleasure (Revelations 4:11). Isn't that a lovely thought? You were made for His pleasure, so in fact you are pleasing to Christ.

He is above all and in all. He is everywhere. Wherever you are…He is. So be still and know Him. Again I say, "Be still."

He is waiting.

\*\*\*

"You are worthy, O Lord, to receive glory and honor and power: for You have created all things, and for Your pleasure they are and were created." Revelation 4:11

# SEPTEMBER

*"For all the promises of God in Him are yea, and in Him Amen, unto the glory of God by us."*

II CORINTHIANS 1:20

# SEPTEMBER 1
## THIS IS THE DAY THAT THE LORD HAS MADE. I WILL REJOICE AND BE GLAD IN IT.

*"Come unto Me, all ye that labor and are heavy laden, and I will give you rest... Learn of Me; for I am meek and lowly in heart:" (Matthew 11:28 & 29b) Jesus says these words to each of us. What better words can we hear as we live in such a cruel and fast pace life?*

*Who is tired? Come to Me.*

*Who has a heavy burden? Come to Me.*

*Learn of Me. Learn about meekness and lowliness of heart.*

*I will give you an easy yoke and a light burden.*

*An easy yoke sounds great! How many of us are struggling with unequally yoked relationships?— husband, wife, boss, co-workers, relatives, children.*

*Well, the yoke does not have to be hard. He said the yoke is easy.*

*"Help us, Jesus, to come to You, to learn of You. Help us, Jesus, help!"*

*Are there any situations He can't handle? No, not one! Hallelujah!*

\*\*\*

*"Take My yoke upon you, and learn of Me; for I am meek and lowly in heart: and you shall find rest unto your souls. (30) For My yoke is easy, and My burden is light." Matthew 11:29–30*

*"Behold, I am the LORD, the God of all flesh: is there any thing too hard for me?" Jeremiah 32:27*

## THIS IS THE DAY THAT THE LORD HAS MADE. I WILL REJOICE AND BE GLAD IN IT.

*This is the day of revelation.*

*He has gifts He wants to give to you. Can you receive them?*

*Let Him saturate your brain with the balm of Gilead (Jeremiah 8:22).*

*Open up your life to the new things He is doing.*

*You can go where He's never been. Go and spread His love. Go and sing of His presence. Let your light shine that men may know Him.*

*Go where you have never been before.*

*He is leading you into new adventures.*

*"Help us, Jesus, to leave the past and old ways and places and embrace something new. The new thing that You are doing."*

\*\*\*

*"Let your light so shine before men, that they may see your good works, and glorify your Father which is in heaven." Matthew 5:16*

*"Behold, I will do a new thing; now it shall spring forth; shall you not know it? I will even make a way in the wilderness, and rivers in the desert." Isaiah 43:19*

*"You have heard, see all this; and will not you declare it? I have shown you new things from this time, even hidden things, and you did not know them." Isaiah 48:6*

*"And He that sat upon the throne said, Behold, I make all things new. And He said unto me, Write: for these words are true and faithful." Revelation 21:5*

> **THIS IS THE DAY THAT THE LORD HAS MADE. I WILL REJOICE AND BE GLAD IN IT.**

*"Oh, Lord have mercy. Our sins are many and our transgressions are far. Our love is cold and our passion has died.*

*"Have mercy and restore to us the joy of Your salvation (Psalms 51:12). Father, make us to fear You. Our hearts have grown weak. We do not fear the one true God, but we walk proudly in our fortunes and do not realize our sicknesses and poverties.*

*"Oh God! open our eyes. We are blind. Do not continue another day allowing us to walk in ignorance—total blindness. We are blind! Oh, God have mercy! Do not turn from us in disgust and remorse, but turn Your face to us and open our eyes.*

*"Have mercy! Bring us to repentance. Open our eyes. How can we cry for help when we are so ignorant that we do not know our sad condition? Have mercy and send a Nathan to us as you did to David that we may see and repent and be saved!*

*"Oh, God, we cry out for Your mercy!"*

\*\*\*

*"Turn us again, O God, and cause Your face to shine; and we shall be saved…(7) Turn us again, O God of hosts, and cause Your face to shine; and we shall be saved…(19) Turn us again, O LORD God of hosts, cause Your face to shine; and we shall be saved." Psalms 80:3, 7, 19*

*"Come, and let us return unto the LORD: for He has torn, and He will heal us; He has smitten, and He will bind us up… (3a) Then shall we know, if we follow on to know the LORD…" Hosea 6:1 & 3a*

## THIS IS THE DAY THAT THE LORD HAS MADE. I WILL REJOICE AND BE GLAD IN IT.

*Listen.*

*Be still and listen. And I will tell you of great and mighty things. This is the day that the LORD made—rejoice.*

*Put on the garment of praise for the spirit of heaviness. That thing that is bothering you, I can handle it.*

*God can handle it. Forget that anxious feeling and replace it with thanksgiving, for God can handle it—whatever it is.*

*Get excited, because your needs are the bedrock of Jesus. He is the Rock. He is able to handle whatever comes up. He is able to fix, repair, make time, solve problems…bring peace, healing, and love.*

*He is love, joy, peace, patience, gentleness, goodness, faithfulness, meekness, self-control (Galatians 5:22–23); and He inhabits the praises of His people! (Psalm 22:3)*

*So begin to praise, and He'll be present with all His traits!*

\*\*\*

*"And when he had consulted with the people, he appointed singers unto the LORD, and that should praise the Beauty of Holiness, as they went out before the army, and to say, Praise the LORD; for His mercy endures for ever. And when they began to sing and to praise, the LORD set ambushments against the children of Ammon, Moab, and mount Seir, which were come against Judah; and they were smitten." II Chronicles 20:21–22*

*Some holy aspirations:*

*"Thy will be done."*

*"Have Thine Own way."*

*"Lord have mercy; Christ have mercy; Lord, have mercy."*

*"Thank You, Father."*

*"For unto you a Child is born; unto you a Son is given and the government shall be upon His shoulders."*

*Your shoulders are not to be carrying…you name the burdens you are carrying. They are not yours to carry. If Jesus is your head, go to Him for the solving of your problems. He is your older brother and Savior. God is your Father. God has provided us fellowship with Himself, His Son and His Spirit.*

*Isn't it wonderful to have His Spirit dwelling within us continually, not as under the Old Testament? Our New Testament is a much better covenant. Let us rejoice today in this fact alone—His Spirit is with and in us continuously today. We cannot be alone, because His Spirit is with us.*

*Whatever your needs are today, immediately go to Him. Experience the mighty provision God has for you.*

\*\*\*

*"Jesus Christ the same yesterday, and today, and for ever." Hebrews 13:8*

## SEPTEMBER 6
### THIS IS THE DAY THAT THE LORD HAS MADE. I WILL REJOICE AND BE GLAD IN IT.

*Have you ever looked at the Son? Look at Him now by reading about Him in My written Word. Oh, He is in every verse. He is throughout the Old Testament, as well as the New. Come unto Me and learn of Me.*

*Why is it that life gets so wrapped up in doing things?*

*Because the fulfilling of your lust is more important than I.*

*If you'll notice the more wrapped up in Me you are, the more natural will flow the issues of life.*

*The more full your life becomes with busyness (cares of life), the more your flesh is being fed.*

*It is a circle Satan has created to keep you from coming to Me and learning of Me. The more you do, the more there is to do. You are sowing wrong seed. You are sowing fleshly seed and not spiritual.*

*Yes, there are things to be done on earth, but they must be done by walking in the Spirit—sowing to your spirit man instead of the soulish man. Come unto Me and learn of Me.*

\*\*\*

*"For he that sows to his flesh shall of the flesh reap corruption; but he that sows to the Spirit shall of the Spirit reap life everlasting." Galatians 6:8*

*"For if you live after the flesh, you shall die: but if you through the Spirit do mortify the deeds of the body, you shall live." Romans 8:13*

## SEPTEMBER 7
## THIS IS THE DAY THAT THE LORD HAS MADE. I WILL REJOICE AND BE GLAD IN IT.

*How is it you have time for other things and not Me? Is the gratification of the flesh so much more satisfying than the gratification of the spirit?*

*You have asked, "Where is my time for myself?"*

*Well, the answer lies in working for Me and not yourself.*

*You seek to satisfy your needs of accomplishment.*

*You get wrapped up in accomplishing this and that. And you gloat over your success.*

*Seek not the rewards of this life. Where your heart is, is where your treasure is. You do not want to lay up treasure on this earth, do you?*

*So why seek and squander yourself in the pursuit of excellence in earthly things. Seek ye first the kingdom of God and His righteousness and all these things shall be added to you. You have strayed from the way and need to refocus. Adjustments must be made on any fine precision instrument, and you are one. So be encouraged and refocus on Life and not the pursuit of life. Jesus is Life.*

\*\*\*

*"For whom the Lord loves He chastens, and scourges every son whom He receives... (10) For they verily for a few days chasten us after their own pleasure; but He for our profit, that we might be partakers of His holiness. (11) Now no chastening for the present seems to be joyous, but grievous: nevertheless afterward it yields the peaceable fruit of righteousness unto them which are exercised thereby." Hebrews 12:6 & 10–11*

## THIS IS THE DAY THAT THE LORD HAS MADE. I WILL REJOICE AND BE GLAD IN IT.

*Oh, come let us worship the Lord together! (Psalm 95:6) Let us come in holy array bringing our tithes and offerings—our love, adoration, and our repentance. Let us come to the house of the Lord to worship and adore Him (Psalm 122:1).*

*How often is it that we come to Him in our quiet time by weeping and moaning for the condition we find our self, our family members, the world? Let's forget about our self, and worship Him instead of worshiping our problems.*

*Do you believe He desires our company? And has He said He'll care for our every need? (Matthew 6:31–33) Then why come to Him in sorry? He has already solved your problem, so why not come to Him rejoicing? Will He find faith when He comes to earth? (Luke 18:8) Let Him find one who believes. Let Him find one that believes His Words instead of believing the mountains in one's way. He has conquered, and He will conquer again if He can find any believers. "And He did not many mighty works there because of their unbelief." (Matthew 13:58) Let it not be that way in our city.*

*Come to Him rejoicing, for He has already leveled the mountains in your life. Get into the flow of the river (Revelation 22:1).*

\*\*\*

*"Every valley shall be exalted, and every mountain and hill shall be made low: and the crooked shall be made straight, and the rough places plain:" Isaiah 40:4*

**THIS IS THE DAY THAT THE LORD HAS MADE. I WILL REJOICE AND BE GLAD IN IT.**

*You who have fallen into sin, repent and be made whole. It is an easy thing to veer off the way. There is no shadow of turning with Me, (James 1:17) but you can have large shadows before you're aware of it. Keep a daily time with Me. This cannot be tampered with, except that you will begin to produce a shadow of turning.*

*Oh, you think you've kept your time with Me, but it has become more haphazard than you realize. I am not a God of law who cannot allow for exceptions, but exceptions must be few and far between.*

*Have I not said, "Seek Me early"? This does not mean just early in the morning. To seek Me early is to seek Me in advance of daily doings. Oh, you thought you were seeking Me, but you were more caught up in accomplishments than in your position in Me.*

*I see you every day with your many necessities, and wonder, "When will she place Me first in her life?"*

*Come unto Me. Come unto Me. Come unto Me, and find rest for your soul. Seek not the things of this world, but of the heavenly world. You will be surprised how your earthly necessities are provided for.*

\*\*\*

*"If you then be risen with Christ, seek those things which are above, where Christ sits on the right hand of God. (2) Set your affection on things above, not on things on the earth." Colossians 3:1–2*

*"But seek you first the kingdom of God, and His righteousness; and all these things shall be added unto you." Matthew 6:33*

*Come unto Me.*

*This means putting our agenda on the back burner. This means glorifying God and not our own self. When we start out a day going after the things that need to be done, we've set other gods before the true God.*

*How is it that the things of this world take precedent over the things of the Spirit? Do not fulfill the lusts of the flesh (Galatians 5:16). And yet, that is what we do when we start out our day accomplishing our "things to be done" list.*

*Well, the first thing "to be done" is to minister to Me. Does that sound egotistical? Well, it is. I know what is best for you, and setting your eyes on earthly matters instead of heavenly matters will lead you down the wrong way. Come away with Me and let the world take care of itself until you have found the peace within My courts.*

*And after having found peace—Go! Go in the might of the Lord and do great exploits. (Daniel 11:32) For then you will know from whence comes your strength.*

*It's neither by might nor by power, saith the Lord, but by My Spirit. (Zechariah 4:6) And you shall know the truth and the truth shall set you free. (John 8:32)*

*I AM the truth. (John 14:6)*

\*\*\*

*"Then he answered and spoke unto me, saying, This is the word of the LORD unto Zerubbabel, saying, Not by might, nor by power, but by My Spirit, says the LORD of hosts." Zechariah 4:6*

*Come unto Me all ye who labor and are
heavy laden and I will give you rest.*

*Are you getting tired of Me saying this? Well then…obey.*

*You grow weary in that your own children veer off from
obeying you, and yet you do the same toward Me. I do
give you many earthly examples of spiritual realities.*

*Yes, you see with your physical eyes, but you also
have spiritual eyes that are seeing the same thing, if
you'd take time to be aware of the spirit world.*

*Yes, it is easier to recognize the physical world,
but the time has come and is now that you must
see, hear, feel, smell, and taste the spirit world
as readily as you do the physical one.*

*Those who worship Me must worship Me in
spirit and in truth. Your life must become
more finely tuned to the Spirit.*

*This is life, that they know the Father.
And He is Spirit. Come unto Me all ye who
are weary and I will give you rest.*

*God has rest and you can enter into His rest if you will.*

\*\*\*

"But the hour comes, and now is, when the true worshippers shall worship the Father in spirit and in truth: for the Father seeks such to worship Him. (24) God is a Spirit: and they that worship Him must worship Him in spirit and in truth." John 4:23–24

## SEPTEMBER 12
### THIS IS THE DAY THAT THE LORD HAS MADE. I WILL REJOICE AND BE GLAD IN IT.

*Do you not know that if I order your life (your day) much more will be accomplished, and besides I will be glorified in it?*

*However when you order your day, you are glorified and little is accomplished, if any. For I have ordained praise to come forth from My children. How much praise comes forth from you?*

*Is not our fellowship a time of therapy? Yes, this is part of our relationship, but when this seems to occupy most of the time together, I begin to feel used—like the son that never comes to the father except for money.*

*Well, I am your Father and I do provide for you, but let us reason together. Let us love and enjoy each other with no other motive except to be together.*

*Put your problems aside for a few moments, and let us walk on the beach together— forget the world and its problems.*

*Come away, My beloved. I desire you. I desire you and not your problems. They have become like idols to you and you shall have no other god before you. No other god! For I am a jealous God and seek those that worship Me in spirit and in truth.*

\*\*\*

*"For you shall worship no other god: for the LORD, whose name is Jealous, is a jealous God:" Exodus 34:14*

## SEPTEMBER 13
### THIS IS THE DAY THAT THE LORD HAS MADE. I WILL REJOICE AND BE GLAD IN IT.

*Come unto Me. You know not what I have in store for you.*

*First read My Word as your body is awakening from a weary night's rest. Yes, weary, because you have lingered too long in this world and neglected the heavenly one.*

*So come unto Me by first reading the written Word. It shall lead you into all truth as My Spirit opens it up to you.*

*After you are awakened, then ask My Spirit to lead you into your morning devotion. It will be different everyday for My Spirit will not always strive with man. No one knows which way the wind will blow except My Spirit and those to whom I reveal Myself. Come unto Me, all ye who labor and are heavy laden.*

*Did you know under the New Covenant, you do not have to labor? Just as I finished My labor, so have you. When you find yourself laboring, know for sure you're off the narrow way and headed off the way. When you find yourself not resting, know for sure you've left the narrow way and headed into the broad way that leads to destruction.*

*I have made life fairly simple. It takes very little observation to realize where you are and where you're going. Love, joy, peace—are these evident in your life? If not, get back on the narrow path, and leave the one upon which you are walking.*

\*\*\*

*"But the fruit of the Spirit is love, joy, peace..." Galatians 5:22a*

## SEPTEMBER 14

### THIS IS THE DAY THAT THE LORD HAS MADE. I WILL REJOICE AND BE GLAD IN IT.

*Oh, how I want My children to praise Me!*

*For in praise, they would come to see My ways, not theirs.*

*Praise raises human beings into another realm of reality—reality that yields fruit—fruit worthy of the kingdom.*

*Come unto Me all ye who labor and are heavy laden and I will give you rest.*

*Come and learn of Me for I am meek and lowly in heart and you will find rest for your soul.*

*Oh, how the soul wanders from one object of endeavor to another! Fulfilling very little in its excursion.*

*Why?*

*Because it is not led by the Spirit of God, but by the spirit of lust.*

*All desires originating from man not sanctified by My Spirit are lustful, in that the desires are to enlarge man's view of himself and not Me.*

*Be careful to walk in the Spirit and not fulfill the desires of the flesh.*

\*\*\*

*"This I say then, Walk in the Spirit, and you shall not fulfill the lust of the flesh." Galatians 5:16*

## THIS IS THE DAY THAT THE LORD HAS MADE. I WILL REJOICE AND BE GLAD IN IT.

*No matter the circumstances, the Lord Almighty requires that we should rejoice. Now we have the option to obey or disobey, but His requirement remains the same.*

*In Philippians 4:4, He says, "Rejoice in the Lord always: again I say, Rejoice!"*

*He also says in I Thessalonians 5:16–18, "Rejoice evermore. (17) Pray without ceasing. (18) In every thing give thanks: for this is the will of God in Christ Jesus concerning you."*

*"Giving thanks always for all things unto God and the Father in the name of our Lord Jesus Christ;" (Ephesians 5:20)*

*These are three verses that admonish us to rejoice. We have the choice.*

*What is your decision? Choose this day whom you will serve.*

*Choose this day life or death; blessings or curses.*

\*\*\*

*"I call heaven and earth to record this day against you, that I have set before you life and death, blessing and cursing: therefore choose life that both you and your seed may live:" Deuteronomy 30:19*

*"Although the fig tree shall not blossom, neither shall fruit be in the vines; the labor of the olive shall fail, and the fields shall yield no meat; the flock shall be cut off from the fold, and there shall be no herd in the stalls: (18) Yet I will rejoice in the LORD, I will joy in the God of my salvation." Habakkuk 3:17–18*

## SEPTEMBER 16
### THIS IS THE DAY THAT THE LORD HAS MADE. I WILL REJOICE AND BE GLAD IN IT.

*This is the day to rejoice. Rejoice! It is a good commandment of our Lord's. How much better than Him saying, "Mourn. Be sad." Let us obey His Word as He has spoken. Obedience is better than sacrifice (I Samuel 15:22).*

*Jesus rejoiced on the day of His capture, which He knew would lead to death. We know God is in control. We can rejoice in that. Scripture also says, "Pray always with perseverance." (Ephesians 6:18) Let your mind be aware of your spirit praying, and then you shall pray with your understanding according to what the Spirit has been doing all along.*

*Seek to know the Father's will for your life today, not in a glancing way, but with a definite posture of seeking His will. The kingdom is not taken by glancing efforts, but by time given to the pursuit of it.*

*Yes, it is not only the quality of time, but also the quantity of time given to the asking, seeking and knocking. His bread is not given to those who do not persist as the woman with the unjust judge (Luke 18:1ff), and the man asking for bread from his neighbor at midnight (Luke 11:5ff).*

*Do not be duped into believing I will reveal My will to those who do not fellowship with Me, giving Me their time and talent.*

\*\*\*

*"And from the days of John the Baptist until now the kingdom of heaven suffers violence, and the violent take it by force." Matthew 11:12*

*This is the day He has made for our repentance and acceptance into the kingdom. You may be saved, and I hope you are, but there is always repentance that can bring one more into the revelation of the Kingdom of God.*

*Do you think for a moment you are aware of the entire Kingdom of God? No. No. Only through Divine revelation do we continue to experience the divine riches of the Kingdom.*

*"Come unto Me and learn of Me," Jesus said. Learn of Jesus, the Author and Finisher of your faith; and without faith it is impossible to please God.*

*Let us pray:*

*"Purge me, O Lord, and cleanse me. Search my heart and see if there be any wicked way in me and lead me into righteousness (Psalm 139:23–24). I cannot know my heart—only You can (Jeremiah 17:9).*

*"So search me and expose my wickedness that I may confess and be set free from the bondages of Satan. I relinquish myself to You, oh Father, and ask for Your purging and cleansing."*

**Be it unto you according to your faith.**

\*\*\*

*"Have mercy upon me, O God, according to Your lovingkindness: according unto the multitude of Your tender mercies blot out my transgressions... (7) Purge me with hyssop, and I shall be clean: wash me, and I shall be whiter than snow." Psalm 51:1 & 7*

# SEPTEMBER 18

## THIS IS THE DAY THAT THE LORD HAS MADE. I WILL REJOICE AND BE GLAD IN IT.

*He alone is our Rock and our Salvation, of whom shall we fear (Psalm 27:1). Though the mountains crumple, we shall not be moved (Psalm 46:2).*

*Move on with the Lord, but do not move from your position of confidence in the Lord. Oh, come and see and taste and feel that the Lord is good (Psalm 34:8). Come to the Fountain that never runs dry (Revelation 21:6). Come to the Rock that is higher than I (Psalm 61:2). Come to the Lord of Host Who is your High Tower.*

*He will come and send His angels to stand guard over you. Fear not. You shall not be overcome. He will be with you through the valley of death and bring you to the mountain of victory.*

*Look not to the right nor left, but keep your gaze forward (Proverbs 4:25). Never wavering from left to right with doubt and unbelief. You want to enter the promised land, do you not? They could not enter because of unbelief (Hebrews 3:18–19). Let us not be like our ancestors and tempt the Lord to anger (Exodus 17:7).*

*Let us TRUST and OBEY for there is no other way! Now set your face and heart to trust Him today. For today is the day of salvation—not yesterday, not tomorrow—but NOW!*

\*\*\*

*"But let all those that put their trust in You rejoice: let them ever shout for joy, because You defend them: let them also that love Your name be joyful in You." Psalm 5:11*

*"...For he that wavers is like a wave of the sea driven with the wind and tossed. (7) For let not that man think that he shall receive any thing of the Lord. (8) A double minded man is unstable in all his ways." James 1:6b-8*

## SEPTEMBER 19
### THIS IS THE DAY THAT THE LORD HAS MADE. I WILL REJOICE AND BE GLAD IN IT.

*He is able to take care of this day. He knew this day before the foundation of the earth because He is eternal—never beginning and never ending—all knowing. In quietness and trust is your strength (Isaiah 30:15). Let us be quiet today in our worries and control. Let us be trusting of God that He can be and is in control of our lives. We now ask:*

*"Oh, Lord, I need help in being a mother, a father, a wife, a husband, a student, a worker, a teacher... Your child today. I desire to walk in Your Spirit today, to experience Your Life in my body and soul today. I give You myself. Potter have Your own way."*

*Trust Me. I AM your Shepherd. I AM the good Shepherd. My rod and My staff shall lead you and you will hear a voice saying, "Walk this way when you turn to the right and the left." (Isaiah 30:21) Fear not. It is My Father's good pleasure to bless you and you shall be blessed. Go forth knowing that you are blessed—coming in and going out, blessed in the field and city, blessed in the closet and market place, blessed in relations and in solitude. (Deuteronomy 28:1–14) Yes, "Blessed" is the name of My children. Should you not trust My Word when I said, "I am always thinking of you and I will never leave you?" (Hebrews 13:5) Yes, trust, believe and rely on Me for I shall surely not disappoint you. Remember to trust in the Lord with all your heart, and don't lean on your own brain. Say to yourself, "God is my leader," and I will direct your path. (Proverbs 3:5–6)*

\*\*\*

*"But now, O LORD, You are our Father; we are the clay, and You our potter; and we all are the work of Your hand." Isaiah 64:8*

## SEPTEMBER 20
## THIS IS THE DAY THAT THE LORD HAS MADE. I WILL REJOICE AND BE GLAD IN IT.

*Hallelujah!*

*For He is good!*

*Our God is good, not as some call good, but good as in all perfection (Matthew 5:48). There is no shadow of turning with our God (James 1:17). He is the same today, yesterday, and forever (Hebrews 13:8).*

*So seek to know Him better today by knowing Him from the past and finding out what He says about the future! He is operating in the present. He is! That means He is ever in proceeding order. Never is He waning or waxing. He is! He says to each of us:*

**Oh, come unto Me.**

**I will give you love and peace.**

**Rest in Me.**

\*\*\*

"You are good, and do good; teach me Your statutes." Psalm 119:68

"And God said unto Moses, I AM THAT I AM: and He said, Thus shall you say unto the children of Israel, I AM has sent me unto you." Exodus 2:14

"Return unto your rest, O my soul; for the LORD has dealt bountifully with you." Psalm 116:7

"Let us therefore fear, lest, a promise being left us of entering into His rest, any of you should seem to come short of it." Hebrews 4:1

"And My people shall dwell in a peaceable habitation, and in sure dwellings, and in quiet resting places;" Isaiah 32:18

## SEPTEMBER 21
### THIS IS THE DAY THAT THE LORD HAS MADE. I WILL REJOICE AND BE GLAD IN IT.

*He is never late. Even when we are late, He is not and He redeems our failings.*

*Isn't it good to know that nothing we do or can do can be so terrible Jesus' redemptive character cannot make it right? Hallelujah! That does not give us the license to purposefully do wrong. It does give us the freedom to walk without fear.*

*He is our Redeemer and He "fixes" our messes. Hallelujah!*

*Oh yes, we do reap what we have sown, but He makes all things work out for good for those who love Him (Romans 8:28). So even our mistakes are turned into good, and our reaping is of good things.*

*Jesus has covered all the bases. Satan cannot win in our lives.*

*Blessed is He who comes in the name of the Lord. Hosanna in the highest! (Luke 13:35)*

*He was slain and now is risen. He sits with the Father in heaven. All glory and honor to Him!*

\*\*\*

*"...Hosanna; Blessed is He that comes in the name of the Lord: (10) Blessed be the kingdom of our father David, that comes in the name of the Lord: Hosanna in the highest." Mark 11:96–10*

*"Which He wrought in Christ, when He raised Him from the dead, and set Him at His own right hand in the heavenly places, (21) Far above all principality, and power, and might, and dominion, and every name that is named, not only in this world, but also in that which is to come." Ephesians 1:20–21*

## SEPTEMBER 22
# THIS IS THE DAY THAT THE LORD HAS MADE. I WILL REJOICE AND BE GLAD IN IT.

*Say with me: "My Father, My Daddy, has made this day. God, my Daddy, is controlling everything that concerns me. Why? Because I am His child. Why? Because He chose me and I surrendered my life, my everything to Him to do as He wills. He knows when I'm going to sit down and when I am going to get up. He knows my thoughts while they are far off from me. He knows what I'm going to say before I say it (Psalm 139)."*

*He said in Deuteronomy 28 that if we listen to His voice and heed His commandments this day, blessings will overtake us. So why not listen? Why not obey? We have no idea what the future brings or this day, except by His Spirit revelation.*

*So, why not surrender your soul (emotions, thoughts, & will) to your Father today? Let's see what He can do today, with a compliant child. Let's see what He will do and wants to do.*

*You know our God is a God of love, joy, and peace. Wouldn't you like to partake of some of those fruits today? Let's spread some love and joy and peace today amongst the earth!*

*Let's experience God today as we give Him permission to unreservedly live His life in us—soul and body.*

*Let's recall at the end of the day what it was like to see God on earth!*

\*\*\*

*"I am crucified with Christ: nevertheless I live; yet not I, but Christ lives in me: and the life which I now live in the flesh I live by the faith of the Son of God who loved me, and gave Himself for me." Galatians 2:20*

## THIS IS THE DAY THAT THE LORD HAS MADE. I WILL REJOICE AND BE GLAD IN IT.

*Be glad and rejoice for God has made a way for you. If you come to Him at each invitation (and He is always inviting you), He will never turn you away.*

*Hang onto His blessings. His blessings are His Son, Jesus. Look at Jesus and see the love Jesus has for you and the Father.*

*Do not let the physical world around you choke out what He has given you. We are all made of dust, but He came to make us live forever and that we will do. Start now to enjoy eternity. He has put it in your heart! (Ecclesiastes 3:11)*

*Hang on!*

*Meditate on what He has done (Malachi 3:16).*

*Keep it in the front of your mind and embrace it to your chest.*

*Yes, protect His blessings by embracing them and holding them close.*

*He told Joshua to meditate on His Word day and night and to keep His Word in his mouth (Joshua 1:8).*

*Let us do the same!*

\*\*\*

*"Then they that feared the LORD spoke often one to another: and the LORD hearkened, and heard it, and a book of remembrance was written before Him for them that feared the LORD, and that thought upon His name." Malachi 3:16*

## SEPTEMBER 24
### THIS IS THE DAY THAT THE LORD HAS MADE. I WILL REJOICE AND BE GLAD IN IT.

*"How is it that we can rejoice when so many are living without knowing You? How is it we can be happy when so many live without loving You? How can we be joyful when so many are content doing their own thing?"*

*Grief and sorrow are also a part of the Kingdom. My Son was sorrowful unto death. He wept for Jerusalem. His heart was broken upon the cross. If you do not bear the sorrow, you cannot share the joy. This heavy burden you feel is for the lost, and well you should feel it. Many are dying and going to hell, because My people just like you have no burden for the lost.*

*Without seeing the need, there is never a movement to help. Even the alcoholic has to recognize his need for help before he can be helped.*

*Don't you see, it is as I said in Philippians; that I may know Him and the power of His resurrection, and may share His sufferings, becoming like Him in His death, that if possible I may attain the resurrection from the dead. (Philippians 3:10–11) Many souls are living lives lost, and may you also feel the burden I feel for them.*

\*\*\*

*"That I have great heaviness and continual sorrow in my heart. (3) For I could wish that myself were accursed from Christ for my brethren, my kinsmen according to the flesh;" Romans 9:3*

*"Brethren, my heart's desire and prayer to God for Israel is, that they might be saved." Romans 10:1*

## SEPTEMBER 25
### THIS IS THE DAY THAT THE LORD HAS MADE. I WILL REJOICE AND BE GLAD IN IT.

*Give all praise and thanksgiving to the Father of all fathers! He cares and has His attention on you.*

*Have you ever been pampered and treated like a china doll? Because the china doll is so precious and fragile, the owner is very careful to handle it gently. Well, you are more precious than any china doll! And you are cared for more gingerly than any physical object.*

*Do we think of ourselves as precious, special, a pearl of great price? (Matthew 13:46)*

*I say, "No!" However, He wants us to know how special and precious we are.*

*"Oh God! to know Your thoughts toward us."*

**You are the pearl of great price that I have given My all for. So see yourself as I see you—worth the price of My Son's suffering and blood.**

**Yes, the price of an object is indicative of its value. Your value was the humbling and death of My only Son. There was no higher price I could pay.**

*No, there was not.*

\*\*\*

*"For I know the thoughts that I think toward you, says the LORD, thoughts of peace, and not of evil, to give you an expected end." Jeremiah 29:11*

## SEPTEMBER 26
### THIS IS THE DAY THAT THE LORD HAS MADE. I WILL REJOICE AND BE GLAD IN IT.

*What can we think of and bring to mind to rejoice in?*

*Sometimes we find ourselves in a tight squeeze. However this is only a smoke screen of the enemy's. You see Satan's work for the most part operates in the physical realm. If he can get you to look at your physical surroundings (people, messy home, unpleasant job, etc.), he can steal your joy.*

*The joy of the LORD is your strength (Nehemiah 8:10). Why get caught up in the world you see with your physical eyes? That is only temporary.*

*These light afflictions cannot compare to the coming glory. You know it is more beneficial to look with your spiritual eyes. That is what God expected of Abraham who is your father. Before it comes into physical existence, it is in the spiritual. So why not focus on the beginning of a thing, the seed?*

*Faith is the substance of things hoped for and the evidence of things not seen. Look not at the way things are, but keep your eyes on the way things will be, for the things that are, are called forth from things that are not (Hebrews 11:1–3). In other words, those things you desire in the physical only come forth in the physical after having been created in the spiritual. Do not grow weary in well doing, for you will reap a harvest if you keep hold of your faith in Christ (Galatians 6:9).*

\*\*\*

*"For our light affliction, which is but for a moment, works for us a far more exceeding and eternal weight of glory: (18) While we look not at the things which are seen, but at the things which are not seen: for the things which are seen are temporal; but the things which are not seen are eternal." II Corinthians 4:17–18*

## SEPTEMBER 27

## THIS IS THE DAY THAT THE LORD HAS MADE. I WILL REJOICE AND BE GLAD IN IT.

*Rejoice, for He has prepared your way!*

*No matter the trouble, He has prepared and gone before you. Fall back into His assuring arms—His experienced arms.*

*Cry out for His grace to abound to you in the situation in which you find yourself (II Corinthians 9:8 & Hebrews 4:16). His grace is sufficient (II Corinthians 12:9).*

*Seek to know Him and not the intricacies of your problem. If you zoom in on your problem, that will be all you can see—bad decision.*

*Instead, zoom in on Jesus, meditate on Him, ponder Him, fret over Him, yearn to know Him, to desire Him, to crave Him, to see Him, hear Him, feel Him, and live in Him. Do not live in your problem. You'll only go round and round.*

*He has the answers. He is the Answer.*

*I know it doesn't make sense to your rational brain that by CONCENTRATING ON JESUS you will solve your problems, but He uses the foolish things to confound the wise.*

*Believe, so you'll understand, that is what He asks.*

\*\*\*

*"But God has chosen the foolish things of the world to confound the wise; and God has chosen the weak things of the world to confound the things which are mighty;" I Corinthians 1:27*

## SEPTEMBER 28
## THIS IS THE DAY THAT THE LORD HAS MADE. I WILL REJOICE AND BE GLAD IN IT.

*Is there anything in which to rejoice?*

*Rejoice in the fact that you love Jesus, because without His movement in you, you would not even be able to love Him.*

*Rejoice that you love Jesus, and that your heart pants for Him in a dry and thirsty land (Psalm 63:1). He will not disappoint you.*

*All those that trust in God will not be disappointed nor ashamed (Psalm 31:1). He will not let you down. It is not in His character.*

*Now, you may feel like God has let you down. God cannot let you down. It is your perception of the situation and not His perception that has you in a tizzy. We need His perspective and truth. Then peace comes like a river.*

*His ways are higher than ours; therefore, they are above ours, better than our ways and surprisingly rewarding.*

\*\*\*

*"O taste and see that the LORD is good: blessed is the man that trusts in Him." Psalm 34:8*

*"You are good, and do good; teach me Your statutes." Psalms 119:68*

*"For My thoughts are not your thoughts, neither are your ways My ways, says the LORD. (9) For as the heavens are higher than the earth, so are my ways higher than your ways, and My thoughts than your thoughts." Isaiah 55:8–9*

> **THIS IS THE DAY THAT THE LORD HAS MADE. I WILL REJOICE AND BE GLAD IN IT.**

*Follow the Lord and He shall give you the things you desire—time with Him.*

*While we are yet here on earth, there are responsibilities to be accomplished. Jesus had His earthly duties, and still all of God's will was done.*

*His Will will be done in your life too. We must be patient and trust Him. He created time. He can create time for you.*

*Seek not time with Him, but seek His will and it will bring you into all good things.*

*He is the Answer, and He has the answer.*

*Be patient and trust—in time you will reap if you faint not.*

\*\*\*

*"And let us not be not weary in well doing: for in due season we shall reap, if we faint not." Galatians 6:9*

*"And we desire that every one of you do show the same diligence to the full assurance of hope unto the end: (12) That you be not slothful, but followers of them who through faith and patience inherit the promises." Hebrews 6:11–12*

*"For you have need of patience, that, after you have done the will of God, you might receive the promise." Hebrews 10:36*

*"Wherefore seeing we also are compassed about with so great a cloud of witnesses, let us lay aside every weight, and the sin which does so easily beset us, and let us run with patience the race that is set before us." Hebrews 12:1*

## SEPTEMBER 30
### THIS IS THE DAY THAT THE LORD HAS MADE. I WILL REJOICE AND BE GLAD IN IT.

*This is a great time to be alive. God is calling for intercessors to usher in the revival. Will you be one?*

*The qualifications are only a desire to know Him and to do His will. It will require quiet time with Him, for we are ignorant and cold-hearted. But in His presence, He will change us and make us like Himself.*

*What is revival except a turning toward God? The time is now. Just as Joshua was ready to go into the Promised Land, we too are ready. Let us go! What are we waiting for? And if you do not feel compelled to go, then cry out in desperation that God would give you a desperate need for Him.*

*You cannot make yourself hungry for God. BUT you can plead with Him to give you a hungry heart! He will.*

*Hallelujah!*

\*\*\*

*"Blessed are they which do hunger and thirst after righteousness: for they shall be filled." Matthew 5:6*

*"Oh that You would rend the heavens, that You would come down, that the mountains might flow down at Your presence, (2) As when the melting fire burns, the fire causes the waters to boil, to make Your name known to Your adversaries, that the nations may tremble at Your presence!" Isaiah 64:1–2*

*"Therefore said He unto them, The harvest truly is great, but the laborers are few: pray therefore the Lord of the harvest, that He would send forth laborers into His harvest." Luke 10:2*

# OCTOBER

"A garden enclosed is My sister, My spouse; a spring shut up, a fountain sealed... ¹⁶Awake, O north wind; and come, thou south; blow upon my garden, that the spices thereof may flow out. Let my Beloved come into His garden, and eat His pleasant fruits."

SONG OF SOLOMON 4:12&16

> **THIS IS THE DAY THAT THE LORD HAS MADE. I WILL REJOICE AND BE GLAD IN IT.**

*Trust and obey.*

*Neglect not the promptings of the Spirit (Acts 7:51).*

*Why hesitate in fear? Lift it up to the Lord for confirmation and then trust.*

*He will never fail you, but will complete what He started (Philippians 1:6).*

*Did He not descend from heaven to save us? And did He not refuse the sword and nails for our sake?*

*Will He not much more lead us, if we ask and surrender to Him? Even if we don't ask and surrender, He will still lead, because we are His children.*

*Do you not lead your children even when they don't ask? We are His children and He is our Father. Be like a little child.*

\*\*\*

*"The LORD is my Shepherd; I shall not want. (2) He makes me to lie down in green pastures: He leads me beside the still waters. (3) He restores my soul: He leads me in the paths of righteousness for His name's sake." Psalm 23:1–3*

*"He that spared not His own Son, but delivered Him up for us all, how shall He not with Him also freely give us all things?" Romans 8:32*

*"Trust in the LORD with all your heart; and lean not unto your own understanding. (6) In all your ways acknowledge Him, and He shall direct your paths." Proverbs 3:5–6*

## OCTOBER 2
### THIS IS THE DAY THAT THE LORD HAS MADE. I WILL REJOICE AND BE GLAD IN IT.

*Sometimes it is a battle to keep our mind on the Lord.*

*How easy it is to concentrate on the problems at hand! When we do that, we exalt the problem to the status of god. Now, we don't admit that we have idols, but we do. What is meditating on a problem, but the exaltation of it? I do not suggest ignoring the problem, but what does God say to do with troubles?*

*Philippians 4:4-7 says (my paraphrase): Rejoice in the Lord always: and again I say, Rejoice. Let your moderation be known unto all men. The Lord is at hand. (He is at hand to solve your problem.) Be careful for nothing (don't worry); but in everything by prayer and supplication with thanksgiving let your requests (your problems) be made known unto God. And the peace of God, which passes all understanding shall keep your hearts and minds through Christ Jesus.*

*Then God says in verse 8 (my paraphrase): Finally think about these things: whatever is true, whatever is honest, whatever is just, whatever is pure, whatever is lovely, whatever is of a good report, if there is any virtue, if there is anything worthy of praise,*

*THINK ON THESE THINGS.*

*Jesus fits into each one of these categories. So think on JESUS!*

\*\*\*

*"Jesus says unto him, I am the Way, the Truth, and the Life: no man comes unto the Father, but by Me." John 14:6*

## THIS IS THE DAY THAT THE LORD HAS MADE. I WILL REJOICE AND BE GLAD IN IT.

*We will be glad, for He has done great things. He is always warring on our behalf and even during those hard times, He is working. We shall reap what we have sown—some to righteousness and some to perdition. Oh, that we would believe the Lord!*

*How can you believe someone if you don't know what they say, what they stand for, what they are capable of and on and on? Jesus said, "Know God—this is eternal life." (John 17:3a)*

*"To Know Him is to Love Him," (Phil Spector, 1958) was the title of a song I listened to as a teenager. This song is applicable to Jesus, His Father and Spirit. To know Them is to love Them. Oh, to know Them and to be known by Them!*

*"Father, our prayer as was Jesus' prayer for us is this—May we know You; and the same love You have for Jesus be in us. Yes and amen."*

\*\*\*

*"And I have declared unto them Your name, and will declare it: that the love wherewith You have loved Me may be in them, and I in them." John 17:26*

*"That He would grant you, according to the riches of His glory, to be strengthened with might by His Spirit in the inner man; (17) That Christ may dwell in your hearts by faith; that you, being rooted and grounded in love, (18) May be able to comprehend with all saints what is the breadth, and length, and depth, and height; (19) And to know the love of Christ, which passes knowledge, that you might be filled with all the fullness of God." Ephesians 3:16–19*

## OCTOBER 4

### THIS IS THE DAY THAT THE LORD HAS MADE. I WILL REJOICE AND BE GLAD IN IT.

*Oh, come and let us worship Jesus! Let us come unto the Lord of Hosts and sing praises unto Him for He is good and His mercy endures for ever. His mercy is new every morning (Lamentations 3:22–23). His mercy is new for every situation. Oh, come and let us sing praises unto Him! Oh, glory to God in the highest! Peace on earth (Luke 2:14). Peace. Peace. What a lovely word!*

*When all the world around us is tumultuous, what a testimony to the Lord when peace reigns within your soul in the midst of a storm. Have you gone somewhere that your Father is not? No! He said He would always be with you. So He is there. Cry out to Him. Don't give up on Him. You may be in a state of hysteria in which case it takes a little time for Him to get your attention. Quiet your mind by slowly saying His name over and over…Jesus, Jesus, Jesus… At that name everyone and everything must submit.*

*Now that the storm is quiet, He says to you, "Where was your faith?" (Luke 8:25) Only believe. Whatsoever things you desire, when you pray, believe you have received them and you shall have whatsoever things you say. Things may not turn out the way you expect, but His Word is true.*

\*\*\*

*"For verily I say unto you, That whosoever shall say unto this mountain, Be removed, and be cast into the sea; and shall not doubt in his heart, but shall believe that those things which he says shall come to pass; he shall have whatsoever he says. (24) Therefore I say unto you, What things soever you desire, when you pray, believe that you receive them, and you shall have them." Mark 11:23–24*

## OCTOBER 5

### THIS IS THE DAY THAT THE LORD HAS MADE. I WILL REJOICE AND BE GLAD IN IT.

*Bless the Lord, oh my soul, for He has done great things. He has done great things! Remember all He has done. Recount His mighty works on your behalf. This is how you can bless the Lord.*

*He longs for your love, for your fellowship. Just as an earthly father desires his children's love, so your heavenly Father desires you. Can you imagine the King of all Ages has a desire for you?*

*He can make anyone or anything, but He has chosen to make you free. Free to be with Him. Free to ignore Him. He could have forced you to be with Him. But He wants a free love. He wants a free fellowship. He even gives you the right to choose eternal life or eternal death.*

*With Jesus' sacrifice, God made it possible for us to choose life. Before Jesus, we were under the reign of Satan. He was a hard taskmaster. Jesus condemned sin, therefore setting us free to walk in the Spirit. Before Christ, we were slaves to sin, now we are slaves to righteousness (Romans 6:16–20). He made a way whereas our flesh could not make a way. The just requirement of the law has been satisfied, and we are free of punishment and free to serve Him.*

*Yes, we can serve Him and not Satan!*

\*\*\*

*"Know you not, that to whom you yield yourselves servants to obey, his servants you are to whom you obey; whether of sin unto death, or of obedience unto righteousness?…(18) Being then made free from sin, you became the servants of righteousness." Romans 6:16 & 18*

## OCTOBER 6

## THIS IS THE DAY THAT THE LORD HAS MADE. I WILL REJOICE AND BE GLAD IN IT.

*Sing unto the Lord a new song (Psalm 98:1). Bring praises into His house. Offer Him a sacrifice of praise for He is worthy (Hebrews 13:15). All power and honor belong to Him. All majesty and praise belong to Him (Jude 1:25).*

*Is it not enough that He has given His all? What else can He do! He has done it all and now why do we sit and lounge in our mess?*

*Oh, seek Him Whom thy soul loves. Seek Him for none else shall satisfy. Seek Him for He has loved you with an everlasting love and desires to commune with you.*

*Who knows the Father, save the Son? He is approachable. Do not believe all the deceptions that have been perpetuated throughout the centuries. His Word is true.*

*What situation in your life is bringing you trouble? Find out what God's Word says about it. And then believe God.*

*Seek Him.*

\*\*\*

*"By night on my bed I sought Him whom my soul loves: I sought Him, but I found Him not. (4) ... but I found Him whom my soul loves: I held Him, and would not let Him go..." Song of Solomon 3:1, 4b*

*"I sought the LORD, and He heard me, and delivered me from all my fears. (5) They looked unto Him, and were lightened: and their faces were not ashamed. (6) This poor man cried, and the LORD heard him, and saved him out of all his troubles." Psalm 34:4–6*

## OCTOBER 7
## THIS IS THE DAY THAT THE LORD HAS MADE. I WILL REJOICE AND BE GLAD IN IT.

*If a child asks his parents for direction, will they not give it? How much more our heavenly Father? If a child asks his parents to let him know what he is doing wrong, will they not correct him? As a matter of fact, no child needs to ask their parents for correction or guidance. That is the parents' job, and they just do it. How much more our heavenly Father will do His job.*

*When a child's heart is surrendered to his parents' will, life is much easier. He can trust and feel safe under his parents' care. How much more we can feel safe in our heavenly Father's care.*

*Out of time spent with the Lord will come guidance and correction; love and companionship; trust and security; a relationship that every child needs with his Parent for a solid foundation in life.*

*Is your life shaky? It may be because you have not been with your Parent enough. You have spent too much time with other people, doing other things. Build your life on the solid Rock.*

\*\*\*

*"Call unto Me, and I will answer you, and show you great and mighty things, which you know not." Jeremiah 33:3*

*"My Beloved spoke, and said unto me, Rise up, My love, My fair one, and come away." Song of Solomon 2:10*

*"He is like a man which built a house, and dug deep, and laid the foundation on a rock: and when the flood arose, the stream beat vehemently upon that house, and could not shake it: for it was founded upon a rock." Luke 6:49*

## OCTOBER 8

## THIS IS THE DAY THAT THE LORD HAS MADE. I WILL REJOICE AND BE GLAD IN IT.

*Rejoice in the Lord always! (Philippians 4:4)*

*That word, "always," seems to be inclusive. What time is there that is outside of "always"? There is no time outside of always.*

*Why then do we disobey our Father?*

*Because we walk in the flesh and not the Spirit? Because we look at the circumstances and not God's Word? Because we are full of the world and not the Word? Because we seek to please man and not God? Because we walk by sight and not faith? Oh, sinners that we surely are!*

*Repent! Repent! Repent! For the Lord is at hand, and His threshing fork is winnowing the chaff from the grain.*

*Therefore we declare, "We will walk in the Spirit. We will look to God's Word. We will be full of His Word. We will seek to please God, and we will walk by faith with His grace and mercy."*

\*\*\*

*"Whose fan is in His hand, and He will thoroughly purge His floor, and gather His wheat into the garner; but He will burn up the chaff with unquenchable fire." Matthew 3:12*

*"Whose fan is in His hand, and He will thoroughly purge His floor, and will gather the wheat into His garner; but the chaff He will burn with fire unquenchable." Luke 3:17*

*"Let us therefore come boldly unto the throne of grace, that we may obtain mercy, and find grace to help in time of need." Hebrews 4:16*

## OCTOBER 9
### THIS IS THE DAY THAT THE LORD HAS MADE. I WILL REJOICE AND BE GLAD IN IT.

*Do you rejoice? That is a strong word. Rejoicing is more than a mild enthusiasm. Rejoicing is exciting. Rejoicing cannot be denied. Some people may have a happy face and disposition, but rejoicing is more than that.*

*David rejoiced as he brought the ark back to Jerusalem (I Chronicles 15:27–28). Did you know the verse above from Psalm 118:24, "This is the day that the Lord has made..." was said at Passover dinners? Jesus would have said this on the night of the last supper. He was rejoicing in the midst of great suffering.*

*Was He rejoicing in the garden? No, He was sweating blood. Weeping may endure for a night, but joy comes in the morning (Psalm 30:5). His morning was three days later.*

*When shall our morning come? It has come, because we died with Him and we have been raised with Him. Our outward body will fade away, but our inward body is being renewed every day.*

*Sing unto the Lord a new song. Make melody in His ears, for He is great and greatly to be praised!*

\*\*\*

*"For which cause we faint not; but though our outward man perish, yet the inward man is renewed day by day. (17) For our light affliction, which is but for a moment, works for us a far more exceeding and eternal weight of glory; (18) While we look not at the things which are seen, but at the things which are not seen: for the things which are seen are temporal; but the things which are not seen are eternal." II Corinthians 4:16–18*

*"Great is the LORD, and greatly to be praised; and His greatness is unsearchable." Psalm 145:3*

# OCTOBER 10
## THIS IS THE DAY THAT THE LORD HAS MADE. I WILL REJOICE AND BE GLAD IN IT.

*Oh! give thanks to the Lord for He is good, His mercy endures forever.*

*No other name, but the name of Jesus. At the name of Jesus, demons flee, sickness disappears. Oh, that we had the faith, knowledge, purity or whatever is needed to speak His name and all things surrender. It is at the name of Jesus that all things on earth, in heaven and below the earth shall bow (Isaiah 45:23 & Romans 14:11).*

*"Father God, do with us what You will in order for Your kingdom to come on earth as it is in heaven. Shall we always be lacking in authority when You said, 'All authority I've given to you?'"*

*Nay, you shall rise up on eagles' wings. Believe My Word and look ever for its manifestation. If you cannot believe, it shall never come. But those that believe shall receive all things whatsoever they have believed. (Mark 11:24)*

\*\*\*

*"And they rose early in the morning, and went forth into the wilderness of Tekoa: and as they went forth, Jehoshaphat stood and said, Hear me, O Judah, and ye inhabitants of Jerusalem; Believe in the LORD your God, so shall you be established; believe His prophets, so shall you prosper." II Chronicles 20:20*

*"For the vision is yet for an appointed time, but at the end it shall speak, and not lie: though it tarry, wait for it; because it will surely come, it will not tarry." Habakkuk 2:3*

*"Behold, I give unto you power to tread on serpents and scorpions, and over all the power of the enemy: and nothing shall by any means hurt you." Luke 10:19*

## OCTOBER 11
### THIS IS THE DAY THAT THE LORD HAS MADE. I WILL REJOICE AND BE GLAD IN IT.

*Oh, let us rejoice! His Word is true. He says, "By His stripes we are healed."*

*"...by Whose stripes you were healed." I Peter 2:24b*

*We are healed. Believe Him. Continue to believe Him until your healing is manifested.*

*He says, "Those that wait on Me shall not be ashamed." We will not be disappointed.*

*"...and you shall know that I am the LORD: for they shall not be ashamed that wait for Me." Isaiah 49:23c*

*All things are possible with God. All things are possible with those who believe.*

*"Jesus said unto him, If you can believe, all things are possible to him that believes. (24) And straightway the father of the child cried out, and said with tears, Lord, I believe; help thou mine unbelief." Mark 9:23–24*

*Continue to believe...*

\*\*\*

*"For the which cause I also suffer these things: nevertheless I am not ashamed: for I know whom I have believed, and am persuaded that He is able to keep that which I have committed unto Him against that day." II Timothy 1:12*

*"Cast not away therefore your confidence, which has great recompense of reward. (36) For you have need of patience, that, after you have done the will of God, you might receive the promise. (37) For yet a little while, and he that shall come will come, and will not tarry." Hebrews 10:35–37*

## OCTOBER 12

## THIS IS THE DAY THAT THE LORD HAS MADE. I WILL REJOICE AND BE GLAD IN IT.

*He has made all wisdom available to us. He said, "Ask for wisdom, not doubting and you'll receive." (James 1:5–6)*

*We do perish for our lack of knowledge (Hosea 4:6). We dwell so much in this world that all His provisions are never received and used by us.*

*"Morning, noon and night, let us find out something about You, Father. Record it. Believe it. Trust it."*

*A little girl watches "Oprah" every day to learn something. Can we not learn something from our Father every day?*

*We shall not exhaust His storehouse. He delights in us. Let us delight in Him.*

*What have we learned today? Whenever we have a question about something, all we have to do is ask God for wisdom, not doubting, and we'll get an answer.*

\*\*\*

*"If any of you lack wisdom, let him ask of God, that gives to all men liberally, and upbraids not; and it shall be given him. (6) But let him ask in faith, nothing wavering. For he that wavers is like a wave of the sea driven with the wind and tossed. (7) For let not that man think that he shall receive any thing of the Lord. (8) A double minded man is unstable in all his ways." James 1:5–8*

## OCTOBER 13
## THIS IS THE DAY THAT THE LORD HAS MADE. I WILL REJOICE AND BE GLAD IN IT.

*Give Him thanks.*

*If you have problems with discouragement or depression, ask God to give you the grace each morning to think of things for which to thank Him. Let's not think about the bad things.*

*Let's try hard to recall good things like; a safe night's sleep, health to get out of bed, a bed to sleep in, a roof over our heads, our children are alive, the hope of a day walking with the Lord. This day may be the day my healing is manifested. This may be the day joy breaks forth in my life, and on and on.*

*In Philippians 4:8, God says to think on these things; whatever is true, whatever is honorable and worthy of respect, whatever is right and confirmed by God's word, whatever is pure and wholesome, whatever is lovely and brings peace, whatever is admirable and of good repute; if there is any excellence, if there is anything worthy of praise, think continually on these things [center your mind on them, and implant them in your heart]. (Amplified Version)*

*Let us fix our minds on praiseworthy thoughts! Let us keep our thoughts and emotions stayed on the Lord. Yes and Amen!*

\*\*\*

*"Finally, brethren, whatsoever things are true, whatsoever things are honest, whatsoever things are just, whatsoever things are pure, whatsoever things are lovely, whatsoever things are of good report; if there be any virtue, and if there be any praise, think on these things." Philippians 4:8*

## THIS IS THE DAY THAT THE LORD HAS MADE. I WILL REJOICE AND BE GLAD IN IT.

*He has healed and restored to life those things dead. What more could we ask for? Except we do not believe. How can I say that we do not believe? Because we still are not doing the things that Jesus did and even greater things.*

*"Verily, verily, I say unto you, He that believes on Me, the works that I do shall he do also; and greater works than these shall he do; because I go unto My Father." John 14:12*

*Those things of God from of old are still true. They have not changed, but we have. God changes not. But we do!*

*Seek the things from above not from below. He has redeemed us from the curse. The curse includes also every sickness and every affliction even the ones not written in the book of the Law (Deuteronomy 28:61). Deuteronomy 28:47–48a says, "Because you serve not the LORD your God with joyfulness, and with gladness of heart, for the abundance of all things; (48a) therefore shall you serve your enemies which the LORD shall send against you..."*

*We say every day, "Rejoice in the Lord," so we should be rejoicing or the curse is open to be visited upon us. Yes, Jesus has redeemed us from the curse (Galatians 3:13). God says, "Rejoice." Jesus' death has given us the power to obey and be blessed! Choose you this day whom you will serve.*

*"Help us, Father, to follow Your Son in all we do and say, in His sweet and holy name we pray, amen and amen."*

\*\*\*

*"If you then be risen with Christ, seek those things which are above, where Christ sits on the right hand of God." Colossians 3:1*

*Let us look for God today. Where is He in our goings and doings and sayings?*

*"Father, we speak blessings to those ministering to the Body of Christ and we bless His Body."*

*Oh! how we need to share Christ—His love, His concern, His attention, His mercy, His compassion, His health, His salvation, His truth, and on and on.*

*"Oh, Lord God Almighty, quicken in us Your passion for the lost and dying. Get us out of our selfish life style and open to us Your heart for the lost. Open our eyes and ears to see and hear. Loosen our feet and hands to go and do. Oh, to have Your eyes!"*

*Is it any wonder so many are dying, while we are living and not seeking to find the lost sheep and bring them in? We declare by faith and His grace that we shall live in His Spirit and do the works He did and even greater works shall we do.*

*We pray as God told us to, "The harvest truly is plenteous, but the laborers are few; (38) Pray therefore the Lord of the harvest, that He will send forth laborers into His harvest." Matthew 9:37–38*

\*\*\*

*"Verily, verily, I say unto you, He that believes on Me, the works that I do shall he do also; and greater works than these shall he do; because I go unto My Father." John 14:12*

## OCTOBER 16

## THIS IS THE DAY THAT THE LORD HAS MADE. I WILL REJOICE AND BE GLAD IN IT.

*Oh, that we would praise the Lord! Bless His Holy name. Let us sing or read the 103rd Psalm today. Meditate on one of the verses that seem to resonate within your heart. Believe it. Receive it and ask God to rid you of unbelief!*

\*\*\*

"Bless the LORD, O my soul: and all that is within me, bless His holy name. (2) Bless the LORD, O my soul, and forget not all His benefits: (3) Who forgives all your iniquities; who heals all your diseases. (4) Who redeems your life from destruction; who crowns you with lovingkindness and tender mercies; (5) Who satisfies your mouth with good things; so that your youth is renewed like the eagle's. (6) The LORD executes righteousness and judgment for all that are oppressed. (7) He made known His ways unto Moses, His acts unto the children of Israel. (8) The LORD is merciful and gracious, slow to anger, and plenteous in mercy. (9) He will not always chide neither will He keep His anger for ever. (10) He has not dealt with us after our sins; nor rewarded us according to our iniquities. (11) For as the heaven is high above the earth, so great is His mercy toward them that fear Him. (12) As far as the east is from the west, so far has He removed our transgressions from us. (13) Like as a father pities his children, so the LORD pities them that fear Him. (14) For He knows our frame, He remembers that we are dust. (15) As for man, his days are as grass: as a flower of the field, so he flourishes. (16) For the wind passes over it, and it is gone; and the place thereof shall know it no more. (17) But the mercy of the LORD is from everlasting to everlasting upon them that fear Him, and His righteousness unto children's children; (18) To such as keep His covenant, and to those that remember His commandments to do them. (19) The LORD has prepared His throne in the heavens; and His kingdom rules over all. (20) Bless the LORD, ye His angels that excel in strength, that do His commandments, hearkening unto the voice of His Word. (21) Bless ye the LORD, all ye His hosts; ye ministers of His, that do His pleasure. (22) Bless the LORD, all His works in all places of His dominion: bless the LORD, O my soul." Psalm 103

## OCTOBER 17

## THIS IS THE DAY THAT THE LORD HAS MADE. I WILL REJOICE AND BE GLAD IN IT.

*After meditating on Psalm 103, it is easy to rejoice. There are so many good words of promise given to us from our Father. We can be rejoicing in Him at all times just as He has commanded.*

*He said His commandments are not grievous. It is our lack of knowledge that makes His commandments hard. He has given us His Spirit—the Spirit of love, wisdom, understanding, counsel, strength, knowledge and the fear of the Lord (Isaiah 11:2–3). But we continue to walk in our reasoning.*

*"Oh! deliver us Lord, from our reasoning and set us in a high place in the Spirit that we can do Your works and spread Your love. Oh, may Your Spirit reign over our flesh and soul!"*

*Glory, hallelujah, as we walk in His anointing! Hallelujah! Hallelujah!*

\*\*\*

*"For this is the love of God, that we keep His commandments: and His commandments are not grievous." I John 5:3*

*"I will bless the LORD at all times: His praise shall continually be in my mouth. (2) My soul shall make her boast in the LORD: the humble shall hear thereof, and be glad. (3) O magnify the LORD with me, and let us exalt His name together." Psalm 34:1–3*

*"And it shall come to pass in that day, that his burden shall be taken away from off your shoulder, and his yoke from off your neck, and the yoke shall be destroyed because of the anointing." Isaiah 10:27*

## THIS IS THE DAY THAT THE LORD HAS MADE. I WILL REJOICE AND BE GLAD IN IT.

*We were made to have communion with God and to have dominion over the earth. Adam and Eve lost it for us, BUT Jesus got it back.*

*Let us not stagger in unbelief, but press in to touch the hem of His garment.*

*Let us rest in His very present care of us (Psalm 46:1). He is here. Always ready to bless His children, but we forget Him and try to do things on our own. So true!*

*He is here. Walk with Him today.*

*Know His presence.*

*Know His love.*

*Know His care.*

*He is here.*

\*\*\*

*"...and, lo, I am with you always, even unto the end of the world." Matthew 28:30b*

*"He staggered not at the promise of God through unbelief; but was strong in faith, giving glory to God; (21) And being fully persuaded that, what He had promised, He was able also to perform." Romans 4:20–21*

*"And besought Him that they might only touch the hem of His garment: and as many as touched were made perfectly whole." Matthew 14:36*

*"Then he answered and spoke unto me, saying, This is the word of the LORD unto Zerubbabel, saying, Not by might, nor by power, but by My Spirit, says the LORD of hosts." Zechariah 4:6*

## THIS IS THE DAY THAT THE LORD HAS MADE. I WILL REJOICE AND BE GLAD IN IT.

Be gone, rejoicing in the things of this world! Rejoice in the Lord!

How can we rejoice when we know so little in Whom we are to rejoice? It is sad and more than sad the state of our spiritual affairs. Has any generation been as lost as this one? We pray:

"Open our eyes, Lord, to our depravity. How can we repent unless You open our eyes? We are deceived. It is Your Spirit that convicts us of our sin. Keep not Your Spirit from us. Uncover our darkness and flood our souls with Your Light. Your Truth will set us free. Make us uncomfortable in our contentment. It is not Godly contentment, but ignorant contentment and perhaps lazy contentment. Oh, for our eyes to be opened, and our ears unstopped! Work in us Your righteousness, for we long to please You and bless You. Work in us Your Love so we can know You, love our brethren, and heap hot coals on our enemies' heads, so that even our enemies are made our allies. We love You, Lord, and desire to love You more and more and more!"

\*\*\*

"Therefore if your enemy hunger, feed him; if he thirst, give him drink; for in so doing you shall heap coals of fire on his head." Romans 12:20

"And this I pray, that your love may abound yet more and more in knowledge and in all judgment; (10) That you may approve things that are excellent; that you may be sincere and without offense till the day of Christ;" Philippians 1:9–10

## THIS IS THE DAY THAT THE LORD HAS MADE. I WILL REJOICE AND BE GLAD IN IT.

*What mighty works of God shall be seen today!*

*Maybe today is the day He gives you faith to believe for your healing. Maybe today is the day your healing is manifested.*

*Maybe today He gives you the boldness to witness to those you see.*

*Maybe today you experience to a greater depth His great love for you.*

*The possibilities of today are endless, just like our God.*

*We are the clay and He is the potter. "Melt us and mold us, Lord."*

*Be sensitive to the Spirit today. Don't run off in a worldly way. Be still inwardly and attentive to His voice. Go in assurance of His constant care and do not doubt. Anything done outside of faith is sin. We cannot please God without faith (Hebrews 11:6). So walk according to faith and not sight. Try operating today in the Spirit and not fleshly reasoning!*

\*\*\*

*"…for whatsoever is not of faith is sin." Romans 14:23c*

*"(For we walk by faith, not by sight:)" I Corinthians 5:7*

*"For if you live after the flesh, you shall die: but if you through the Spirit do mortify the deeds of the body, you shall live. (14) For as many as are led by the Spirit of God, they are the sons of God." Romans 8:13–14*

> MADE. I WILL REJOICE AND BE GLAD IN IT.

*...For today is the day of salvation (II Corinthians 6:2d).*

*Salvation from sin, sickness, disease, mourning, fear, worry, distress, unrest, sorry, anxiety, questions, doubts, anger, frustration, hatred, unforgiveness, rebellion, lust, greed, gluttony, idolatry, murder, lack, impatience, ungodly thinking, immorality, useless words, selfishness, disobedience, ignorance, unbelief, distrust, confusion, blindness, deafness, tumors, cowardice...*

*Look to the rock from which you were hewn. Look to Abraham and to Sarah your mother (Isaiah 51:2). See how God worked in their lives. He is the same yesterday, today, and forever (Hebrews 13:8).*

*He is trustworthy. Trust Him.*

*He is the Rock and He died for you. Love Him. Trust Him.*

*We say, "Jesus, we trust in You."*

\*\*\*

*"Hearken to Me, you that follow after righteousness, you that seek the LORD: look unto the rock whence you are hewn, and to the hole of the pit whence you are digged. (2) Look unto Abraham your father, and unto Sarah that bare you: for I called him alone, and blessed him, and increased him." Isaiah 51:1–2*

*"He only is my rock and my salvation; He is my defense; I shall not be greatly moved... (6) He only is my rock and my salvation: He is my defense; I shall not be moved. (7) In God is my salvation and my glory: the rock of my strength, and my refuge, is in God." Psalm 62:2, 6–7*

# OCTOBER 22

## THIS IS THE DAY THAT THE LORD HAS MADE. I WILL REJOICE AND BE GLAD IN IT.

*Oh, hallelujah for days of rest and relaxation! Should not all our days be as such? He has rested from His work and has provided for our rest. Now let us walk in it!*

*But how you ask?*

*Sit at His feet listening to Him as Mary did in the Bible (Luke 10:39). How can you listen to Him? Try reading the red words in the Bible—Jesus' words. The Holy Spirit will speak to your heart giving you direction for the moment. It may not be for the whole day. Therefore as you walk out the day, take time to turn your face to Him again, seeking His direction. Tell Him you love Him and want His will in your life today. He'll honor your desire to follow Him. He'll guide and lead you.*

*Ask Him each morning, "How can I walk in the rest You've provided for me, so my life is not a reproach unto my Father in the eyes of the world watching?"*

\*\*\*

*"And she had a sister called Mary, which also sat at Jesus' feet, and heard His Word…(41) And Jesus answered and said unto her, Martha, Martha, you are careful and troubled about many things; (42) But one thing is needful: and Mary has chosen that good part, which shall not be taken away from her." Luke 10:39, 41–42*

## OCTOBER 23
## THIS IS THE DAY THAT THE LORD HAS MADE. I WILL REJOICE AND BE GLAD IN IT.

*Why not rejoice?*

*The other option is so depressing, disobedient, and defeating. His commandment is to rejoice.*

*"Oh, God! turn our hearts to You so we cry out like David—'Purge me with hyssop, and I shall be clean: wash me, and I shall be whiter than snow.'" (Psalm 51:7)*

*For we know we were born in sin, and in sin did our mother conceive us (Psalm 51:5). But Christ came, cleansed us, and made us new. There are enough reasons to rejoice in any circumstance and all through the day. Study His Word and find out all the reasons to rejoice. Renew your mind to the truth, and cast down the lies with which you've been living.*

*Don't consort with the enemy, it only leads to death. God's words are life to those that find them and healing to all their flesh.*

\*\*\*

*"My son, attend to My words; incline your ear unto My sayings. (21) Let them not depart from your eyes; keep them in the midst of your heart. (22) For they are life unto those that find them, and health to all their flesh." Proverbs 4:20–22*

*"And be not conformed to this world: but be transformed by the renewing of your mind, that you may prove what is that good, and acceptable, and perfect, will of God." Romans 12:2*

*"Casting down imaginations, and every high thing that exalts itself against the knowledge of God, and bringing into captivity every thought to the obedience of Christ;" II Corinthians 10:5*

## MADE. I WILL REJOICE AND BE GLAD IN IT.

*How is it that our lives have wandered so far from the Truth?*

*When man's reasonings replace God's wisdom, man falls far from the glory of God. The foolishness of God is compared to the greatness of man. In other words, the greatest reasoning of man is foolishness on God's level (I Corinthians 1:25).*

*If we walk by faith in His Word, then we can walk on His level—way above the level of man. We have walked in such poverty for so long. We have become accustomed to lack. The lack of health, wealth, joy, peace, security, and on and on! Let us burst out of our deceptive world, and begin to live according to the Kingdom of God (Romans 14:17), according to our inheritance He has left to us.*

*Why go mourning, O my soul, hope in God for He has surely made a way (where there seems to be no way) to His glory and not man's!*

\*\*\*

*"Why are you cast down, O my soul? And why are you disquieted within me? Hope in God: for I shall yet praise Him, who is the health of my countenance, and my God." Psalm 42:11 & Psalm 43:5*

*"Because the foolishness of God is wiser than men; and the weakness of God is stronger than men." I Corinthians 1:25*

*"For the kingdom of God is not meat and drink; but righteousness, and peace, and joy in the Holy Ghost." Romans 14:17*

*Have you been searching the Scriptures for words that lead you into joy and rejoicing? Paul, in Philippians chapter four, says to think on whatever is: true, honorable, just, pure, lovely, gracious, excellent and worthy of praise.*

*All these things are true of Scripture and true of Jesus. Jesus is the Truth. He is honorable, just, pure, lovely, gracious, excellent, and worthy of praise. The first commandment says to love the Lord your God with all your heart, soul and body. Love Him. Think about Him. Spend time with Him. Learn of Him.*

*When you love someone, you want to be with him, get to know him, help him if he has a need. Do you know our Father has a need and that need is for us to work with Him to save a lost and dying generation? He has chosen to have a need for us to work with Him. Without us working with Him, the work will not get done. Pray for laborers for the harvest.*

\*\*\*

*"Therefore said He unto them, The harvest truly is great, but the laborers are few: pray therefore the Lord of the harvest, that He would send forth laborers into His harvest." Luke 10:2*

*"I must work the works of Him that sent Me, while it is day: the night comes, when no man can work." John 9:4*

## THIS IS THE DAY THAT THE LORD HAS MADE. I WILL REJOICE AND BE GLAD IN IT.

*Be glad for I have overcome the enemy, death, and hell.*

*Rejoice! Ours is the victory, but we have to enforce the victory. We have to maintain order, or the enemy will cause havoc. He is ready to kill, steal, and destroy. Do not allow him. We have the power. We've been given the authority, and we've been chosen to the position. The position brings with it definite occurrences of skirmishes and battles. Once we've been assigned priest, the devil looks at us as a target to annihilate. So think it not strange when diverse problems come upon us. We shall go through trials and tribulations, but our faith must be tried as gold.*

**Come unto Me all ye who labor and are heavy laden, and I will give you rest.**

\*\*\*

"I am He that lives, and was dead; and, behold, I am alive for evermore, Amen; and have the keys of hell and of death." Revelation 1:18

"Behold, I give unto you power to tread on serpents and scorpions, and over all the power of the enemy: and nothing shall by any means hurt you." Luke 10:19

"Wherein you greatly rejoice, though now for a season, if need be, you are in heaviness through manifold temptations: (7) That the trial of your faith, being much more precious than of gold that perishes, though it be tried with fire, might be found unto praise and honor and glory at the appearing of Jesus Christ:" I Peter 1:6–7

"These things I have spoken unto you, that in Me you might have peace. In the world you shall have tribulation: but be of good cheer; I have overcome the world." John 16:33

*Let us not waver between faith and unbelief. Let us capture and put down every thought that is against the knowledge of Jesus Christ. Oh! for more knowledge of Christ, His Father and the Spirit.*

*"Stir in us a hunger for You, Lord. Let us not rest in our ignorance, for much is to be done for Thy Kingdom to come. We are your sons and daughters, servants and slaves, warriors and victors.*

*"Oh! come Lord Jesus and instill in us Your love, Your life. Oh! to love with the love of Jesus. Be ever moving in our hearts to further Thy Kingdom to come upon earth. Let our mind and body be ever moving in the Spirit, not lounging in the world.*

*"Come Lord Jesus and wake us, stir us, move us!"*

\*\*\*

*"Wherefore He says, Awake you that sleep, and arise from the dead, and Christ shall give you light. (15) See then that you walk circumspectly, not as fools, but as wise, (16) Redeeming the time, because the days are evil. (17) Wherefore be you not unwise, but understanding what the will of the Lord is." Ephesians 5:14–17*

*"And that, knowing the time, that now it is high time to awake out of sleep: for now is our salvation nearer than when we believed. (12) The night is far spent, the day is at hand: let us therefore cast off the works of darkness, and let us put on the armor of light… (14) But put you on the Lord Jesus Christ, and make not provision for the flesh, to fulfill the lusts thereof." Romans 13:11–12 & 14*

*"Casting down imaginations, and every high thing that exalts itself against the knowledge of God, and bringing into captivity every thought to the obedience of Christ; (6) And having in a readiness to revenge all disobedience, when your obedience is fulfilled." II Corinthians 10:5–6*

† 

## OCTOBER 28

## THIS IS THE DAY THAT THE LORD HAS MADE. I WILL REJOICE AND BE GLAD IN IT.

*Oh, hallelujah for another day to praise and worship our Savior, our King, our Friend, our Lover! He is all in all, and we are all in all in Him.*

*What you have need of, He has supply of. Come unto the throne of grace and receive mercy and grace in your time of need (Hebrews 4:16). He is able.*

*What is belief? It is faith in action in the spiritual world. Yes, belief is faith in action. Without faith you cannot please God, and without belief you cannot receive. When you pray, believe that you have received and you shall have it (Mark 11:24).*

*Children ask expecting to receive. When the answer is, "No," there is crying initially, but it soon ends. The desire may be forgotten by the child, but not by the parent. If the desire is beneficial, the parent shall give to the child at the right time. But if the desire is detrimental, the child shall never receive that desire, but something beneficial in its place.*

*When you are a child of God, once you have demonstrated a desire, the Father never forgets. But the satisfaction of that desire must wait for God's perfect timing and way. However, you may be called upon to elicit many faith-filled actions prior to manifestation of the desire.*

\*\*\*

*"He has made every thing beautiful in His time: also He has set the world in their heart, so that no man can find out the work that God makes from the beginning to the end." Ecclesiastes 3:11*

*"Therefore I say unto you, What things soever you desire, when you pray, believe that you receive them, and you shall have them." Mark 11:24*

## OCTOBER 29
## THIS IS THE DAY THAT THE LORD HAS MADE. I WILL REJOICE AND BE GLAD IN IT.

*Let us continue from the point of our departure yesterday. God never forgets our heart's cry. He is ever in the process of maturing us to the place of receiving from Him the manifestation of our desires.*

*Abide in Christ. Abide in His Words, and you shall ask and you shall receive. Ask and keep on asking. That way the Father and you stay connected, and the desire fulfilled will give glory to God.*

*Never has man fulfilled his own desires and been satisfied, because pride comes before a fall; but God exalts the humble (I Peter 5:6). Humility realizes every good and perfect gift is from above (James 1:17).*

*Think it not strange when diverse trials come your way (James 1:2). They are God's course for maturing His children. Growing up in Christ does not make you an adult. It makes you a child in His kingdom. You shall always be a child to God. As I have often said, "My children shall always be my babies." That is true in some ways, but in other ways our children also become our friends and co-workers in the Kingdom, just as we do with Christ.*

\*\*\*

*"If you abide in Me, and My words abide in you, you shall ask what you will, and it shall be done unto you." John 15:7*

*"And said, Verily I say unto you, Except you be converted, and become as little children, you shall not enter into the kingdom of heaven." Matthew 18:3*

*"My brethren, count it all joy when you fall into divers temptations; (3) Knowing this, that the trying of your faith works patience." James 1:2–3*

## THIS IS THE DAY THAT THE LORD HAS MADE. I WILL REJOICE AND BE GLAD IN IT.

*Treat each person you meet as if this could be their last day. Would you not be kind and patient with such a person who would be leaving this earth and going on—to eternal life or eternal death?*

*"Oh! Father open our eyes and heart so we shall see and discern what is going on in the lives of those You send us to."*

*This is the day that the LORD has made. What is it today that we must do? This is not a fearful threatening, but it is a call to treat each person we meet with love, patience, joy, kindness, goodness, and gentleness.*

*Oh, to be loving as our Father is loving to us! Let us experience His love so that we may extend that love to others in this vale of tears. We have the key to Life. Let us use it to open the door of Life to those dying!*

*"Bring us home to Your love, Lord! Let us not rest until we are resting in Your love!"*

*Then we shall spread that love around like light and salt (Matthew 15:13–15). We shall no longer be dark and bland. Awake, O harp and lyre and sing the song of Moses!*

\*\*\*

*"And they sing the song of Moses the servant of God, and the song of the Lamb, saying, Great and marvelous are Your works, Lord God Almighty; just and true are Your ways, You King of saints." Revelation 15:3*

## THIS IS THE DAY THAT THE LORD HAS MADE. I WILL REJOICE AND BE GLAD IN IT.

*Have you made Jesus Lord of your life? More specifically, have you made Jesus Lord of your time, activities, desires?*

*The time is now!*

*If you hear His voice, harden not your heart (Hebrews 3:15). He is calling for passion and desire on the part of His children. No longer is it sufficient to go to church and be blessed. The revival fires are flickering and causing hearts to languish over the lost here and abroad.*

*Seek not the acceptance of your loved ones. Seek the words from Jesus, "Well done, good and faithful servant." Have you asked Him to be Lord?*

*Now continue seeking Him, so He is Lord of your life.*

*Now continue knocking, until He blesses you with fire.*

*His love is fire; and it is His love that will consume the world bringing in the Kingdom of God.*

\*\*\*

*"His lord said unto him, Well done, you good and faithful servant: you have been faithful over a few things, I will make you ruler over many things: enter you into the joy of your lord." Matthew 25:21*

*"…He shall baptize you with the Holy Ghost, and with fire:" Matthew 3:11c*

# NOVEMBER

"The fig tree puts forth her green figs, and the vines with the tender grape give a good smell. Arise, My love, My fair one, and come away."

SONG OF SOLOMON 2:13

**THIS IS THE DAY THAT THE LORD HAS MADE. I WILL REJOICE AND BE GLAD IN IT.**

*Words of wisdom pour forth from our Savior's mouth and oh, that we could hear them! "Speak, Lord, for your servant listens."*

*Do we listen or do we rush into and out of prayer—rush into and out of life? Do people pass us without our blessings or intercessions being offered to God?*

*Let us not flippantly walk or run through life, ignoring those around us. That includes your husband, wife, children, children's friends, and your friends, as well as those at work, gas station, grocery store...*

*God has blessed us with knowledge of Himself, so that we would be a blessing to others.*

*Pass it on! Don't be a dammed up river. Let it flow. Let the river of Life flow out of you!*

\*\*\*

*"For the LORD gives wisdom: out of His mouth comes knowledge and understanding." Proverbs 2:6*

*"And I will make of you a great nation, and I will bless you, and make your name great; and you shall be a blessing." Genesis 12:3*

*"He that believes on Me, as the scripture has said, out of his belly shall flow rivers of living water." John 7:38*

## NOVEMBER 2
### THIS IS THE DAY THAT THE LORD HAS MADE. I WILL REJOICE AND BE GLAD IN IT.

*For what things have I given unto you that you should bemoan the fact that I am your God?*

*Do not all good and perfect gifts come from Me? (James 1:17)*

*What is it that disturbs your peace and puts you off course?*

*Those whose mind is stayed on Me have perfect peace. (Isaiah 26:3)*

*Read my Word, Psalm 51, and repent for the foolish way in which you allow your mind to wonder and wander.*

*Meditate on My Words day and night and you shall have prosperity.*

*What words shall you eat? Those of the world and Satan or those of Life?*

*Choose you this day which you shall serve!*

\*\*\*

"This book of the law shall not depart out of your mouth; but you shall meditate therein day and night, that you may observe to do according to all that is written therein: for then you shall make your way prosperous, and then you shall have good success." Joshua 1:8

"It is the Spirit that quickens; the flesh profits nothing: the words that I speak unto you, they are spirit, and they are life." John 6:63

"I call heaven and earth to record this day against you, that I have set before you life and death, blessing and cursing therefore choose life; that both you and your seed may live." Deuteronomy 30:19

## NOVEMBER 3
## THIS IS THE DAY THAT THE LORD HAS MADE. I WILL REJOICE AND BE GLAD IN IT.

*Rejoice in the LORD always and again I say rejoice. (Philippians 4:4)*

*Say not what your mind is thinking, but what your spirit is revealing. We walk by faith and not by sight (II Corinthians 5:7). Is it not enough that Jesus has died and conquered sin and death? We must believe His triumph or we shall believe the enemy, thus be deceived.*

*Look not to the right nor left (Proverbs 4:27). Be always ever, focused upon the face of your Lover. It is He to Whom your freedom can be accredited. He came to set us free, and we are free. No longer linger in the enemy's camp of bondage—whether to fear, frustration, anger, jealousy, insufficiency, etc.*

*Whatever is causing you to have a life lived without love, joy, peace, patience, kindness, gentleness, faithfulness, meekness, and self-control, ask God to forgive you and renounce it so you can live the life Jesus has provided for you.*

*"Lord, I repent for my lack of joy. I repent for my undercurrent of anxiety. I repent for not rejoicing. Please forgive my mess. Wash me in Jesus' Blood and cleanse me from my sins that I may sing of Your righteousness all the days of my life! In Jesus' precious name, amen and amen."*

\*\*\*

*"Finally, brethren, whatsoever things are true, whatsoever things are honest, whatsoever things are just, whatsoever things are pure, whatsoever things are lovely, whatsoever things are of good report; if there be any virtue, and if there be any praise, think on these things." Philippians 4:8*

## THIS IS THE DAY THAT THE LORD HAS MADE. I WILL REJOICE AND BE GLAD IN IT.

*Oh, sing for joy all you His people! Shout unto God with a voice of triumph, for He has caused our enemies to be at peace with us! (Proverbs 16:7) He has made us to be the head and not the tail (Deuteronomy 28:13a).*

*Tell Satan that he is under your feet, because that is where Jesus has banished him—under your feet. NOW! Do not let thoughts of defeat linger in your mind. Satan has been defeated. However he is the deceiver and would like for you to believe he's a threat to your life. No! He is as a roaring lion, seeking whom he may destroy (I Peter 5:8b). He can seek, but he cannot destroy you. You have authority and dominion over him and all his threats and deceptions.*

*Seek not to know the sons of men, but seek to know the Son of Man. It is He Who has caused you to reign in the heavenlies, far above all rule and authority; for what Jesus accomplished, He shares with His brothers and sisters (Ephesians 1:3–6).*

*So when fear or frustration roar in your life today, tell them you are not impressed with them, but that you are impressed with a sound mind and power that God has given you (II Timothy 1:7). We do not have a spirit of fear which leads to fear and frustration, but we have God's Spirit of love, power, and a sound mind—a mind in control.*

\*\*\*

*"And have put all things under His feet, and gave Him to be the head over all things to the church, (23) Which is His body, the fullness of Him that fills all in all." Ephesians 1:22–23*

> **THIS IS THE DAY THAT THE LORD HAS MADE. I WILL REJOICE AND BE GLAD IN IT.**

*Hallelujah! All His answers are yea and amen (II Corinthians 1:20). His answers are correct, right, just, peaceable, lovable and receivable. You can receive His Words. Even hard words are healing and health to us (Proverbs 4:22). Oh, for any word from our Savior!*

Pray with me: "Lord, I want some definite clear words from my Father today. I will eat these words. I will meditate on these words. I will not let these words get stolen or choked out by the cares of this world. I will cherish and nourish these words. So they'll grow into a big tree bringing comfort, deliverance and life to many. Only by Your grace and mercy will I do this.

"Speak for Your servant listens."

\*\*\*

"For all the promises of God in Him are yea, and in Him Amen, unto the glory of God by us." II Corinthians 1:20

"But he that received seed into the good ground is he that hears the word, and understands it; which also bears fruit, and brings forth, some a hundredfold, some sixty, some thirty." Matthew 13:23

"Another parable put He forth unto them, saying, The kingdom of heaven is like to a grain of mustard seed, which a man took, and sowed in his field: (32) Which indeed is the least of all seeds: but when it is grown, it is the greatest among herbs, and becomes a tree, so that the birds of the air come and lodge in the branches thereof." Matthew 13:31

## THIS IS THE DAY THAT THE LORD HAS MADE. I WILL REJOICE AND BE GLAD IN IT.

*You have heard "Rejoice for the day of the Lord is here." But I say weep and mourn for the great and terrible Day of the Lord. For those that weep shall return with singing.*

*It is a sad day when the children weep for the sins of their parents. But that day is no longer here. For the Lord has caused the sins of the parents to be upon their own heads and not the children. Christ came for freedom—freedom for His children. The curse has been broken and you are free! (Galatians 3:13) Free to come and go as you please!*

*Christ has set us free. Be no longer yoked to the laws of man. Their binding ways have restricted the move and movements of God.*

*Look to Jesus! Sing, O barren one! Sing! For the Lord has set you free—free!*

\*\*\*

*"And the LORD shall utter His voice before His army: for His camp is very great: for He is strong that executes His Word: for the day of the LORD is great and very terrible; and who can abide it?" Joel 2:11*

*"He that goes forth and weeps, bearing precious seed, shall doubtless come again with rejoicing, bringing his sheaves with him." Psalm 126:6*

*"The soul that sins, it shall die. The son shall not bear the iniquity of the father, neither shall the father bear the iniquity of the son: the righteousness of the righteous shall be upon him, and the wickedness of the wicked shall be upon him." Ezekiel 18:20*

*"Sing, O barren, you that did not bear; break forth into singing, and cry aloud..." Isaiah 54:1a*

**THIS IS THE DAY THAT THE LORD HAS MADE. I WILL REJOICE AND BE GLAD IN IT.**

*Rejoice, and again I say rejoice!*

*Can you go wrong when you rejoice? Paul said he had learned how to be content in all circumstances (Philippians 4:11). Have you? Why not begin to practice being content this day. There are always many things to be thankful for. Concentrate on those things and not the grumbling circumstances.*

*Seek ye first the kingdom of God. Do not seek all that is wrong in your life. Seeking salvation for all the problems only buries you deeper into the mire.*

*Seeking God's kingdom (loving Him with all your heart, soul, and body) will result in the answers coming to you concerning your problems.*

*He said, "Seek ye first the Kingdom of God and His righteousness and all these other things would be added to you."*

*Believe Him!*

\*\*\*

*"Not that I speak in respect of want: for I have learned, in whatsoever state I am, therewith to be content." Philippians 4:11*

*"But seek ye first the kingdom of God, and His righteousness; and all these things shall be added unto you." Matthew 6:33*

## NOVEMBER 8
### THIS IS THE DAY THAT THE LORD HAS MADE. I WILL REJOICE AND BE GLAD IN IT.

*Oh, rejoice and sing a song of love to Your Lover! He is the Lover of your soul, the Wounded Warrior, the Knight in shining armor, the one and only Savior, Brother and King!*

*Let us think on these things. Let us think about Him today—His humility, His suffering, His servanthood, His compassion, His passion, His power and strength, His courage and perseverance for us.*

*Let us think about His Spirit that walks with us, talks to us, leads us, convicts us, helps us, comforts us, reveals to us—Jesus!*

*Let us think on these things from above.*

\*\*\*

*"If you then be risen with Christ, seek those things which are above, where Christ sits on the right hand of God. (2) Set your affection on things above, not on things on the earth. (3) For you are dead, and your life is hid with Christ in God." Colossians 3:1–3*

*"Let Him kiss me with the kisses of His mouth: for Your love is better than wine… (4:9) You have ravished My heart, My sister, My spouse; you have ravished My heart with one of your eyes, with one chain of your neck." Song of Solomon 1:2 & 4:9*

*"His eyes were as a flame of fire, and on His head were many crowns; and He had a name written, that no man knew, but He Himself. (13) And He was clothed with a vesture dipped in blood: and His name is called The Word of God… (15) And out of His mouth goes a sharp sword, that with it He should smite the nations: and He shall rule them with a rod of iron: and He treads the winepress of the fierceness and wrath of Almighty God. (16) And He has on His vesture and His thigh a name written, KING OF KINGS, AND LORD OF LORDS." Revelation 19:12–13; 15–16*

# NOVEMBER 9
## THIS IS THE DAY THAT THE LORD HAS MADE. I WILL REJOICE AND BE GLAD IN IT.

*Go, and get the peace of the Lord.*

*He will keep you in perfect peace whose mind is stayed on Him, because you trust in Him (Isaiah 26:3). Trust—a big word—full of meaning—void of fear, doubt, insecurity, anxiety. Trust in the Lord with all your heart (Proverbs 3:5–6). Those that trust in the Lord shall not be ashamed (Psalm 25:2).*

**You that trust Me have been perfected. Jesus, My only begotten Son, trusted Me with His life. Would you not think His life is more precious than yours, since the salvation of the world was in Him? He being fully human trusted Me. Can you not do the same?**

**Walk in fear and trust in yourself, or walk in faith and trust in Me. The choice is yours. I've made the way possible for you to choose. I've done everything, but I cannot or better said, I will not decide for you. Life is a two way street—you and I. We are both important. We are both indispensable for life. I made you independent of Myself, but with the choice of being fully dependent upon Me or going it on your own—the choice is yours.**

**Freedom or Slavery. You choose. Choose Life.**

\*\*\*

*"O keep my soul, and deliver me: let me not be ashamed; for I put my trust in You." Psalm 25:20*

*"I call heaven and earth to record this day against you, that I have set before you life and death, blessing and cursing: therefore choose life, that both you and your seed may live:" Deuteronomy 30:20*

## NOVEMBER 10
### THIS IS THE DAY THAT THE LORD HAS MADE. I WILL REJOICE AND BE GLAD IN IT.

*It has come to Me that you linger too long in the things of this world and not enough time in the things of the Spirit. Can you practice walking and talking in the Spirit versus the flesh?*

*"How, Lord?"*

*It is easy. Keep your thoughts on Me, the Lover of your soul. Find manna for each day and eat it. Eat it throughout the day. Don't just eat it once, but eat it again and again throughout the day. As you eat it, more and more will appear to be eaten, like the oil for the widow woman and the loaves and fishes for the multitude. But if you don't eat it, it will not multiply. That, My child, is walking in the Spirit, much like the Israelites in the desert.*

*Go in peace to serve Me!*

\*\*\*

"For they that are after the flesh do mind the things of the flesh; but they that are after the Spirit the things of the Spirit. (6) For to be carnally minded is death; but to be spiritually minded is life and peace." Romans 8:5–6

"Evening, and morning, and at noon, will I pray, and cry aloud: and He shall hear my voice." Psalm 55:17

"Seven times a day do I praise You because of Your righteous judgments." Psalm 119:164

## THIS IS THE DAY THAT THE LORD HAS MADE. I WILL REJOICE AND BE GLAD IN IT.

*Declare with me: This is the day my Father has made for me. No matter the circumstances, my Father made this day for me. He has taken care of me through the night, and all is well for the coming day.*

*Do not neglect to give thanks and rejoice in what your Father did for you today. "Oh! sing unto the Lord. He has triumphed gloriously. The horse and rider has been cast into the sea" (Exodus 15:21). And so should your cares and woes.*

*Do not linger in fear, but trust in your Daddy. He cares for you. Does not a good earthly father do all he can to take good care of his children?*

*Yes.*

*Well we, being evil, do good for our children; how much more does our heavenly Father, with all resources available, take good care of us.*

*Meditate on His good care and purposes for you, and trust will grow.*

\*\*\*

*"If you then, being evil, know how to give good gifts unto your children, how much more shall your Father which is in heaven give good things to them that ask Him?" Matthew 7:11*

*"For I know the thoughts that I think toward you, says the LORD, thoughts of peace, and not of evil, to give you an expected end." Jeremiah 29:11*

*"For you have not received the spirit of bondage again to fear; but you have received the Spirit of adoption, whereby we cry, Abba, Father." Romans 8:15*

## THIS IS THE DAY THAT THE LORD HAS MADE. I WILL REJOICE AND BE GLAD IN IT.

*"It is time for us to rejoice in Your work, Father."*

Seek not pleasure, but seek My Kingdom and pleasure shall surely reign. For a word from Me or a walk with Me is more pleasurable than many mountain streams bubbling over with My praises. Do you not know My words are life? So why do you live each day with little few of My words sustaining thee?

My kingdom is not lacking. My Kingdom is overflowing, if only I could get My children to receive their blessings.

Come to Me and I shall show and tell you great and mighty things.

Only come, My child. Listen and obey and you shall see My glory and live in My kingdom—ruling and reigning.

\*\*\*

*"Call unto Me, and I will answer you, and show you great and mighty things which you know not." Jeremiah 33:3*

*"And has made us unto our God kings and priests: and we shall reign on the earth." Revelation 5:10*

*"It is the Spirit that quickens; the flesh profits nothing: the words that I speak unto you, they are spirit, and they are life." John 6:63*

*"And after the earthquake a fire; but the LORD was not in the fire: and after the fire a still small voice. (13) And it was so, when Elijah heard it, that he wrapped his face in his mantle, and went out, and stood in the entering in of the cave. And, behold, there came a voice unto him, and said, What are you doing here, Elijah?" I Kings 19:12–13*

## THIS IS THE DAY THAT THE LORD HAS MADE. I WILL REJOICE AND BE GLAD IN IT.

*Be glad! Let your face know there is reason to be glad.*

*God has made us and takes care of His creation—just as we take care of our offspring! Can we not rest in His care? Must we be like the Israelites who did not enter into the Promised Land because of unbelief? (Hebrews 3:19)*

*No, we will trust our Father, our Daddy. He loves us.*

*Rest.*

*Believe.*

*Trust in the Lord with all your heart (Proverbs 3:5–6). Trust in your Daddy. He is your Daddy. He is not like earthly fathers who can fail and make mistakes. He cannot fail. He cannot make a mistake.*

*Let go. Release all fear, pain, grief, sorrow, anger… and trust your Daddy to take care of it.*

*Trust. Rely. Fall back on Him with all abandon. He will not disappoint. Believe. He will not disappoint. Release all and rest.*

\*\*\*

*"Let us therefore fear, lest, a promise being left us of entering into His rest, any of you should seem to come short of it… (10) For he that is entered into his rest, he also has ceased from his own works, as God did from His. (11) Let us labor therefore to enter into that rest, lest any man fall after the same example of unbelief." Hebrews 4:1, 10–11*

## NOVEMBER 14
### THIS IS THE DAY THAT THE LORD HAS MADE. I WILL REJOICE AND BE GLAD IN IT.

*Let us give thanks unto the Lord, His mercy endures for ever.*

*He is sovereign and all knowing. He knows the beginning unto the end. Why rebel at His direction? Submit yourself and lay down your life!*

*He has good things in store for you. He has a future of hope. Yield yourself to His leading and do not be angry. Surrender and you will see the glory of the Lord. What better vision could there be?*

*He is ready to bring us into victorious living. Are we ready to surrender?*

\*\*\*

*"For whosoever will save his life shall lose it: but whosoever will lose his life for My sake, the same shall save it." Luke 9:24*

*"Remember the former things of old: for I am God, and there is none else; I am God, and there is none like Me, (10) Declaring the end from the beginning, and from ancient times the things that are not yet done, saying, My counsel shall stand, and I will do all My pleasure: (11) Calling a ravenous bird from the east, the man that executes My counsel from a far country: yes, I have spoken it, I will also bring it to pass; I have purposed it, I will also do it." Isaiah 46:9–11*

*"Verily, verily I say unto you, Except a corn of wheat fall into the ground and die, it abides alone: but if it dies, it brings forth much fruit. (25) He that loves his life shall lose it; and he that hates his life in this world shall keep it unto life eternal. (26) If any man serve Me, let him follow Me; and where I am, there shall also My servant be: if any man serve Me, him will My Father honor." John 12:24–26*

† 

## NOVEMBER 15

## THIS IS THE DAY THAT THE LORD HAS MADE. I WILL REJOICE AND BE GLAD IN IT.

*Oh, come and let us worship the King,
for He has done mighty things.*

"Give us passion, Father, for You. We are so consumed with our everyday lives—with all the problems. We become overwhelmed with the brush fires and do not go to the Burning Bush. You are the answer to our problems. Yet, we go about our busyness neglecting You.

"Oh, Father, I cry out for us who are so consumed with life that You are a very small portion of our life. Shake us to the point of awareness. Father, it is only You Who can rescue us from our dying ways. The thorns are choking out the seeds' growth.

"You've done it before, Lord, do it again. I see so many hurting and painful people. How many You must see, and how Your heart must break. You have made the way to fullness of joy and yet we do not turn to You. Oh God, forgive! Oh God, have mercy! Oh God, turn us!"

\*\*\*

"O LORD, I have heard Your speech, and was afraid: O LORD, revive Your work in the midst of the years, in the midst of the years make known; in wrath remember mercy." Habakkuk 3:2

"Turn us again, O God of hosts, and cause Your face to shine; and we shall be saved." Psalm 80:7

"You will show me the path of life: in Your presence is fullness of joy; at Your right hand there are pleasures for evermore." Psalm 16:11

## NOVEMBER 16
### THIS IS THE DAY THAT THE LORD HAS MADE. I WILL REJOICE AND BE GLAD IN IT.

*For the Lord has done great things for us. You can say with me: My desires, He accomplishes. He manifests my desires, and I thank Him for answered prayer.*

*"Forgive me, Father, for being downcast. Ever continue to grow in me faith and trust in You in the midst of ugly, difficult times; so that I may say, 'He has been found faithful and trusting in my time of trial.'"*

*Never forget, "My God reigns." He is mighty. He is almighty. He cares about the little things in your life. For example, time with your teenage child is precious, but cannot be obtained without His orchestration.*

*He cares and He takes care of you.*

*Relax, and rest in His love today. He really does have all things in His control!*

\*\*\*

*"For You are great, and do wondrous things: You are God alone." Psalm 86:10*

*"I will extol You, my God, O King; and I will bless Your name for ever and ever. (2) Every day will I bless You; and I will praise Your name for ever and ever. (3) Great is the LORD, and greatly to be praised; and His greatness is unsearchable." Psalm 145:1–3*

*"Why are you cast down, O my soul? And why are you disquieted within me? Hope thou in God: for I shall yet praise Him, who is the health of my countenance, and my God." Psalm 42:11*

> **THIS IS THE DAY THAT THE LORD HAS MADE. I WILL REJOICE AND BE GLAD IN IT.**

*Forget the past. It is over. Only Jesus can redeem what has been done and what has not been done. Glory to His Name!*

*Every day and many times during the day, do we die. We die to our hopes and dreams, but Christ resurrects them. I have tried to bring into existence my visions, but have failed miserably. Now I see… all I can do is die to them and trust my God to work it out.*

*He is the one who will orchestrate the situations in life to bring to pass His good pleasure. If you relinquish your dreams to Him, He is big enough to carry them and powerful enough to manifest them.*

*Tenacious is His description of you. Do not let go of your dream. But do let go and let God do the work. You will know what your part is. The Holy Spirit is your guide. Keep your eyes on pleasing Jesus.*

*Major in the major circumstances in life and do not get stuck in the minor ones. Ask for wisdom to know the difference.*

\*\*\*

*"But let patience have her perfect work, that you may be perfect and entire, wanting nothing. (5) If any of you lack wisdom, let him ask of God, that gives to all men liberally, and upbraids not; and it shall be given him." James 1:4–5*

*"For it is God which works in you both to will and to do of His good pleasure. (14) Do all things without murmurings and disputings: (15) That you may be blameless and harmless, the sons of God, without rebuke, in the midst of a crooked and perverse nation, among whom you shine as lights in the world; (16) Holding forth the word of life; that I may rejoice in the day of Christ, that I have not run in vain, neither labored in vain." Philippians 2: 13–16*

## THIS IS THE DAY THAT THE LORD HAS MADE. I WILL REJOICE AND BE GLAD IN IT.

*...For He has done mighty things of which we know not. But He is willing to reveal Himself to us. Are we willing to make the sacrifice of our time?*

*"Early I shall seek Thee—early."*

*"And in the morning, rising up a great while before day, He went out, and departed into a solitary place, and there prayed." Mark 1:35*

*Be not dismayed when God awakens you early. He is worth whatever He is calling you to. Knowledge of Him is beyond all other desires. You have called and cried out for knowledge of Him. Surrender your notions and see how He blesses you. Then submission will be a pleasure to your heart for you shall see Him. He is worthy. Beyond all pleasures of life, knowing Him makes all else pale. "And this is life, that you know God," said Jesus (John 17: 3).*

**Know Me and live. Know the flesh and die. The choice is yours. Always has been and always will be.**

\*\*\*

*"O God, You are my God; early will I seek You: my soul thirsts for You, my flesh longs for You in a dry and thirsty land, where no water is;" Psalm 63:1*

*"My son, attend to My words; incline your ear unto My sayings. (21) Let them not depart from your eyes; keep them in the midst of your heart. (22) For they are life unto those that find them, and health to all their flesh. (23) Keep your heart with all diligence; for out of it are the issues of life... (25) Let your eyes look right on, and let your eyelids look straight before you. (26) Ponder the path of your feet, and let all your ways be established. (27) Turn not to the right hand nor to the left: remove your foot from evil." Proverb 4:20–23 & 25–27*

## THIS IS THE DAY THAT THE LORD HAS MADE. I WILL REJOICE AND BE GLAD IN IT.

*Have you cried out lately to know the Father? To do the works He did and even greater works? To hunger and thirst for Him? Well, He is answering your prayers. Fear not, you will be sufficient for that to which He is calling you.*

*Fear not, only trust.*

*He will open doors, and you will easily walk through.*

**Wait for My Word. Then you will have the assurance I am telling you to do this thing. Only step out when you are positive of what I have called you. You will know. You will know—fear not—only believe.**

**There is no fear in perfect love. When you are doing what My Spirit is leading you to do, there is peace! It may be stormy on the outside, but there is strength and assurance on the inside.**

**Seek Me, and continue to knock. I will be found, and I will open the door.**

\*\*\*

"There is no fear in love; but perfect love casts out fear: because fear has torment. He that fears is not made perfect in love." I John 4:18

"After this I looked, and, behold, a door was opened in heaven: and the first voice which I heard was as it were of a trumpet talking with me; which said, Come up hither, and I will show you things which must be hereafter." Revelation 4:1

## NOVEMBER 20
### THIS IS THE DAY THAT THE LORD HAS MADE. I WILL REJOICE AND BE GLAD IN IT.

*Have I not said and will I not do? Yes. Amen and amen. Doubt not, only believe. When the going is rough, build your persevering muscles—build your stubborn muscles on a Godly cause—be good and not evil.*

*Have I not said? Will I not do? Doubt not, it only leads to evil. Doubting is fretting about the Father's will. And are not all good and perfect gifts from above? I can, I do, and I will control the peripheral circumstances in your life to bring all things to your good, for your good and not harm. Do not be afraid to fail. This at least shows effort on your part. Do not go forward ignorantly, but do not hold back for fear of failing.*

*If a child never tried to talk, until he could speak plainly, he would never talk. If a child never walked, until he could walk without falling, he would never walk. Our efforts must be exercised or they will not come to fruition. Go for it! Fail or succeed, there will be blessings in the exercise of obedience.*

\*\*\*

*"Though He were a Son, yet learned He obedience by the things which He suffered: (9) And being made perfect, He became the author of eternal salvation unto all them that obey Him;" Hebrews 5:8–9*

*"And we know that all things work together for good to them that love God, to them who are the called according to His purpose." Romans 8:28*

## NOVEMBER 21
### THIS IS THE DAY THAT THE LORD HAS MADE. I WILL REJOICE AND BE GLAD IN IT.

*Oh sing hallelujahs to the Lord, for He is worthy of our praise! His renown has gone forth into all nations, and we are just waiting for the manifestation in man (Romans 8:19).*

*He has called all things beautiful in His time. He has made all things beautiful, so rest in His love and care. He has prepared them for you before the foundation of the world. Can you not enjoy the banquet table He has prepared for you?*

*Lie back, and drink in His love. He is willing to penetrate your body and soul with His love. Have you not felt it?*

*Oh, delay not a minute longer! Present yourself before the King, and He will come.*

\*\*\*

"By night on my bed I sought Him whom my soul loves: I sought Him, but I found Him not. (2) I will rise now, and go about the city in the streets, and in the broad ways I will seek Him whom my soul loves: I sought Him, but I found Him not… (4) It was but a little that I passed from them, but I found Him whom my soul loves: I held Him, and would not let Him go…" Song of Solomon 3:1–2 & 4a

"For I reckon that the sufferings of this present time are not worthy to be compared with the glory which shall be revealed in us. (19) For the earnest expectation of the creature waits for the manifestation of the sons of God." Romans 8:18–19

"Let Him kiss me with the kisses of His mouth: for Your love is better than wine. (3) Because of the savor of Your good ointments Your name is as ointment poured forth, therefore do the virgins love You. (4) Draw me, we will run after You: the King has brought me into His chambers: we will be glad and rejoice in You, we will remember Your love more than wine: the upright love You." Song of Solomon 1:2–4

## THIS IS THE DAY THAT THE LORD HAS MADE. I WILL REJOICE AND BE GLAD IN IT.

*Never give up. Once God has placed that desire or desires in your heart, He plans to bring these things forth into your life. He begins and He ends. You have to hang in there; hang on, don't let go. You will inherit the promises, if you do not give up. It is enough said, "Do not let go!"*

\*\*\*

*"Be not deceived; God is not mocked: for whatsoever a man sows, that shall he also reap. (8) For he that sows to his flesh shall of the flesh reap corruption; but he that sows to the Spirit shall of the Spirit reap life everlasting. (9) And let us not be weary in well doing: for in due season we shall reap, if we faint not." Galatians 6:7–9*

*"There failed not ought of any good thing which the LORD had spoken unto the house of Israel; all came to pass." Joshua 21:45*

*"Being confident of this very thing, that He which has begun a good work in you will perform it until the day of Jesus Christ:" Philippians 1:6*

*"Cast not away therefore your confidence, which has great recompense of reward. (36) For you have need of patience, that, after you have done the will of God you might receive the promise. (37) For yet a little while, and He that shall come will come, and will not tarry. (38) Now the just shall live by faith: but if any man draw back, my soul shall have no pleasure in him. (39) But we are not of them who draw back unto perdition; but of them that believe to the saving of the soul." Hebrews 10:35–39*

*"Cause me to hear Your lovingkindness in the morning; for in Thee do I trust: cause me to know the way wherein I should walk; for I lift up my soul unto Thee." Psalm 143:8*

**THIS IS THE DAY THAT THE LORD HAS MADE. I WILL REJOICE AND BE GLAD IN IT.**

*Oh! hallelujah and give thanks to the God of all the earth and heaven. He created all things for His pleasure. We were created for His pleasure. Just as our children give us pleasure, we give God pleasure. Especially small children give pleasure to their parents. They are so dependent upon the parents—so trusting. Our hearts go out to them, because of their utter dependence upon us for life. We feed, clothe, and shelter them. Without this physical care, they would perish.*

*When we depend on our Father for food, clothes and shelter, He is overjoyed to meet our needs. Unless you are like little children, you cannot enter the kingdom of heaven (Matthew 18:3).*

*"Lord, show us how to be little children—trusting, depending upon You for food, clothes, home, love, and everything!"*

\*\*\*

*"And said, Verily I say unto you, Except you be converted, and become as little children, you shall not enter into the kingdom of heaven. (4) Whosoever therefore shall humble himself as this little child, the same is greatest in the kingdom of heaven." Matthew 18:3–4*

*"You are worthy, O Lord, to receive glory and honor and power: for You have created all things, and for Your pleasure they are and were created." Revelation 4:11*

*"The LORD takes pleasure in them that fear Him, in those that hope in His mercy." Psalm 147:11*

*"For the LORD takes pleasure in His people: He will beautify the meek with salvation." Psalm 149:4*

## THIS IS THE DAY THAT THE LORD HAS MADE. I WILL REJOICE AND BE GLAD IN IT.

*Come out from the shadows and exalt My Name as you go forth in power and authority. Let not circumstances sway you. They are only temporary, but My Word endures forever and never returns void. Go for it, My child, and do not look back but always forward with your eyes on Me.*

*Strive to know Me. The glory has been shown round about, but the day is coming that My Glory shall fill the earth.*

*Seek not those things that are temporal. They will pass away. Seek to know the True and Only God.*

\*\*\*

"If you then be risen with Christ, seek those things which are above, where Christ sits on the right hand of God. (2) Set your affection on things above, not on things on the earth. (3) For you are dead, and your life is hid with Christ in God. (4) When Christ, who is our life, shall appear, then shall you also appear with Him in glory." Colossians 3:1–4

"For our light affliction, which is but for a moment, works for us a far more exceeding and eternal weight of glory." II Corinthians 4:17

"Enlarge the place of your tent, and let them stretch forth the curtains of your habitations: spare not, lengthen your cords, and strengthen your stakes; (3) For you shall break forth on the right hand and on the left; and your seed shall inherit the Gentiles, and make the desolate cities to be inhabited." Isaiah 54:2–3

"...but this one thing I do, forgetting those things which are behind, and reaching forth unto those things which are before, (14) I press toward the mark for the prize of the high calling of God in Christ Jesus." Philippians 3:13b–14

> **THIS IS THE DAY THAT THE LORD HAS MADE. I WILL REJOICE AND BE GLAD IN IT.**

*Give thanks to the Lord for He is good and His mercy extends to all generations (Psalm 100:5). Yes, He is merciful, but He expects us to cry out for His mercy. It is the same as when He says, "Ask," but at the same time He knows the needs and answers while we are yet speaking. Still He expects us to ask. He extends mercy. He is mercy. Yet He expects us to ask for mercy.*

*But don't just ask for mercy, because it is the thing to do. Let us cry out for God to give us that depth of knowing our need for His mercy. Then from our spirit, we'll truly cry out, "Lord have mercy. Christ have mercy. Lord have mercy."*

*It is not enough to voice our need for mercy. What is needed is a cry from the depth of our heart initiated by God's Heart.*

\*\*\*

*"And it shall come to pass, that before they call, I will answer; and while they are yet speaking, I will hear." Isaiah 65:24*

*"But You, O Lord, are a God full of compassion, and gracious, longsuffering, and plenteous in mercy and truth." Psalm 86:15*

*"Surely goodness and mercy shall follow me all the days of my life: and I will dwell in the house of the LORD for ever." Psalm 23:6*

*"Behold, as the eyes of servants look unto the hand of their masters, and as the eyes of a maiden unto the hand of her mistress; so our eyes wait upon the LORD our God, until that He have mercy upon us. (3) Have mercy upon us, O LORD, have mercy upon us: for we are exceedingly filled with contempt." Psalm 123:2–3*

## NOVEMBER 26
### THIS IS THE DAY THAT THE LORD HAS MADE. I WILL REJOICE AND BE GLAD IN IT.

*Seek Me early or you will not seek Me at all. Rise early for the time is short. Come unto Me and I will show you great and mighty things, but you must come.*

*Come before the clattering of the world imposes its way upon you. The world is merciless, and I am mercy. Seek not to sandwich Me into a day that has already begun. Life will not let you rest, but I will.*

*That still small voice is smashed easily by the clamor of the day's busyness. Don't think I will compete with the call of family and business. I will not. Time is Mine. I will not share it with others.*

*Come unto Me when all is quiet, and you can give Me your full attention. I am a jealous God, and I will not share the throne with other gods. Give Me your best and your first fruits. Plan for time with Me. Do not sneak Me into time you should be doing something else. I will not share My time with others. I will not be squeezed into what is left over or made to happen.*

*Our time together will be quiet and unhindered by the cry of the world or it will not be at all.*

\*\*\*

"For you shall worship no other god: for the LORD, whose name is Jealous, is a jealous God:" Exodus 34:14

"For the LORD your God is a consuming fire, even a jealous God." Deuteronomy 4:24

# NOVEMBER 27
## THIS IS THE DAY THAT THE LORD HAS MADE. I WILL REJOICE AND BE GLAD IN IT.

*Just as Joseph was proficient in interpreting dreams, you too can sustain a running communication with Me, your Father. I have not ceased to use dreams as a means of communication with My children.*

*Simply before sleeping, yield your body and soul to My occupation during the night. I already bless you in your sleep, because I never sleep and I am always working to bring you from glory to glory. This way you shall know further into the ways of the Lord, and in understanding you shall reign over confusion and ignorance.*

*I watch over you day and night. Not one moment of time is wasted with Me, and since you are My child the same goes for you.*

\*\*\*

"I will bless the LORD, who has given me counsel: my reins also instruct me in the night seasons." Psalm 16:7

"Behold, He that keeps Israel shall neither slumber nor sleep." Psalm 121:4

"But we all, with open face beholding as in a glass the glory of the Lord, are changed into the same image from glory to glory, even as by the Spirit of the Lord." II Corinthians 3:18

## THIS IS THE DAY THAT THE LORD HAS MADE. I WILL REJOICE AND BE GLAD IN IT.

*"Oh God! our friends, our families are waning in life. Let them and me know there is more to life than living in this physical world. Let us come unto You and receive Life that we may distribute it to those waning. There is more to life than this physical world. You said to keep our mind on things above, to walk by faith."*

*Let us pray:*

*"Oh God! let me make a difference in the dead and dying world around me. Do not let me rest as others are dying. Let me not relax my passion for You as sin and sickness are rampant. You must have mercy upon me. Without Your mercy, I am lost and undone."*

\*\*\*

*"Then said I, Woe is me! For I am undone; because I am a man of unclean lips, and I dwell in the midst of a people of unclean lips: for mine eyes have seen the King, the LORD of hosts…(8) Also I heard the voice of the Lord, saying, Whom shall I send, and who will go for us? Then said I, Here am I; send me." Isaiah 6:5 & 8*

*"And as you go, preach, saying, The kingdom of heaven is at hand. (8) Heal the sick, cleanse the lepers, raise the dead, cast out devils: freely you have received, freely give." Matthew 10:7–8*

*"If you then be risen with Christ, seek those things which are above, where Christ sits on the right hand of God. (2) Set your affection on things above, not on things on the earth." Colossians 3:1–2*

*"And Jesus came and spoke unto them, saying, All power is given unto Me in heaven and in earth. (19) Go ye therefore, and teach all nations, baptizing them in the name of the Father, and of the Son, and of the Holy Ghost: (20) Teaching them to observe all things whatsoever I have commanded you: and, lo, I am with you always, even unto the end of the world. Amen." Matthew 28:18–20*

**THIS IS THE DAY THAT THE LORD HAS MADE. I WILL REJOICE AND BE GLAD IN IT.**

*"You love us and have given Your all. What more can You give?"*

There is no more to give, but there's continued training. Just as I said, "Train up a child," I train you. I AM the husbandman and you are the branches. My job is to hold your hand and your job is to surrender your pull. Come along with Me. I will keep you and stir you and maintain you.

With your will surrendered to Me, all things are possible. I AM the One that ignites the fire, feeds the fire, and manages the fire. My Son baptizes with the Holy Spirit and fire. This is the fire of which I have spoken. The fire that burns within your breast to know Me, the One True God.

\*\*\*

*"And this is life eternal, that they might know You the only true God, and Jesus Christ, whom You have sent." John 17:3*

*"I am the true vine, and My Father is the husbandman… (4) Abide in Me, and I in you. As the branch cannot bear fruit of itself, except it abide in the vine; no more can you, except you abide in Me… (5c)…for without Me you can do nothing." John 15:1, 4, 5c*

*"John answered, saying unto them all, I indeed baptize you with water; but one mightier than I comes, the latchet of whose shoes I am not worthy to unloose: He shall baptize you with the Holy Ghost and with fire:" Luke 3:16*

*"Verily, verily, I say unto you, Except a corn of wheat falls into the ground and dies, it abides alone: but if it dies, it brings forth much fruit." John 12:24*

## THIS IS THE DAY THAT THE LORD HAS MADE. I WILL REJOICE AND BE GLAD IN IT.

*Go to Him Whom thy soul loves. He is standing with an open heart, anticipating the receiving of your body into His.*

*Love is not only a spiritual experience. Love is also a physical and emotional experience. If you have not physically and emotionally experienced God loving you, then cry out for that experience. He is able to manifest in the physical as well as the spiritual. Your body and soul have need of tender touches and loving embraces. There is no sexual insinuation here. God loves your spirit, soul, and body. He is real, and He can really bless you physically and emotionally.*

*Oh, go to Him Whom thy soul loves! He yearns to show you His love, to pour out His love upon you. You see, He is love and love yearns to give and give and give and give. Love is not satisfied to keep to itself. Love must be spread out and shared.*

**"I must be shared!"** *says the Lord Almighty.*

***

*"That Christ may dwell in your hearts by faith; that you, being rooted and grounded in love, (18) May be able to comprehend with all saints what is the breadth, and length, and depth, and height; (19) And to know the love of Christ, which passes knowledge, that you might be filled with all the fullness of God." Ephesians 3:17–19*

*"[That you may really come] to know [practically, through experience for yourselves] the love of Christ, which far surpasses mere knowledge [without experience]: that you may be filled [through all your being] unto all the fullness of God [may have the richest measure of the divine Presence, and become a body wholly filled and flooded with God Himself]!" Ephesians 3:19 (The Amplified Bible)*

# DECEMBER

"For unto us a Child is born, unto us a Son is given:
and the government shall be upon His shoulder: and
His name shall be called Wonderful, Counselor,
The mighty God, The everlasting Father,
The Prince of Peace."

ISAIAH 9:6

## DECEMBER 1
### THIS IS THE DAY THAT THE LORD HAS MADE. I WILL REJOICE AND BE GLAD IN IT.

*He has come to save and He shall. His work is never done until His children are in His fold. God never gives up, because God is love. He says He'll not always strive with man (Genesis 6:3), but that is the man who has gone beyond God's reach of conviction. There is a hard heart, but for those who have a flicker, He will not put it out, but will fan it and stoke it to revive the fire.*

*The fire is love, so be not afraid of the fire. The fire is love. It was love on the day of Pentecost with tongues of fire, and it will be love on the day of revival in each of our lives. God will bring us forth from the shadows, as we, like the ones in the upper room, wait on Him with fixed attention and passion for our Lover.*

\*\*\*

*"A bruised reed shall He not break, and smoking flax shall He not quench, till He send forth judgment unto victory." Matthew 12:20*

*"And now, Lord, what wait I for? My hope is in You." Psalm 39:7*

*"For since the beginning of the world men have not heard, nor perceived by the ear, neither has the eye seen, O God, beside You, what He has prepared for him that waits for Him." Isaiah 64:4*

*"Who is among you that fears the LORD, that obeys the voice of His servant, that walks in darkness, and has no light? Let him trust in the name of the LORD, and stay upon his God." Isaiah 50:10*

## THIS IS THE DAY THAT THE LORD HAS MADE. I WILL REJOICE AND BE GLAD IN IT.

*Oh! Hallelujah! He has triumphed and made a way for us. He has leveled the mountains and raised the valleys. He has straightened the road (Isaiah 40:4).*

*Oh! Hallelujah! Shout to the Lord! Sing praises to His name. Make known His good deeds. For He has loved us, and we can love others.*

"Oh! Father, without Your anointing, we cannot love. Our hearts are cold and selfish. It is You that must move upon and within us to love as we should—to love as You love. What is the difference between Your love and human love?"

**Wisdom, cry out for wisdom. It cries out for you. Seek not the things of this world, but keep your mind on things above, where dust and rust do not corrupt. Come unto Me, and I will give you rest. Be not like My children in the desert who perished for unbelief. Cry out, "Help mine unbelief!" Those that cry will be heard. Those that mutter have much to learn.**

\*\*\*

"Wisdom cries without; she utters her voice in the streets... (23) Turn you at My reproof: behold, I will pour out My Spirit unto you, I will make known My words unto you." Proverbs 1:20 & 23

"Lay not up for yourselves treasures upon earth, where moth and rust do corrupt, and where thieves break through and steal: (20) But lay up for yourselves treasures in heaven, where neither moth nor rust do corrupt, and where thieves do not break through nor steal; (21) For where your treasure is, there will your heart be also." Matthew 6:19–21

"And straightway the father of the child cried out, and said with tears, Lord, I believe; help Thou mine unbelief." Mark 9:24

> **THIS IS THE DAY THAT THE LORD HAS MADE. I WILL REJOICE AND BE GLAD IN IT.**

*Walk in love.*

*But you cannot walk in love unless you walk in Me. Stay attached to the vine. You must commune with Me for love is to be found nowhere else. It is not an effort of the mind to be loving. You cannot be loving without being in Me, because I am Love and there is no love outside of Me. To the extent that you are in Me is the extent to the love in your life.*

*You remember, I said the difference between human love and My love is wisdom. Jesus is Wisdom.*

*Oh! My children you seek much and go to and fro, but if I could get you to come unto Me how your life and the lives of those around you would be changed.*

*Come to the fountain and drink. It is free. Come, I say, and drink. You'll not be disappointed.*

\*\*\*

"Ho, everyone that thirsts, come to the waters, and he that has no money; come, buy, and eat; yes, come, buy wine and milk without money and without price… (3) Incline your ear, and come unto Me: hear, and your soul shall live; and I will make an everlasting covenant with you, even the sure mercies of David." Isaiah 55:1 & 3

"But of Him are you in Christ Jesus, who of God is made unto us wisdom, and righteousness, and sanctification, and redemption: (31) That, according as it is written, He that glories, let him glory in the Lord." I Corinthians 1:30–31

## DECEMBER 4
### THIS IS THE DAY THAT THE LORD HAS MADE. I WILL REJOICE AND BE GLAD IN IT.

*Oh, sing unto the Lord! Every day, every moment is new to the Lord and those who are called by His name. His mercies never cease (Lamentations 3:22–23).*

*He is coming and His coming could be at any moment. He is speaking and calling His children to attention.*

*Will we attend to His voice? Will we listen and obey? Will we take His call seriously? Or will His seed fall on shallow, rocky, thorny soil? (Matthew 13:18–23) Cry out for good soil.*

*"Oh, prepare the way, Lord! We are the way. We are the path. We are the soil. Prepare us to receive the Christ, once again and again and again!"*

*Where have we gone wrong—living in this world for so long and not in the Spirit? We have made our abode in the earthly things and neglected the things of heaven.*

*The time is now to follow Jesus—no turning back, no looking back! Go forward young soldier, onward Christian soldier.*

\*\*\*

*"And that, knowing the time, that now it is high time to awake out of sleep: for now is our salvation nearer than when we believed." Romans 13:11*

*"While we look not at the things which are seen, but at the things which are not seen: for the things which are seen are temporal; but the things which are not seen are eternal." II Corinthians 4:18*

## DECEMBER 5
### THIS IS THE DAY THAT THE LORD HAS MADE. I WILL REJOICE AND BE GLAD IN IT.

*Oh, hallelujah! Sing unto the Lord a new song. Sing praises unto His name. Make known His deeds among the nations (I Chronicles 16:8).*

*He is worthy of our trust. Do not shame our Father with fear and doubt. He is love and love cast out fear. He is our Shepherd. Why should we doubt?*

*Let us walk in full assurance today that He is looking upon us to do good and not harm, and to give us a future (Jeremiah 29:11). Walk in trust today.*

*You cannot trust fully unless you're walking. So do not lie paralyzed, but be up and onward!*

\*\*\*

*"O sing unto the LORD a new song: sing unto the LORD, all the earth. (2) Sing unto the LORD, bless His name; show forth His salvation from day to day. (3) Declare His glory among the heathen, His wonders among all people. (4) For the LORD is great, and greatly to be praised: He is to be feared above all gods." Psalm 96:1–4*

*"Fight the good fight of faith, lay hold on eternal life, whereunto you are also called, and have professed a good profession before many witnesses." I Timothy 6:12*

*"And the LORD said unto Moses, Wherefore do you cry unto Me? Speak unto the children of Israel, that they go forward:" Exodus 14:15*

*"Offer the sacrifices of righteousness, and put your trust in the LORD." Psalm 4:5*

*"There is no fear in love; but perfect love casts out fear: because fear has torment. He that fears is not made perfect in love." I John 4:18*

## DECEMBER 6
### THIS IS THE DAY THAT THE LORD HAS MADE. I WILL REJOICE AND BE GLAD IN IT.

*Seek Me with all your heart, and all these things shall be yours. Seek first the Kingdom of God. (Matthew 6:33)*

*Seek first to know My will. Seek first to do My will, and I shall be there to bring it to pass. No greater joy have I than to see My children following after My Son. (III John 1:4) I said I would give the nations for His inheritance and I shall. (Psalm 2:8)*

*You have become a nation unto yourself as you bring other children into the Kingdom with you. Cry out for more souls. I shall answer your cry.*

*It is the desire of My heart also for more and more nations to come under the rule and reign of My Son. He has come, did come and is coming for a Bride without spot or wrinkle.*

*Fast to know and do My will. It shall be done unto you according to your faith. (Matthew 9:29)*

\*\*\*

*"But the days will come, when the Bridegroom shall be taken away from them, and then shall they fast in those days." Mark 2:20*

*"Therefore said He unto them, The harvest truly is great, but the laborers are few: pray therefore the Lord of the harvest, that He would send forth laborers into His harvest." Luke 10:2*

*"That He might present it to Himself a glorious church, not having spot, or wrinkle, or any such thing; but that it should be holy and without blemish." Ephesians 5:27*

## DECEMBER 7
### THIS IS THE DAY THAT THE LORD HAS MADE. I WILL REJOICE AND BE GLAD IN IT.

*Have you tried something new lately?*
*Practice doing new endeavors.*

*God is speaking, and we must follow. Do not be afraid. We will miss His voice and leading at times, but we will not learn His voice if we do not continue to try. This is learning.*

*Go ahead...make mistakes. It is okay with Him. He had rather you walk in faith than fear, even if it means failure at times.*

*The bad steward buried his treasure because of fear (Matthew 25:26). Remember anything not done in faith is sin (Romans 14:23b).*

*To what new thing is God calling you today? Venture out and take the plunge. Go ahead! You may succeed and what a testimony to God's glory when you do.*

*And if you fail, He turns that into good also—because you are called by Him and love Him! Selah.*

\*\*\*

*"And we know that all things work together for good to them that love God, to them who are the called according to His purpose." Roman 8:28*

*"Behold, I will do a new thing: now it shall spring forth; shall you not know it? I will even make a way in the wilderness, and rivers in the desert." Isaiah 43:19*

*"Enlarge the place of your tent, and let them stretch forth the curtains of your habitations: spare not, lengthen your cords, and strengthen your stakes;" Isaiah 54:2*

## DECEMBER 8
## THIS IS THE DAY THAT THE LORD HAS MADE. I WILL REJOICE AND BE GLAD IN IT.

*Sing hallelujah and praises to your King and Savior for He alone reigns in your heart and mine!*

*I wonder what this means? One thing I know that it means is a peaceful mind and emotions. The upsetting people and situations in your life do not disturb your peace when Jesus reigns in your heart.*

*Oh! that we could experience this more often—His peace that goes right over our minds and emotions. The tension in others does not affect us when Jesus reigns in our heart.*

*How often is this your experience?*

*Admit your lack. Blessed are the poor, for they shall be filled.*

*"Oh God, reveal our lack to us so that we shall be filled!"*

\*\*\*

*"You will keep him in perfect peace, whose mind is stayed on You: because he trusts in You." Isaiah 26:3*

*"Blessed are they which do hunger and thirst after righteousness: for they shall be filled." Matthew 5:6*

*"I am crucified with Christ: nevertheless I live; yet not I, but Christ lives in me: and the life which I now live in the flesh I live by the faith of the Son of God, who loved me, and gave Himself for me." Galatians 2:20*

*"And the work of righteousness shall be peace; and the effect of righteousness quietness and assurance for ever." Isaiah 32:17*

## THIS IS THE DAY THAT THE LORD HAS MADE. I WILL REJOICE AND BE GLAD IN IT.

*This is the day to come out from the shadows. Come out and come forth! There is work to do that only you can do. I have made the iron for the coals (Isaiah 54:16) and you have been made for such a time as this. (Esther 4:14) Shrink not from the calling I have upon your life.*

*"What is that calling, Lord?"*

*You shall know as you fast and pray, seek and knock, go and do, be still and silent. Life will bring to the forefront your calling as you rest in Me. Yes—even in your fasting, praying, seeking, knocking, going, doing, being—you can rest. Rest is simply relaxing, immersed in Spiritual trusting.*

\*\*\*

"He brought them out of darkness and the shadow of death, and brake their bands in sunder. (15) Oh that men would praise the LORD for His goodness, and for His wonderful works to the children of men!" Psalm 107:14–15

"For if you altogether hold your peace at this time, then shall there enlargement and deliverance arise to the Jews from another place; but you and your father's house shall be destroyed: and who knows whether you are come to the kingdom for such a time as this?" Esther 4:14

"For he that is entered into his rest, he also has ceased from his own works, as God did from His. (11) Let us labor therefore to enter into that rest, lest any man fall after the same example of unbelief." Hebrews 4:10–11

"Commit your way unto the LORD; trust also in Him; and He shall bring it to pass… (7) Rest in the LORD, and wait patiently for Him:" Psalm 37:5 & 7a

## DECEMBER 10

## THIS IS THE DAY THAT THE LORD HAS MADE. I WILL REJOICE AND BE GLAD IN IT.

*Rejoice! He is in control.*

*He came to give us freedom and freedom we have! Now do we walk in freedom? Not enough! There is more freedom, more walking in the Spirit available to us.*

*We must seek Him with our whole heart. Repentance must come before Life Everlasting can raise His head and shout, "It is finished," in our lives. We must knock until the Lord Almighty rains down His Spirit of repentance. Our eyes and ears and heart must be opened to hear, see, and feel what God is doing.*

*"Oh God, let Your Spirit brood over us until You can say, 'Let there be light,' in the dark areas of our lives."*

\*\*\*

*"Cast away from you all your transgressions, whereby you have transgressed; and make you a new heart and a new spirit: for why will you die, O house of Israel? (32) For I have no pleasure in the death of him that dies, says the Lord GOD: wherefore turn yourselves, and live." Ezekiel 18:31–32*

*"Or despise you the riches of His goodness and forbearance and longsuffering; not knowing that the goodness of God leads you to repentance?" Romans 2:4*

*"In those days came John the Baptist, preaching in the wilderness of Judaea. (2) And saying, Repent ye: for the kingdom of heaven is at hand." Matthew 3:1–2*

*"From that time Jesus began to preach, and to say, Repent: for the kingdom of heaven is at hand." Matthew 4:17*

## DECEMBER 11
### THIS IS THE DAY THAT THE LORD HAS MADE. I WILL REJOICE AND BE GLAD IN IT.

*Read your Bible and seek the Lord.*

*Those who seek Me shall find Me. My Son said, "This is eternal life to know the Father. And no one knows the Father but the Son and no one knows the Son except to whom the Father reveals Him." (Matthew 11:27)*

*Seek to know Me and the power of My might shall be distributed to you. Love is my strong right arm. It is love that propels the worlds in their orbits.*

*Seek to know Me and the power of My might shall propel you into the worlds and nations that I have planned for you.*

*Seek to know Me and your worlds shall crumble before your eyes and be established in My Kingdom for such a time as this.*

*Everything that was must become new. That is the way of My Kingdom. A wheat seed must fall to the ground and die before it brings life. So it is with the old. You must have new wineskins to hold the new wine.*

*Look not to the right nor left. I am doing a new thing. Look only unto the Author and Finisher.*

\*\*\*

*"Neither do men put new wine into old bottles: else the bottles break, and the wine runs out, and the bottles perish: but they put new wine into new bottles, and both are preserved." Matthew 9:17; also in Mark 2:22 and Luke 5:37–38*

## DECEMBER 12
### THIS IS THE DAY THAT THE LORD HAS MADE. I WILL REJOICE AND BE GLAD IN IT.

*Oh, come let us adore Him! For He has saved us and He continues to save us from depression, discouragement, and distractions.*

*It is time to walk into the destiny to which He has called us. You can. I can. Let us go forward walking in the Spirit of the Most High God. Through adoration and praise, worship and gazing upon Him and His attributes, will we come to know our destinies to which He has called us. He once said to me, "When you are walking in your destiny, you will have favor."*

*Some may say, "We do have His favor." And I say, "Yes, we do, positionally. But there is an experiential favor that will be manifested as we walk more fully into our purpose."*

*As Hosea said, "Then shall we know, if we follow on to know the LORD: His going forth is prepared as the morning; and He shall come unto us as the rain, as the latter and former rain unto the earth." (Hosea 6:3)*

*Let us follow on to know the Lord today. Let us follow our heart and not our head. Let us continually say, "Your will be done, Lord, Your will be done." He will answer that prayer.*

\*\*\*

*"Your kingdom come. Your will be done in earth, as it is in heaven." Matthew 6:10*

*"But now, O LORD, You are Our father; we are the clay, and You our potter; and we all are the work of Your hand." Isaiah 64:8*

## DECEMBER 13
## THIS IS THE DAY THAT THE LORD HAS MADE. I WILL REJOICE AND BE GLAD IN IT.

*Rejoice in the Lord and again I say, Rejoice in the Lord! It is something so hard to do as we walk out this life upon earth. We must turn our eyes upon the Lord and think of His beautiful face, His beautiful peace, His beautiful care of us… We can go on and on. But we rather enjoy pondering the bad and sad stuff of life. We cannot! We must discipline our minds to think upon Him and His majesty (II Corinthians 10:5). But what is His majesty? Once again, we must make new wineskins to receive the new wine that He has for us (Mark 2:22).*

*"We are waiting, Lord, for Your return on earth. But even more, Your return to our hearts, so that we love and adore You with all of our mind, body, strength and soul. Oh, to love You with the love that You deserve!*

*"We can only know You as we read, study, ponder, meditate upon Your Word. That is the only record we have of You. And by Your Spirit dwelling within us, we can know You. Yes, we can.*

*"So Father, Son and Holy Spirit have Your way with us this day. Reveal Yourself to us, so that we can commune with You, live with You, talk with You, walk with You. Where You go, we shall go! Amen and amen."*

\*\*\*

*"And Ruth said, Entreat me not to leave you, or to return from following after you; for whither you go, I will go; and where you lodge, I will lodge; your people shall be my people, and your God my God:" Ruth 1:16*

*I have made this day for your joy—your full joy.*

*Seek not to understand My ways, but seek to know Me. From knowing Me, springs eternal life; and this life can be bestowed among the brethren.*

*Do not look around in disbelief, but look around with full assurance that I am with you and on your side. I seek your victory in all situations.*

*Some may seem not so victorious, but so did Joseph's life seem that way initially. No life under My care can be defeated or lack in effectiveness.*

*What is wrong with you and many of My children is doubt—not only doubt, but also unbelief. Times have not changed so from biblical times.*

*Continue in your work and you shall reap, if you faint not.*

\*\*\*

"And let us not be weary in well doing: for in due season we shall reap, if we faint not." Galatians 6:9

"Take heed, brethren, lest there be in any of you an evil heart of unbelief, in departing from the living God." Hebrews 3:12

"And straightway the father of the child cried out, and said with tears, Lord, I believe; help Thou mine unbelief." Mark 9:24

Here we are in the season of Advent—watching and waiting for the return of our Lord Jesus. We are focusing on His first coming and watching for His second coming.

The angel said in Acts 1:11, "...You men of Galilee, why stand you gazing up into heaven? This same Jesus, which is taken up from you into heaven, shall so come in like manner as you have seen Him go into heaven."

In Revelation 19:11–16, we have another picture of Jesus' second return. John says, "(11) And I saw heaven opened, and behold a white horse; and He that sat upon him was Faithful and True, and in righteousness He does judge and make war. (12) And His eyes were as a flame of fire, and on His head were many crowns; and He had a name written, that no man knew, but He Himself. (13) And He was clothed with a vesture dipped in blood: and His name is called The Word of God. (14) And the armies which were in heaven followed Him upon white horses, clothed in fine linen, white and clean. (15) And out of His mouth goes a sharp sword, that with it He should smite the nations: and He shall rule them with a rod of the fierceness and wrath of Almighty God. (16) And He has on His vesture and on His thigh a name written, KING OF KINGS, AND LORD OF LORDS."

Jesus says in Revelation 22:20, "...Surely I come quickly." And our response in the same verse is, "Amen. Even so, come, Lord Jesus."

\*\*\*

"He which testifies these things says, Surely I come quickly. Amen. Even so, come, Lord Jesus." Revelation 22:20

† 

## DECEMBER 16

## THIS IS THE DAY THAT THE LORD HAS MADE. I WILL REJOICE AND BE GLAD IN IT.

*For wherein is your joy? Let it be emanating from the throne of God. It is He Who is our utmost joy. There is no joy outside of Him.*

*Thus explaining the lack of smiling faces you meet in your world—those faces in the grocery store, abounding on the highways, in your place of employment, and even in your churches behind their masks.*

*Oh! seek Me for discerning the needs of My children, and come before My throne to receive from Me their supplies.*

*Do you not know? Are you not aware? I yearn and wait for My saints to bring to My throne lost and lonely sheep. I was once a Shepherd, and I still have a shepherd's heart. You know I must tend to My sheep and lose none except the son of perdition.*

\*\*\*

*"...and none of them is lost, but the son of perdition; that the scripture might be fulfilled." John 17:12c*

*"But let all those that put their trust in You rejoice: let them ever shout for joy, because You defend them: let them also that love Your name be joyful in You." Psalm 5:11*

*"As a shepherd seeks out his flock in the day that he is among his sheep that are scattered; so will I seek out My sheep, and will deliver them out of all places where they have been scattered in the cloudy and dark day... (15) I will feed my flock, and I will cause them to lie down, says the Lord GOD. (16) I will seek that which was lost, and bring again that which was driven away, and will bind up that which was broken, and will strengthen that which was sick; but I will destroy the fat and the strong; I will feed them with judgment." Ezekiel 34:12, 15–16*

## DECEMBER 17
### THIS IS THE DAY THAT THE LORD HAS MADE. I WILL REJOICE AND BE GLAD IN IT.

*Come unto Me, and I will fill your heart with the joy that I have created before the worlds were. Come unto Me and receive the love that I created before the worlds were. I AM joy and love and the peace that passes your reasoning mind.*

*Oh! is it not good to experience something that you have nothing to do with? To experience something that did not originate within you. The world is so full of man's creations and pride, that to experience something other than man's creations is so welcoming and refreshing and so defeating of the pride that destroys.*

*Come unto Me and receive all things necessary for life and liberty. Liberty in My Spirit.*

*Oh, would that you would come and rest in My arms. Come and receive. This time of Advent is a time to come and keep coming for the refreshing that your body and soul has so much need of.*

*Come for I have everything that you desire and need, but can find nowhere else. Look to Me and receive all.*

\*\*\*

"My Beloved spoke, and said unto me, Rise up, My love, My fair one, and come away. (11) For, lo, the winter is past, the rain is over and gone; (12) The flowers appear on the earth; the time of the singing of birds is come, and the voice of the turtle is heard in our land; (13) The fig tree puts forth her green figs, and the vines with the tender grape give a good smell. Arise, My love, My fair one, and come away." Song of Solomon 2:10–13

## DECEMBER 18
### THIS IS THE DAY THAT THE LORD HAS MADE. I WILL REJOICE AND BE GLAD IN IT.

*There is much noise and talk circulating when My children should be seeking Me. Do not be afraid to seek Me with all your heart. It may mean sloppy efforts at first, but with no beginning there is no finish.*

*Seek ye first My kingdom, and all things shall be added unto you. You have no idea or conception of the passion I have for you. My heart burns for you with an everlasting flame. It never wanes. It never fades or dims!*

*My love is beyond human conception. But I desire to make My love known to you, and My desires are always fulfilled.*

*You will know My love for you.*

\*\*\*

"Set me as a seal upon your heart, as a seal upon your arm: for love is strong as death; jealousy is cruel as the grave: the coals thereof are coals of fire, which has a most vehement flame. (7) Many waters cannot quench love, neither can the floods drown it: if a man would give all the substance of his house for love, it would utterly be condemned." Song of Solomon 8:6–7

"Behold, as the eyes of servants look unto the hand of their masters, and as the eyes of a maiden unto the hand of her mistress; so our eyes wait upon the LORD our God, until that He have mercy upon us." Psalm 123:2

"I wait for the LORD, my soul does wait, and in His Word do I hope. (6) My soul waits for the Lord more than they that watch for the morning: I say, more than they that watch for the morning." Psalm 130:5–6

## DECEMBER 19
## THIS IS THE DAY THAT THE LORD HAS MADE. I WILL REJOICE AND BE GLAD IN IT.

*"Oh! how hard it is to trust in You, Lord, while in the storm! The storm of holiday activities causes great demands on one's body, mind, and emotions."*

*Let not the clamor of the world distort the reality of your relationship with your Father, with Jesus and with the Holy Spirit. Satan and the world has crowded themselves into the celebration of His birth and left us running to maintain our sanity.*

*Linger not in the things of this world for they shall disappoint you and fall short of satisfying your needs during this busy season. Carve out and demand the same amount of time for you and God. Short cuts can be taken in other places of your life. Store up for yourself riches in heaven where moth nor rust do not corrupt.*

**Look for Me in this season. I am there and I am coming.**

\*\*\*

*"And, behold, I come quickly; and My reward is with Me, to give every man according as his work shall be... (20) He which testifies these things says, Surely I come quickly. Amen. Even so, come, Lord Jesus." Revelation 22:12 & 20*

*"For the Son of man is as a man taking a far journey, who left his house, and gave authority to his servants, and to every man his work, and commanded the porter to watch. (35) Watch ye therefore: for you know not when the master of the house comes, at even, or at midnight, or at the cockcrowing, or in the morning: (36) Lest coming suddenly he finds you sleeping. (37) And what I say unto you I say unto all, Watch." Mark 13:34–37*

*God has revealed a mighty thing to me—Love is giving. It cannot be taken from someone. Love always gives. It does not take. To take is to steal when there's no permission involved. Taking, without permission, is stealing.*

*Be sure to ask before taking something from someone. That includes taking their time, their emotions, their body, their sleep, their space, and on and on. I guess that is what boundaries are all about. Satan takes.*

*Christ gives, and then we freely give in return. But Satan takes and takes and takes and that is stealing.*

*Do not be involved in stealing. Do not allow someone to steal from you. God does not expect you to hand over your valuables without your assent.*

\*\*\*

"For even the Son of man came not to be ministered unto, but to minister, and to give His life a ransom for many." Mark 10:45

"And she had a sister called Mary, which also sat at Jesus' feet, and heard His Word... (41) And Jesus answered and said unto her, Martha, Martha, you are careful and troubled about many things: (42) But one thing is needful: and Mary has chosen that good part, which shall not be taken away from her." Luke 10:39, 41–42

"For God so loved the world, that He gave His only begotten Son, that whosoever believes in Him should not perish, but have everlasting life." John 3:16

*He has called us to a holy life—a life
wholly given up and over to Him.*

*You ask, "Where can I give over more of myself to Him?"
Ask Him and He will begin to reveal it to you.*

*In Deuteronomy 30, He began to lead His people into victory.
Sometimes victory is not all at once, but gradual. His ways
are different for each person. God is certainly not boring. He
will not allow you to figure Him out. It is not because He
wants to remain a mystery. It is because He has made us all
different. He knows what works best for each person.*

*This also turns out to be a safety valve; protecting us
from the wiles of the enemy—pride and presumption.
A complete leaning upon the Holy Spirit will keep
the enemy in check and keep you in peace.*

*"Speak, Holy Spirit, and move in our lives to produce
righteous fruit worthy for the Master."*

\*\*\*

*"Let the wicked forsake his way, and the unrighteous man his thoughts:
and let him return unto the LORD, and He will have mercy upon him;
and to our God, for He will abundantly pardon. (8) For My thoughts
are not your thoughts, neither are your ways My ways, says the LORD.
(9) For as the heavens are higher than the earth, so are My ways higher
than your ways, and My thoughts than your thoughts." Isaiah 55:7–9*

## DECEMBER 22
### THIS IS THE DAY THAT THE LORD HAS MADE. I WILL REJOICE AND BE GLAD IN IT.

*Hallelujah! He is risen and alive today. He is no longer a character in a book or a character of history. He is flaming with life in the Holy Spirit baptized believer.*

*Oh! do not stop with Jesus as your Savior and Lord, but invite, request Him to be your baptizer with the Holy Spirit and fire.*

*If this does not coincide with your denominational beliefs, just ask your Father for the truth. He will reveal it to you, but don't deny it based on denominational doctrine.*

*Ask Jesus to baptize you with the Holy Spirit and fire. He will do it. You may not notice anything different immediately, but He will not forget your request. He will begin leading you in that direction, and one day you'll look back and recognize His hand in fulfilling this request.*

*Seek out those that are excited and hungry for more of God. Do not be satisfied with little or enough of God. Desire more than enough, so His Spirit spills out on people and situations wherever you go!*

\*\*\*

*"I indeed baptize you with water unto repentance: but He that comes after me is mightier than I, whose shoes I am not worthy to bear: He shall baptize you with the Holy Ghost, and with fire." Matthew 3:11*

*"John answered, saying unto them all, I indeed baptize you with water; but One mightier than I comes, the latchet of whose shoes I am not worthy to unloose: He shall baptize you with the Holy Ghost and with fire:" Luke 3:16*

## DECEMBER 23
## THIS IS THE DAY THAT THE LORD HAS MADE. I WILL REJOICE AND BE GLAD IN IT.

*This is the day that I have made for you. Rejoice!*

*Go about your life today rejoicing! Not doubting! Not grumbling! Not sad! But REJOICING! You shall be led by My Spirit, and you shall know the joy of your salvation. (Psalm 51:12) You shall see love and experience it.*

*You shall not be offended, but offenses shall bounce off of you. You shall give and not take. You shall bless and not curse, for the Lord your Maker has called you forth for such a time as this.*

*This is the day to rejoice and see the enemy scatter. I have said, "You shall never worry again." Why not meditate upon this word today. My Words are life to those that find them and healing to all their flesh.*

*Be sober and alert for the devil would like to devour you, but I have defeated him, so REJOICE! My Words are life! "You shall never worry again." Chew on those words, taste them, savor them, and then clasp them to your heart and do not let them go.*

*My Words are life!*

\*\*\*

*"My son, attend to My Words… (21a) Let them not depart from your eyes…(22) For they are life unto those that find them, and health to all their flesh." Proverbs 4:20a, 21a & 22*

*"Therefore take no thought, saying, What shall we eat? Or, What shall we drink? Or, Wherewithal shall we be clothed?" Matthew 6:31*

## DECEMBER 24
### THIS IS THE DAY THAT THE LORD HAS MADE. I WILL REJOICE AND BE GLAD IN IT.

*Make your declaration to rejoice!*

*Declare that your will, will align itself with your spirit to glorify God in your body.*

*Die to a life of "self" and purposefully set your spirit to reign over your soul and body, so that your emotions, will, thoughts, desires are submissive to your spirit which is in communion with the Holy Spirit.*

*Pray in the Holy Spirit to edify your spirit— to increase, feed, and supply your spirit.*

*Oh, for our spirit to be in control of our soul and body!*

*This can happen as you willfully surrender to your spirit.*

*His desire is for you. Let your desire be for Him.*

\*\*\*

*"I am my Beloved's, and His desire is toward me." Song of Solomon 7:10*

*"But you, beloved, building up yourselves on your most holy faith, praying in the Holy Ghost, (21) Keep yourselves in the love of God, looking for the mercy of our Lord Jesus Christ unto eternal life." Jude 20–21*

*"This I say then, Walk in the Spirit, and you shall not fulfill the lust of the flesh… (25) If we live in the Spirit, let us also walk in the Spirit." Galatians 5:16 & 25*

*"Then said Jesus unto His disciples, If any man will come after Me, let him deny himself, and take up His cross, and follow Me. (25) For whosoever will save his life shall lose it: and whosoever will lose his life for My sake shall find it." Matthew 16:24–25*

## DECEMBER 25
## THIS IS THE DAY THAT THE LORD HAS MADE. I WILL REJOICE AND BE GLAD IN IT.

*What can be said about the glorious day of salvation? When Jesus was born, it was the beginning day of salvation (being saved) from sin, sickness and poverty.*

*You have believed in salvation from sin and sickness. Now is the time to step into salvation from poverty. Just as it was with sin and sickness, it shall be with poverty. You must believe I ended, finished it on the cross and resist Satan when he comes at you with poverty just like you resist him when he comes at you with sin and sickness. Resist him and he will flee. To date, you have not been mentally ready to open up to My mind of financial prosperity. You have been sick financially and accepting it, not realizing you were sick. Now confess your sickness and be made whole! Pray this prayer:*

*"Father, I confess I am sick financially. You want me prosperous, being a blessing to others. I repent for believing a lie and living in deception. Please forgive me for accepting this state and cleanse me so I can receive Your gift to me of salvation in my finances. Be it done unto me according to Your will. Open unto me the flood gates of heaven, so that I cannot contain all the blessings. Thank You for forgiving me, cleansing me, and filling me with Yourself, in the name of Your Son, Jesus, amen and amen."*

\*\*\*

*"Let them shout for joy, and be glad, that favor my righteous cause: yes, let them say continually, Let the LORD be magnified, which has pleasure in the prosperity of His servant." Psalm 35:27*

## THIS IS THE DAY THAT THE LORD HAS MADE. I WILL REJOICE AND BE GLAD IN IT.

*You see I have many, MANY blessings I am holding for you until you can receive them.*

"Why can't I receive them, Father?"

*Because you are not looking to receive them. You must be expecting, looking for, anticipating, hoping, believing for something before you can receive it or else it goes right past you. If you're not looking for something, you won't find something. What are you expecting? You'll receive it.*

"Don't You ever give without Your children expecting it?"

*Yes, I do. But with the mature, I follow the better way! And that is when the child looks to Me and expects. Then the blessings have multiple effects and are better utilized. Let Me open your soul to what I desire to give you, and then exercise your faith to receive. I will be glorified, and you will be blessed. Let Me bless you. Let Me fulfill My desires for you. Let Me receive My joy from blessing you. Look to Me, and you will receive to overflowing.*

\*\*\*

"Hitherto have you asked nothing in My name: ask, and you shall receive, that your joy may be full." John 16:24

"Delight yourself also in the LORD: and He shall give you the desires of your heart." Psalm 37:4

> **THIS IS THE DAY THAT THE LORD HAS MADE. I WILL REJOICE AND BE GLAD IN IT.**

*Oh! how the year has gone, and yet there is much in which to rejoice!*

*He has mighty secrets to give to you—only believe and expect.*

*What have you given Him for His birthday?*

*If you have not already asked Him what He wants for His birthday, do so now. Find out what He wants. You shall be surprised. Whatever it is, He will be working in your life to make it a reality.*

*Let us praise Him and above all…let us listen to what He has to say.*

*We think and talk too much and leave little time for our Father to converse with us. Now be still and come before Him.*

*He has something to say…*

\*\*\*

*"And the LORD came, and stood, and called as at other times. Samuel, Samuel. Then Samuel answered, Speak; for your servant hears." I Samuel 3:10*

*"And after the earthquake a fire; but the LORD was not in the fire: and after the fire a still small voice." I Kings 19:12*

*"Call unto Me, and I will answer you, and show you great and mighty things, which you know not." Jeremiah 33:3*

*"And therefore will the LORD wait, that He may be gracious unto you, and therefore will He be exalted, that He may have mercy upon you: for the LORD is a God of judgment: blessed be all they that wait for Him." Isaiah 30:18*

## DECEMBER 28
### THIS IS THE DAY THAT THE LORD HAS MADE. I WILL REJOICE AND BE GLAD IN IT.

*Set aside an hour at lunch time to commune with Me. Eat My Word instead of bread. Come and sup with Me. I have meat you know not of.*

*I have meat I want to share with you that will leave you full and not wanting.*

*Come and buy from Me. It does not cost silver nor gold… but it costs your will and your faith.*

*Come expecting Me to show and to feed.*

*Come expecting the Lord of Lord's to dine with you.*

*Come expecting the Lover of your soul.*

*Come expecting to be fed and nourished.*

*Come and you will not be disappointed.*

*Come with anticipation of good things.*

*Come with excitement and you will not be disappointed.*

*Come with your Bible and notebook.*

*Come and I shall feed you!*

\*\*\*

*"Ho, every one that thirsts, come to the waters, and he that has no money; come, buy, and eat; yes, come, buy wine and milk without money and without price." Isaiah 55:1*

## DECEMBER 29
### THIS IS THE DAY THAT THE LORD HAS MADE. I WILL REJOICE AND BE GLAD IN IT.

*"Hallelujah! Father, You love us. What does it mean to love someone?"*

*I AM love.*

*God is love (I John 4:8 & 16). Who am I? I am whatever I do. You are whatever you do. And whatever you do begins with whatever you think. From thought, comes action. I think I am prosperous, therefore I am.*

*You are just now realizing and accepting the fact that it is okay to be prosperous financially. I have expected you to be rich all along, but you have accepted mediocre wealth. STOP! Your blessings are overabundant! Not just enough! Wake-up! Be expecting money to flood into your bosom! I purchased it all back for you on the cross. Do not, do not go any further with lack and an impoverished mentality.*

*Follow Me, listen and obey. I will lead you into the place I purchased for you. It is easy as you lean your ear to hear My voice and obey.*

\*\*\*

*"The LORD is my Shepherd; I shall not want. (2) He makes me to lie down in green pastures: He leads me beside the still waters." Psalm 23:1–2*

*"The blessing of the LORD, it makes rich, and He adds no sorrow to it." Proverbs 10:22*

*"And God is able to make all grace abound toward you; that you, always having all sufficiency in all things, may abound to every good work;" II Corinthians 9:8*

† 

## DECEMBER 30
## THIS IS THE DAY THAT THE LORD HAS MADE. I WILL REJOICE AND BE GLAD IN IT.

*"Come, Lord, and speak the words of life that position us into Your will for our life."*

*Words of life well up from your spirit and must needs be spoken in order to carry purpose to them. Speak aloud those words that arise from your chest. Those are words of life welling up from the Spring of Life. Those words spoken will bring life to a dying world, a dying situation.*

*"Come, Lord, and bring to us Words of Life for our life's situations that we will speak to them and life will manifest."*

*You may not see immediate manifestation, but if you believe and not doubt whatsoever things you say shall come to pass. Now speak those words of life that you need… your children and spouse need! Speak and doubt not! God said, "Let there be light: and there was light."*

*Speaking is as important as believing, for without action faith is dead. And without faith it is impossible to please God. Enough said.*

*Now go and speak life into every dark and dreary situation, and see God move!*

\*\*\*

*"For verily I say unto you, That whosoever shall say unto this mountain, Be removed, and be cast into the sea; and shall not doubt in his heart, but shall believe that those things which he says shall come to pass; he shall have whatsoever he says." Mark 11:23*

## DECEMBER 31
## THIS IS THE DAY THAT THE LORD HAS MADE. I WILL REJOICE AND BE GLAD IN IT.

*"Have you called me to this place of resentment? This place of resentment—for me to surrender my flesh to You? Or is Satan at work here? I must know!*

*"Cleanse my heart. Expose my sin! You have many ways of waking us. Is this You, Lord, or is this the enemy?"*

**By their fruits you will know them. Is this a fruitful time? Have I come to sup with you? Yes, your flesh is angry and rebelling, but your spirit is abounding.**

**You have sought to seek Me early. Well, your desires have come to pass. I can use the things of Satan to fulfill My purposes on earth. Your enemy, My enemy is not Satan, but your unsurrendered will.**

**I have defeated Satan, but only you can defeat the selfish, controlling will. I have made available the power—the ability—to overcome your will, but you must assent to the Spirit reigning and not you!**

\*\*\*

*"And He said to them all, If any man will come after Me, let him deny himself, and take up his cross daily, and follow Me." Luke 9:23*

*"Verily, verily, I say unto you, Except a corn of wheat falls into the ground and dies, it abides alone: but if it dies, it brings forth much fruit. (25) He that loves his life shall lose it; and he that hates his life in this world shall keep it unto life eternal." John 12:24–25*

*"He that loves father or mother more than Me is not worthy of Me: and he that loves son or daughter more than Me is not worthy of Me. (38) And he that takes not his cross, and follows after Me, is not worthy of Me." Matthew 10:37–38*

*Thank you, Valerie Powell Mangold, my sister, for encouraging me in my writing ministry and your time of editing this book. Thank you for sharing it with your friends as you saw their needs may be met by these words of inspiration from our Father.*

*Thank you, Rita Barnett, for your deep heart-felt desire and prayers for this book's publication. It happened!*

*My appreciation and thanks go to Deborah Newman, with Washed By the Word Ministries, for her time and effort in editing and proofing the manuscript.*

*Always my thanksgivings go to my most excellent husband, Charles Glover, for his support and continued belief in me!*

*And lastly, I give thanks to God for all my patrons who support my ministry with their prayers and finances. May you receive a prophet's reward according to Scripture:*

> *"He that receives a prophet in the name of a prophet shall receive a prophet's reward; and he that receives a righteous man in the name of a righteous man shall receive a righteous man's reward." Matthew 10:41*

www.ingramcontent.com/pod-product-compliance
Lightning Source LLC
Chambersburg PA
CBHW021114300426
44113CB00006B/148